The Rise of Weaponized Flak in the New Media Era

Intersections in Communications and Culture

Global Approaches and Transdisciplinary Perspectives

Cameron McCarthy and Angharad N. Valdivia
General Editors

Vol. 35

The Intersections in Communications and Culture series
is part of the Peter Lang Media and Communication list.
Every volume is peer reviewed and meets
the highest quality standards for content and production.

PETER LANG
New York • Bern • Berlin
Brussels • Vienna • Oxford • Warsaw

Brian Michael Goss

The Rise of Weaponized Flak in the New Media Era

Beyond the Propaganda Model

PETER LANG
New York • Bern • Berlin
Brussels • Vienna • Oxford • Warsaw

Library of Congress Cataloging-in-Publication Data

Names: Goss, Brian Michael, author.
Title: The rise of weaponized flak in the new media era:
beyond the propaganda model / Brian Michael Goss.
Description: New York: Peter Lang, 2019.
Series: Intersections in communications and culture:
global approaches and transdisciplinary perspectives; vol. 35 | ISSN 1528-610X
Includes bibliographical references and index.
Identifiers: LCCN 2019024946 | ISBN 978-1-4331-4259-8 (hardback: alk. paper)
ISBN 978-1-4331-4258-1 (paperback: alk. paper) | ISBN 978-1-4331-4260-4 (ebook pdf)
ISBN 978-1-4331-4261-1 (epub) | ISBN 978-1-4331-4262-8 (mobi)
Subjects: LCSH: Mass media and propaganda—United States. | Mass
media—Political aspects—United States. | Press and propaganda—United
States. | Press and politics—United States. | Communication in
politics—United States.
Classification: LCC P96.P722 U64 2019 | DDC 303.3/75—dc23
LC record available at https://lccn.loc.gov/2019024946
DOI 10.3726/b15978

Bibliographic information published by **Die Deutsche Nationalbibliothek**.
Die Deutsche Nationalbibliothek lists this publication in the "Deutsche
Nationalbibliografie"; detailed bibliographic data are available
on the Internet at http://dnb.d-nb.de/.

The paper in this book meets the guidelines for permanence and durability
of the Committee on Production Guidelines for Book Longevity
of the Council of Library Resources.

© 2019 Peter Lang Publishing, Inc., New York
29 Broadway, 18th floor, New York, NY 10006
www.peterlang.com

All rights reserved.
Reprint or reproduction, even partially, in all forms such as microfilm,
xerography, microfiche, microcard, and offset strictly prohibited.

Printed in the United States of America

CONTENTS

List of Tables   vii
Acknowledgments   ix

Part I: Introducing Flak

Chapter 1: 1988/2016: From PAC and Flak to Hack and Flak   3
Chapter 2: "Bow the Knee to This New Dictatorship": The Many Faces of Flak   23

Part II: Flak Mills

Chapter 3: "We Are Those Experts": Heartland Institute and the Think Tank as Flak Mill   57
Chapter 4: "Transcendent Truth" in Disguise: Project Veritas' Flak Traps   97

Part III: Flak Issues and Conclusions

Chapter 5: Voters as "Thieves and Fraudsters": Flak against Elections   131

Chapter 6: "Indoctrination," "Persecution," "Control": Flak Goes to College 161
Chapter 7: Conclusion: Play to Win 197

Index 203

TABLES

Table 5.1: Less is more—or packing and cracking to transform
            a minority of voters into a majority of seats   155
Table 6.1: Content analysis of CR (15 April–May 15, 2017)   175

ACKNOWLEDGMENTS

As concerns the genesis of this volume, I will acknowledge that one title that I floated for it was *Political Ebola*. Instead, *The Rise of Weaponized Flak* finally won out over the perhaps more colorful if morbid and commercially suspect title.

As for people who have helped summon the book into being, I will name names. I thank the members of the Professional Development Advisory Committee at Saint Louis University-Madrid and its chair, Dave Howden, for granting me a teaching release in Spring 2019. The release enabled locked-on focus and completion of the book in a timely fashion.

While the book was in progress, I had the chance to rehearse and refine evidence and arguments through a series of presentations at different moments in the two-and-a-half-year sojourn through flak. I thank my colleagues Simona Elena Rentea and Joan Pedro Carañana for scheduling me three times (2016–2018) to deliver presentations for the Humanities and Social Sciences Division Research Seminars as I prepared the book proposal and while writing was in progress. *Mulțumiri* to Emilia Parpala-Afana and her colleagues at University of Craiova, Romania for giving me hospitality and the opportunity to address the Comparativism, Identity and Communication Conference as a plenary speaker. In Spring 2019, Tony Ozuna enabled the chance to present findings at Anglo-American University in Prague, Czech Republic—with further support from Rob Warren and Andrew Giarelli who brought their students *en masse*. Arne Saeys was hands-on in arranging a Faculty of Social Sciences lecture later in Spring 2019 at the University of Antwerp, Belgium, in a room that memorably overlooked the final resting place of P.P Rubens in Saint Jacob's Church.

Prior to crisscrossing Europe with the message on flak, I benefitted from the generosity that Intersections in Communication and Culture Series Editor Cameron McCarthy has afforded me, as well as countless other scholars, during his dazzling career. Cameron has been an encourager in first asking me to consider a book proposal more than ten years ago; the volume in your hands now is our fourth collaboration with Peter Lang. Speaking of Lang, although she is relatively new to the firm, Acquisitions Editor Erika Hendrix inspired total confidence as she shepherded the book to endgame and nailed even obscure questions with good cheer.

More thanks: a hand to Paul A. Vita, Director of the Saint Louis University-Madrid campus for his consistent support over many years, after bringing me to my first academic post coming out of University of Illinois. Anne Dewey and Cary Barney were among the first people I met on arrival at SLU's distinctive and ahead-of-its-time international campus; their encouragement, wisdom, and example have been vital to my career trajectory. Daniel Chornet's arrival on our campus in 2006 propelled our department forward and heralded a rigorous and positive culture within it. As noted, many people have now heard me present this book's content at different moments of progress toward completion, but my colleague Dale Fuchs was brave enough to read an advanced draft. Students in my *Political Communication* course have also sharpened my concept of flak over the years; shout outs are in order for Ema Debeljak, Luis Garanzo Asensio, Paula Otero Santos, Bracey Parr, Nada Tahiri and Jennyfer D. Zuili.

El gran amigo John Kayan has listened to soliloquies on the emergent theory of flak across untold trajectories through *zonas de marcha* while Cristina Domingo Zaragoza has been similarly regaled at her kitchen table.

Finally, I hope the contents of the book on the written page are equal to the lofty artistic accomplishment of the cover artists: Paul Francis Goss (cover painting) and Lua Fischer (author photograph).

Brian Michael Goss
May 2019
Madrid, Spain

Part I
INTRODUCING FLAK

· 1 ·

1988/2016: FROM PAC AND FLAK TO HACK AND FLAK

Introduction: Remembering 1988

The year 1988 witnessed two events of considerable interest to the study of flak as a sociopolitical force.

The first event was the publication of Edward Herman and Noam Chomsky's *Manufacturing Consent* in which the authors introduced their propaganda model. In presenting their structuralist account of the behavior of news media in the contemporaneous United States, Herman and Chomsky's objective was to illuminate "a propaganda system at work where the media are private and formal censorship is absent" (1988, p. 1); a system far more supple and decentered than the then-terminally ill Soviet system. Herman and Chomsky were interested in how a force that steers the conduct of news workers is exerted without evident force for having been embedded within a framework of robust formal freedoms.

In explaining the paradox, Herman and Chomsky (1988) posit five systemic filters that condition the performance of news workers and the resultant news narratives. In their account, the filters behave in concert to palpably but un-coercively bring news into alignment with powerful (capitalist, nationalist) interests. Herman and Chomsky characterize news as filtered from the start through oligopolistic ownership patterns. Thereafter, news is conditioned by commercial imperatives (transacting the delivery of an audience to advertisers in exchange for revenue), sourcing patterns (massively tilted toward elite information brokers) and unswerving ideological opposition to the communist Other (recall that this was 1988!). These constraints play out within a news milieu structured by professional procedures that shunt reporting toward prevailing consensus and its circumscribed controversies. With the filters deeply insinuated into the news media industry and internalized by news workers, journalism is generally, if imperfectly, textured by the status quo.

Alongside these four filters, Herman and Chomsky also propose one more filter that limits the autonomy of news organizations: flak. In contrast with the first four filters, Herman and Chomsky's "classic" version of flak construes it as a set of disciplinary mechanisms exerted from outside news organizations. In their characterization, flak consists of "negative responses to a media statement or program" (1988, p. 16). Flak goes into motion when the other filters, in effect, slip-up and ideologically wayward reporting is broadcast or published. Vintage 1988 flak could be mobilized through "letters, telegrams, phone calls, petitions, lawsuits, speeches and bills before Congress, and other modes of complaint, threat, and punitive action" (1988, p. 16). Herman and Chomsky stress the gravity of flak: if "produced on a large scale, or by individuals or groups with substantial resources, it can be both uncomfortable and costly," with the professional and personal implications that follow. Efforts to discipline news media with flak may—or may not—be immediately successful, but news organizations need to be mindful of the costs of disapprobation or harassment. That said, at least in their "Introduction," Herman and Chomsky (1988) devote relatively little attention to flak.

Today, as in 1988, flak can be understood as ideologically purposeful, enacted with the objective of delegitimizing, disabling or dismantling the careers and activities of its targets. In this volume, I will further posit flak as having slipped the propaganda model leash to become a significant force in its own right. In this view, the practices of flak have claimed a more central place in contemporary sociopolitical processes, far beyond disciplinary mechanisms directed against news media. Contemporary flak arguably works through media far more massively than against it.

Since the publication of *Manufacturing Consent* in 1988, the advent of new media platforms has altered news in ways that are being debated even as they unfold (Curran, Fenton & Freedman, 2016; Fenton, 2010; Morozov, 2011; Peters & Broersma, 2013). On one hand, the new media era has facilitated notable improvements in the news environment. The new media order has loosened the demands of the simplistic objectivity doctrine and, for many platforms, enabled a measure of independence from media conglomerates. At the same time, the seemingly filter-less new media environment has been conducive to the growth of flak campaigns. New media has smoothed the way toward proliferation of flak-dedicated channels, specialized in the production of ideologically-driven harassment against individuals, organizations, and political causes.

Accuracy in Media (AIM, founded 1969) presented Herman and Chomsky's lead example of flak when they introduced the propaganda model. In AIM's appraisal, then and now, mainstream news media channels are not sufficiently monochrome, self-censorious and *Pravda*-like in enforcing a right-wing line. While AIM continues its dreary brand of antagonism (Goss, 2009), it is now more of a relic in what has become a crowded flak industry. To take a couple of examples of newer flak players, the Heartland Institute (founded 1984) and Project Veritas (founded 2009) are themselves media presences through their products and (niche as well as mainstream) media appearances. The remit of the flak new-wavers extends beyond ostensible media critique to produce ideologically radioactive flak against the usual litany of targets: "liberals," universities, climate science, marginal populations, and effective State regulatory intervention in the economy.

In the effort to thoroughly characterize flak and draw attention to its techniques and impact, I am not positing flak as "the clue that solves all crimes." As I have previously argued (Goss, 2013), the propaganda model's amalgam of concentrated ownership patterns, rampant commercialism, elite sourcing and dichotomized narrative forms (Us/Them) continue to shape the news. I also acknowledge that flak presents a relatively limited—but influential and growing—place within the sociopolitical arena. However, flak's impact is likely misunderstood in large part because flak campaigns are rarely identified as such. Flak's impact can be observed, even as flak itself remains largely unmentioned and shrouded in shadows. To my knowledge, there are no previous book-length treatments of flak as political harassment. To begin to remedy this previous lack of scrutiny, I will now drill down further into defining the contours of flak.

Beyond Bullshit: Defining the Term

As Terry Eagleton (1991) points out, ideology can be considered in at least some situations as a normatively neutral term, as everyone carries ideologies just as everyone hosts bacteria. To characterize something as flak is, as I am defining it, never neutral and always a criticism in the first instance. Flak is (pick one or more) weaponized, instrumentalized, contrived, spoofed, counterfeit, simulated—or, in Harry Frankfort's terms, encrusted with bullshit that even the cynical flak merchant may not even believe (2005).

What more specifically is flak? In the brutal concision of a few words, I define it as centered on *tactics and strategies toward political harassment*. Flak is enacted by powerful entities—or backed by powerful players in the wings—toward consequential sociopolitical objectives. It is distinct from good faith criticism (of a speech, of a bill) as well as from indiscriminant trolling against whomever is convenient. In this view, flak is a multidimensional form of weaponized political activity intended to attract notice, while it impedes or abolishes the effectiveness of its targets. Flak strategies and tactics toward these ends are not simply expressions of personal antipathy, but are driven by purposeful, ideologically-defined goals with tangible impact in the sociopolitical domain. Campaigns of astringent disparagement and delegitimation are perhaps the most straightforward tactics toward disabling a target's (or targets') effectiveness. These campaigns often aggressively kick-off by asserting the target to be, irreducibly and in essence, a problem (i.e., problematizing) or even criminal. It follows that the conduct of flak is regularly tendentious as well as contentious, and is often brazen about making moves (claims, actions) far outside of proportion or basis in evidence.[1]

As for power that I have characterized as nourishing flak, it can assume distinctly different forms with their associated modalities. Power can be analyzed in terms of its coercive, economic, political, and symbolic dimensions (Flew, 2007, pp. 4–8). While coercive power is not directly in play in this discussion, I posit flak as imbued with power's palpable economic, political, and symbolic dimensions. These dimensions can be converted into each other and then back again in an almost infinite loop. A tycoon or an industry consortium can exert economic power to fund "think tanks" or flak mills ostensibly characterized by intellectual rigor and authority. In turn, think tank symbolic power can be marshaled to reinforce the funders' bottom-line and economic power. Politicians can, for their part, rally to the think tank flak campaigns with slogans and bills (symbolic and political power). At the same time, flak memes can be peppered over the symbolic realm of discourse in media—and reinforce the same array of economic and political powers; and so on, ad infinitum.

In this view, power is not inert, nor is it simply some discrete force that one person exercises, cudgel-like, to make another person do something; the internalization of multidimensional power relations penetrate far deeper into a person's subjectivity and partly constitute him or her as, for example, a member of a socioeconomic class. While attentive to political and economic forms of power in the backstory of flak campaigns, I will largely focus on the symbolic dimensions of flak by analyzing flak discourses.

About those discourses: I am dwelling in the opening pages of this volume on flak's origins in the propaganda model to emphasize that my arguments are in no measure nostalgic for the late twentieth model of U.S. journalism. In terms compatible with the propaganda model, researchers have demonstrated that U.S. news media was failing to educate the public on high-consequence issues to a shocking extent during the era of professionalized, objective journalism; high-consequence issues that include, for example, the 1991 assault on Iraq (Clark, 1992; MacArthur, 1993) and the subsequent sanctions regime against Iraqi civilians during the 1990s (Gordon, 1999; Goss, 2002).

In this view, the RAND Corporation' recently minted concept of "truth decay" contributes a clever name to current scholarship on news (Kavanaugh & Rich, 2018). However, the truth decay analysis does not extend far enough in making its critique of what has been and what is wrong with news. To some extent, truth decay seeks to contain a contemporary crisis of authority and reassert "official" parameters of truth. In this manner, RAND's formulation of truth decay implies a nostalgic desire to re-enthrone the status quo antebellum of ostensibly "trusted" twentieth-century news; an outcome that is neither possible, nor desirable. A flak-grounded analysis harbors no nostalgia for the U.S. news model of the twentieth century that, metaphorically speaking, outfitted systemically skewed news in a "reassuring" suit-and-tie.

Having situated flak with respect to its eruption beyond its conceptual origins in the propaganda model, I will step back to examine what another series of events in 1988 augured for a future of heightened flak. I will then trace the path of flak's development to the new media era in 2016. The upshot of this discussion is to look in some detail at how flak, past and present, behaves in vivo, before fashioning a more systematic theoretical mapping of flak in Chapter 2.

1988: Duke of Hazard

The 1988 U.S. presidential election furnished a high-profile rehearsal for new logics of political discourse in which flak would become increasingly prevalent; a glimpse of an internet-memed future still to come.

In the summer of 1988, Michael S. Dukakis, Massachusetts governor and Democratic nominee for the U.S. presidency, appeared well-positioned to challenge for the White House. His standing in polls against sitting Vice-President George H.W. Bush was high with a steep 17-point advantage with voters by late July (DeCosta-Klipa, 2016). It may not be surprising that a decisive margin of voters pivoted to quasi-incumbent in Bush as summer gave way to autumn. However, the manner in which 1988's electoral turnaround played out is of interest. Specifically, the case of William Horton presents a keynote flak discourse that delivered for Bush against Dukakis. Kathleen Jamieson Hall's account of the 1988 election posits it as unusual to that moment in modern campaigning for its bare-knuckle qualities (1992). With the benefit of decades of hindsight, I suggest that the 1988 campaign can be construed as the missing-link to contemporary, flak-saturated politics.

The main blows at Dukakis' campaign concerned the Commonwealth of Massachusetts' prison furlough program. In the fall of 1988, the public was led to believe that the program was a shocking aberration, designed by the apparently depraved governor himself. In fact, Massachusetts' furlough program originated with Francis W. Sargent, Dukakis' Republican predecessor as governor (Jamieson, 1992, p. 20). Television ads about the furloughs conveyed flak memes with 30-second gut-punch force. "By juxtaposing words and pictures" in an audiovisual slight-of-hand, one TV ad primed the false inference that 268 first degree murderers had jumped furloughs in Massachusetts (Jamieson, 1992, p. 19). Another ad focused on the case of William Horton and implied that he was a poster-boy for the Dukakis-orchestrated mayhem supposedly unleashed during his governorship in Massachusetts (1975–1979, 1983–1991). The ad described Horton's furlough activities as "kidnaping," "stabbing" and "raping" (quoted in Jamieson, 1992, p. 17). In turn, the eruption of a new form of weaponized discourse wrong-footed Dukakis' campaign. The campaign initially ignored the ads as beneath contempt. By the time Dukakis pivoted to response, the flak toxins had circulated widely and the ads were recognized by a majority of voters who saw and recalled them (Jamieson, 1992, p. 36).

It is also important to notice that the ads were not the direct products of the Bush campaign. As Jamieson details, the ads originated with Bush-allied political action committees (PACs). Bush's campaign was thusly insulated from backlash if the ads were judged to have breached the perimeter of good taste and/or honesty. There were further unstated but visceral aspects to the Horton case as well. To wit, Horton is African-American, his victims

Euro-Americans, with all of the baggage that these optics have long mobilized in the US.

Once the inflammatory ads were in circulation, it became fair game to comment on and elaborate their content—as Bush obligingly did for the *New York Times* (Jamieson, 1992, p. 22). Even reporting that was critical of the ads fell into the sticky trap of reanimating their premises about Horton's menace and proximity to Dukakis' putatively skewed vision of law-and-order. In 1988, ads from PACs were the figurative crash-test dummies for flak memes that could jar public opinion—while simultaneously furnishing the beneficiaries of those memes with some distance from them. Distance, in turn, removed hints of grubby self-interest and provided cover should the delegitimizing flak discourse generate backlash.

Thirty years after Bush-Dukakis, what entities serve the flak purpose of injecting flak memes into wider public discourse? The answer is as large as the internet. YouTube or ostensible transparency, document-dump web sites can be conscripted to flak discourses and carry their flak memes far and wide— even all the way into mainstream media. Mark Turnbull, a managing director of Cambridge Analytica (CA), explained the logic while the now defunct company was practicing its dark political arts:

> We just put information into the bloodstream to the internet and then watch it grow, give it a little push now and again over time to watch it take shape. And so this stuff infiltrates the online community and expands but with no branding—so it's unattributable, untrackable. (quoted in Dallison, 2018, para. 13)

Following coverage of CA's previously secret methods—tenaciously pursued in the United Kingdom by *The Guardian*'s Carole Cadwalladr in the face of flak (Guardian News and Media Press Office, 2018)—the firm claimed insolvency. However, strategically (and clandestinely) injecting flak toxins into the political bloodstream is a practice that did not originate, nor will it end, with CA—although the firm added a data-driven thrust to these practices.

Fact-Checking the Flak

Returning to Dukakis-Bush 1988, one may ask what was wrong with the Horton ads. After all, it is a fact that Horton skipped the furlough from a Massachusetts prison, went AWOL to Maryland, slashed a man and raped his finance while holding them captive for hours; heinous crimes, by any standard.

To begin, *contra* the implications of the ad, "first degree murderers" were not eligible for furlough in Massachusetts. Moreover, jumping furlough was defined as being more than four hours late returning to prison—a rare event that occurred in 0.0036–percent of cases. Horton presented the *sole instance* (and *not* one of 268) of someone committing further serious crimes on furlough out of 76,455 furloughs in Massachusetts during three-term governor Dukakis' administration (Jamieson, 1992, p. 20).

The rationale of the furlough program was that prisoners who have limited release into the community prior to the end of their sentence are less likely to re-offend. If keeping people out of jail is the objective—as it should be, given the social and financial costs of incarceration—then there are empirically-backed logics for furloughs. These logics were also widely accepted by the 1980s. Jamieson observes that during the Reagan-Bush era, a similar furlough system was in place in the federal prison system—and Horton would have been eligible for a federal furlough at the time. Most U.S. states had similar furlough programs, including California during Reagan's governorship decades earlier. Yet, through the ideological alchemy of flak discourse, the Horton case was not a horrific instance that could regrettably have happened anywhere—but the efflux of the peculiar social laboratory convened in elitist Massachusetts by Harvard geek *cum* madman Dukakis.

To summarize, the 1988 flak discourse did not merely criticize, but crafted baldly misleading memes toward the strategic end of disabling Dukakis' campaign. Moreover, as it circulates, flak generates an aura of truth via sheer repetition, challenging the truth to catch up with its hoary discourse. As for Dukakis, he was sufficiently delegitimized by the 1988 campaign that he not only lost the election despite his summer lead in polls; he never ran for office again and was effectively retired from politics at age 57.

Audience Effects

In explaining the impact of the ads, Jamieson suggests that audiences to politics are often semi-distracted, observing from the corners of their eyes, scavenging fragments of discourse from the all-enveloping media environment. Moreover, information is not received in straightforward ways by audiences. Information is sculpted and reshaped while jostled within memory—not "filed away," then immaculately retrieved from a filing cabinet in the mind (Loftus & Loftus, 1980). Moreover, during electoral campaigns, information is collated through one's pre-standing sociopolitical beliefs and is more likely to be accepted if it is compatible with those beliefs (Flynn, Nyhan, & Reifler, 2017; Lazarsfeld, Berelson, & Gaudet, 1969, pp. 87–93).

Jamieson documents how these audience effects played out in 1988 via focus group data:

> 1: "We should ship all our criminals to the college liberals in College Station [Texas]."
> 2: "Or Austin. Crime's not statistics, honey."
> 4: Dukakis supporter (37-year old male): "But Bush's guy killed a pregnant woman, a halfway house, a parole place. That's no different from Dukakis, Massachusetts."
> 1: "That's not his [Bush's] fault." (Jamieson, 1992, p. 32)

And that is that: in indignant language, Dukakis is symbiotically tied to Horton. Bush is, by assertion, remote from the federal furlough machine and thus exonerated. In this case, flak memes around Dukakis may have stuck more readily for their repetition across media channels during the fall of 1988—as well as for their tightly tailored fit with decades of right-wing discourse about "law-and-order." It is an issue on which Republicans took ownership through aggressive repetition during the Nixon era—even as officials of Nixon's government were ushered into prison. Massachusetts/*Dukakisista* policies on furloughs were unremarkable by national standards, but readily articulated to long-standing flak discourses of the right vis-à-vis crime.

Nineteen eighty-eight's election witnessed startling memes, indirectly sourced through PACs then picked up by more mainstream media platforms; memes that were dishonest and played upon the audience's vulnerabilities as concerns keeping facts straight in a media-saturated world. All of this was further complicated by audience members' pre-standing ideologies. In each of these respects, the 1988 election's flak campaign anticipated the state of play for contemporary flak. Nonetheless, the practices of flak are not static—and there are indeed striking contemporary imprimaturs on it in a new media environment.

The Twenty-First Century's Planet of Flak

The 1988 campaign can be regarded in retrospect as a dress rehearsal for flak campaigns to come. A brief and necessarily partial look at the 2016 U.S. presidential election illuminates characteristics of the new flak order. Most obviously, the practices of flak have intensified since 1988. During the 2016 electoral debates, for example, Trump's talking points consists of rote concatenation of already established flak memes toward Hillary Clinton—in contrast with Bush in 1988 who ran on rarefied rhetoric and largely left the flak to subordinates and PAC players. Moreover, flak has been fully intertwined with the ongoing "communications revolution" of new media platforms. Along with its quantity and higher profile, flak is also more globalized at present than in 1988 in ways that will quickly become apparent.

Deep-context accounts of the 2016 election have already arrived via journalism (Harding, 2017) and academic investigation (Snyder, 2018) that pull together a wider narrative than I am attempting here. For the eager student of contemporary flak, the Intelligence Community Assessment (ICA) on the 2016 election is an original source of interest. The report was released in January 2017, two months after the 2016 election and weeks before Trump's team assumed office. The report collates the judgments of the Federal Bureau of Investigation (FBI), Central Intelligence Agency (CIA), and National Security Agency (NSA). I do not take it as my "job" to valorize the work of the alphabet-soup agencies as I work in the (more transparent, if disorderly) environment of a university—but am mindful of the agencies' research acumen, their formidable tools and workforce. In this case, their work clearly previewed the more elaborate findings of special counsel Robert S. Mueller III's full report in 2019.

ICA's report opens with blunt statements about the stakes around its investigation:

> Russian efforts to influence the 2016 U.S. presidential election represent the most recent expression of Moscow's longstanding desire to undermine the U.S.-led liberal democratic order, but these activities demonstrated a significant escalation in directness, level of activity, and scope of effort compared to previous operations.
>
> *We assess Russian President Vladimir Putin ordered an influence campaign in 2016 aimed at the U.S. presidential election. Russia's goals were to undermine public faith in the U.S. democratic process, denigrate Secretary Clinton, and harm her electability and potential presidency. We further assess Putin and the Russian Government developed a clear preference for President-elect Trump.* We have high confidence in these judgments. (original emphasis; Intelligence Community Assessment, 2017, p. ii)

These are bracing statements about the ambition of Russian activities and objectives. It bears further mention that Russia is not Canada; the MI6 intelligence service of the United States' closest ally, the United Kingdom, recently "reclassified Russia as a 'tier one' threat, alongside Islamic terrorism" by 2017 (Edwards, 2017, para. 1).

The U.S. intelligence community's account of Russian activity also squares with the characterization of flak discussed earlier. To wit, ICA appraises the

Kremlin as undertaking a delegitimization effort in support of Russia's strategic objectives—and its flak targets were not only personalized vis-à-vis Clinton, but ultimately directed at the bigger target of fundamental faith in the U.S. electoral system that makes the nation governable. ICA's further maintains that Russia, a hostile foreign power, assessed that Trump's ascendency was compatible with Russian interests. While Russian agents hacked material from "some Republican-affiliated targets," ICA concludes that Russia exclusively weaponized stolen material against Democrats (2017, p. 3).[2]

Had Clinton prevailed in the November 2016 election, Russia was also prepared to pour high-octane fuel on any brushfires of discontent in the United States over the result. Russian intelligence had already prepared the #DemocracyRIP hashtag to look like the work of indignant Americans, for the purpose of mobilizing doubts about Clinton, in particular—and the probity of U.S. electoral results, in general (2017, p. 2). Toward these strategic ends, Russian intelligence endowed its activities with the façade of being organic, U.S. domestic opposition, and not the work of a hostile foreign government.

Alongside cyber operations to spearfish and penetrate the Clinton campaign's computer networks, ICA reports that the Russian flak offensive featured more "above board" flak tactics. *RT* (formally called *Russia Today*) was the Kremlin-sponsored, English-language television network that answered the call (2017, pp. 6–12). RT went to the ramparts for Trump and against Clinton with repetition on flak memes about "her leaked emails [...], poor physical and mental health, and ties to Islamic extremism" (2017, p. 4). RT's most popular video, viewed more than nine million times, circulated under the flak claim, *How 100-Percent of the Clintons' Charity Went to … Themselves* (2017, p. 4).[3] RT ventured far beyond straightforward criticism of Clinton as claims were not only made in apparent bad faith but were loaded to delegitimize and even criminalize the target. Moreover, Russia's campaigns were not rolled up after the election in 2016. ICA assess that Russia's program of spearfishing U.S. government officials, thinks tanks and nongovernmental organizations continued, in the effort to gain advantages over the its foe, the United States (Intelligence Community Assessment, 2017, p. 5).

Mueller's GRU(e)some Indictment

A year-and-a-half later in 2018, *The United States of America versus Viktor Borisovich Netyksho, et al.* presents further interesting reading for the student of flak around the 2016 election. A product of the Robert S. Mueller III special counsel investigation, the indictment provides operational detail about the activities flagged in the ICA's report in 2017. Mueller (2018) mainly focuses on the Main Directorate of the General Staff of the Armed Forces of the Russian Federation, known in the west by the acronym GRU; a notoriously severe outfit even by the standards of military intelligence. However, in this episode, GRU was more concerned with killing campaigns and reputations via flak than people.

According to Mueller's indictment, GRU operatives hacked email accounts "of volunteers and employees of the U.S. presidential campaign of Hillary Clinton," including her campaign chair John Podesta (2018, p. 2). Once email accounts were compromised, Russian military intelligence stole documents, logged keystrokes, and made screen shots of Clinton campaign workers' computers. All of this was undertaken by a "tier one" threat, eager to weaponize the information it was gathering to flak against its disfavored candidate. Toward this strategic end, "By in or around June 2016," Russia's GRU had "gained access to approximately 33 DNC [Democratic Party National Committee] computers" (Mueller, 2018, p. 10).

In line with a flak strategy, the stolen communications were subjected to "stage releases" for political impact at crucial intervals of the 2016 campaign. The objective was "to interfere" with the election—and to do so in ways that flaked Clinton to Trump's advantage (Mueller, 2018, p. 2). Document dumps of the pilfered materials were made through "fictitious online persons"—Guccifer 2.0 and DCLeaks—in order to conceal Russia's hand. Mueller's indictment notes that GRU agents "created the online persona Guccifer 2.0" that was "falsely claimed to be a lone Romanian hacker" (2018, p. 14). DCLeaks, launched in June 2018, was proclaimed with similar speciousness to have been "started by a group of 'American hacktivists' when it was in fact started by the [GRU] Conspirators" (2018, p. 13). In both cases, the GRU fronts were designed to exude the "white hat" prestige of being concerned (h)ac(k)tivists. DCLeaks' hashtag was subsequently used to organize flash mobs against Clinton as well as to post images from #BlacksAgainstHillary in an attempt to demobilize a core Democratic Party constituency.

GRU also employed these fronts to recruit other players to spread the hacked booty and damage Clinton's campaign: "the Conspirators, posing as Guccifer 2.0, transferred approximately 2.5 gigabytes of data stolen from the DNCC [Democratic Party National Congressional Committee] to a then-registered state lobbyist and online source of political news" (2018, p. 16). Through the Guccifer 2.0 persona, GRU shared its ill-begotten wares with two reporters and "a person who was in regular contact with senior members of the presidential campaign of Donald J. Trump" (2018, p. 16). The stolen booty was also shared with an organization named in the indictment as "Organization 1," understood to be WikiLeaks. In turn, Mueller's indictment cites communications between GRU/Guccifer 2.0 and WikiLeaks about how to make the pilfered material "have a much a higher impact" (2018, p. 18)—a central flak objective since flak, by definition, does not seek to "inform" but to delegitimize and disable.

WikiLeaks made good on its promise for impact through timing. It released a tranche of GRU-stolen materials three days before the Democratic Party convention in July 2016. The timing furnished enough news cycles before the convention to provoke internal dissension and the resignation of the party's chairperson—and generally conjured rainclouds of distraction over Clinton's formal nomination as the first woman standard-bearer for a major U.S. party. The revelations from the vast trove of stolen materials were damp squibs, what I will later conceptualize as faux (or phantom) flak. However, within the regime of faux flak, the mere suggestion that "something bad" was in the lode of documents was *in itself* enough to nourish finger-wagging flak-memes about wrongdoing.

Stone Cold Flak

Mueller (2018) focuses on GRU's processes of hacking material later used for flak purposes. Mueller's subsequent indictment in January 2019, *United States of America versus Roger Jason Stone, Jr.* (2019) sheds further light on the GRU's development of flak narratives against Clinton to be channeled to the U.S. public.

Mueller assesses Stone as implicated in an effort to obtain and then disseminate "emails damaging to the Clinton campaign" (Mueller, 2019, p. 2). Toward this end, Stone was in contact with "a senior, Trump campaign official," among other interlocutors, discussing the timing and likely influence of the document dumps while he also coordinated with WikiLeaks (2019, p. 3). "Impact [of the document dumps] planned to be very damaging," the indictment's "Person 1" (Jerome Corsi) explains to Stone as the clandestine flak campaign played out in summer 2016. Person 1 further elaborates the flak campaign talking points to Stone: "Would not hurt to start suggesting HRC [Hillary Rodham Clinton] old, memory bad, has stroke—neither he nor she well [...] setting stage for [Clinton] Foundation debacle" (quoted in Mueller, 2019, pp. 4–5).

In these flak meme rehearsals, Clinton is not simply wrong on some or even most all issues—but is broadly unfit for office due to physical and moral decrepitude. Stone and his interlocutors eagerly anticipated "October Surprise" weaponized flak memes to blow up in Clinton's face in the endgame of the election and sink the Democrats' campaign. In the event, no full-blown scandals arose from the dissemination of the Clinton campaigns' hacked emails. However, that is not the standard that flak merchants need to meet. The news itself of 50,000 documents released to the public (too much material for anyone to read in short order) is *in and of itself* taken as casting suspicion on the victim, regardless of whether the emails reveal anything beyond office bitching and operational details. The very fact of hacks and subsequent leaks also lent themselves to residual flak "fringe benefits." That is, news narratives projected Clinton's campaign as a loose or sinking ship, on the defensive, needing to raise its voice over the din about emails in the effort to get its message out.

Impacts: Flak Delivers More Than Pizza

One revelation in the hacked emails concerned a pizza restaurant that Clinton campaign chair John Podesta frequented. This explosive discovery prompted the meme that the—non-existent—basement of the pizza establishment was the site of a child pornography ring. Among other clues, "child porn" and "cheese pizza" share the acronym "CP" (the phrase "one could not make these things up" comes to mind here). In short order, the pizza restaurant was stormed by an armed gunman, thankfully without fatalities, as flak to murder an election campaign almost spiraled into murdering people (Pilkington, 2019).

Pizza aside, Kathleen Hall Jamieson (2018) analyzes the 2016 election at book length in *Cyberwar*; a volume that she pointedly titled in order to emphasize the stakes. In Jamieson's appraisal, Russia's interventions in the 2016 election far exceed anodyne characterizations such as meddling—and they were likely decisive to the electoral outcome. As in her analysis of 1988, Jamieson does not employ the term flak in her discussion. However, her analysis squares with a flak-based understanding of the campaign to slime Clinton with delegitimizing memes and to prop up Trump.

Jamieson argues that Russia's covert activities in the run-up to the election were not necessarily designed to change votes from "blue" to "red"; a tall order, as it implicates changing minds and even subjectivities to switch party allegiances in a narrow timeframe. Instead, demobilizing core Democratic constituencies from voting was a reachable goal in a flak framework—and one less vote for a candidate amounts to the same in the final electoral tally as one more vote in the other candidate's column. Votes could be siphoned off by raising doubts about Clinton among wavering voters who leaned Democrat with whom Clinton's campaign was assaying to close the deal in the campaign endgame. Targeted flak in these cases could crucially drain motivation to vote, or nudge voters away from Clinton toward a third-party candidate. Moreover, social media data exhaust was sufficient to identify voters with a wavering profile.

Jamieson argues that the U.S. media system unwittingly channeled the Kremlin's flak campaign that denigrated Clinton and put wind under the wings of Trump's often faltering campaign. This was in part due to the U.S. media's fixation on melodramatically narrating elections through the lens of which side is apparently winning or losing the momentum game. By contrast with the United States in 2016, Jamieson observes that Russian interventions (for Marine Le Pen, against Emmanuel Macron) fell flat in France's 2017 election. French journalists largely ignored hacked information, rather than copiously laundering it into the news hole, as they instead tracked issues.

Jamieson (2018) cites examples of memes drawn from the hacked material that were insinuated into the 2016 election discourse during candidate debates witnessed by 60–70 million viewers. In one of several such moments during the debates, Clinton was asserted to advocate for "open borders," based on the hacked materials; in the hacked source material, she was referring to an energy grid in South America. Clinton's comments were subsequently, selectively and disingenuously, cut-and-pasted into the debate to signify purported retreat from any form of border control around the United States. The meme was purportedly grounded in Clinton's unguarded words and authentic views—rather than a disingenuous flak-glossed version of them—that also chimed with Trumpian border fetishism. In turn, the meme also resonated with the decades-long construction of Clinton as two-faced and harboring hidden agendas. By contrast, Trump gained a boost in the agora of personality perceptions when unashamed boorishness was conflated with authenticity.

Jane Mayer reports that more front-page *New York Times* space was devoted to Clinton's emails during a week in October when undecided voters were making up their minds than was devoted to both candidates' policy packages during months of campaign coverage; the emails had, in turn, become a flak shorthand code for "something amiss" with Clinton. Mainstream news narrative constructions that seek two-sides-of-every-issue "symmetry" further enabled flak—to Kremlin specifications, laundered through WikiLeaks, and favorable to Trump's interests. In particular, Trump was on the ropes on 7 October as the Director of National Intelligence announced an assessment of Russian interference in the U.S. election. Hours later, Trump's audio-recorded enthusiasms for assaulting women by genital grab was published. A flak response to these well-grounded narratives was swift: thirty minutes after the genital grab recording's release, WikiLeaks shifted the narrative arc of the news by publishing purloined emails from Podesta's account. The stories about the two campaigns were, in turn, treated as symmetrical in their suggestions of wrongdoing—and the sensation of private emails, with the promise of scandal *somewhere* within them, blunted the body blows to Trump's campaign with a flak *deus-ex-machina*.

On the basis of her study, Jamieson concludes that it is "'likely'" that Russia's flak-oriented interventions to problematize and delegitimize one candidate flipped the result of the 2016 U.S. presidential election (quoted in Mayer, 2018, para. 9). James Clapper, the US' Director of National Intelligence in 2016, similarly posits that "it stretches credulity to think the Russians didn't turn the election outcome" (quoted in Mayer, 2018, para. 3). The George W. Bush-era director of the Central Intelligence Agency, Michael Hayden, appraised the Russian intervention as "the most successful covert influence operation in history" (quoted in Mayer, 2018, para. 47). And flak was written into the Russian intervention's genetic makeup. At the same time, it should not be forgotten that Trump claimed 60-million votes; that is alarming in itself given the candidate's policy package, record and conduct, although it likely would not have put him over the electoral hump without the flak enabled by the Kremlin's helping hands.

Conclusion

Thus far, I have proceeded through paired case studies of flak in the electoral arena while flagging, on the fly, features of the flak regime. In the following chapter, I will extend the arc of this introduction by fleshing out flak in further detail, addressing its scope and sub-types while marking flak's important differences from other concepts (scandal, activism). The upshot of these efforts will be to turn the scrutiny away from flak targets and toward flak merchants and practices, to pull flak out its shadowy origins.

At the same time, the focus in this volume may seem one-sided in suggesting that flak campaigns are associated with the political right. I acknowledge the association in this volume—but have no apology to make for it. That is, left-wing flak does exist. A figure such as Walter Palmer—notorious midwestern dentist and killer of Cecil the Lion in Zimbabwe—can be said to be a subject of left-leaning flak, on the assumption that animal rights is a more left-oriented issue. However, in gazing out onto the world, I am seeing one side of the political spectrum that is taking ownership over the practices of flak along with exhibiting undisguised contempt for fair play that puts political faction (and not country) first. Some of the discourses and actions that I have in mind include Senate Republicans' refusal to honor lawful precedent in acting on presidential nomination for the Supreme Court in 2016 during Barack H. Obama's last year on office (Faris, 2018).

The right has also become comfortable in routinely criminalizing its political opponents on flimsy, flak-driven grounds. In this vein, Michael Flynn, one of 2016's leading campaign rally chanters of the "lock her [Clinton] up" flak mantra, has so far evaded prison time as a felon via plea bargaining. As a former Republican operative, Elise Jordan, observed with disgust, Republican candidates involved in close election races in 2018 lividly screamed fraud at their opponents. With the exception of Martha McSally during her narrow Senate loss in Arizona, Republicans succumbed to the flak reflex to criminalize their opponents when election results were tight, drawing as they did so upon flak tropes that I will elaborate in Chapter 5 (Jordan, 2018).

What I am calling right-wing does not implicate classically conservative traditionalists and communitarians who preserve the rhythms of life through slow, measured change; the kind of people who inhabit the idealized worlds of Norman Rockwell images, although Rockwell's fictional people can have their real world concomitants. A figure such as John S. McCain III, Republican Party candidate for president in 2008, may fit this bill for his communitarian respect for the nation's traditions; a flawed politician for whom I, for one, would not vote but who engendered respect even from ideological opponents for "conserving" the nation's better political practices that include owning up to errors. By the end of his life, it is fair to assess that a conservative such as McCain was an awkward fit in an increasingly right-wing party.

The flak campaigns that I focus on in this book, in one way or another, all come back to a resolute right-wing concern with re-enthroning primitive, illiberal hierarchy. Right-wingers are not conservative, nor concerned with exalting community or gradual reform; explosive and destructive movement is their bag. The flak campaigns that I examine assay, for example, to de-tax and de-regulate capitalism to law-of-the jungle specifications that extend the continued authority of pollution industries. Flak is similarly deployed to broadly attack universities that are engines of positive innovations, such as scientific discoveries, as well as enabling social mobility for students. Right-wing flak is also mobilized to denigrate access to the franchise that gives voice via the vote to the masses; votes that are, in turn, a channel of political accountability to the wider public. By contrast, flak memes construct voting as a fount of criminality for the flak strategic objective of culling the voter rolls.

I focus on flak by the political right given that, on each of these significant issues, flak has found a far more comfortable home on that side of the political spectrum. In this view, flak has been weaponized for the rightist objective of sabotaging progress toward equality and reinvigorating hard-core, pre-liberal social stratification.

Notes

1. Flak typically does not engender illegal activity in the United States in large part because speech laws and their interpretation have tended toward a strong version of classical liberalism. Libel is, by design, exceedingly difficult to prove under US law (Campbell, 2003, pp. 545–549). Robust liberalism in speech rights readily enables flak campaigns that may paradoxically channel illiberal ideologies.
2. In my appraisal, the infinitely better candidate in 2016 faced extraordinary obstacles in having her campaign's communications hacked then leaked. I posit that Clinton's campaign nevertheless let the public down in failing to drive a stake into an opposing candidate unprecedented in lack of qualifications and fitness for office.
3. Despite extensive document dumps around the Clinton Foundation, it has not been shown to be athwart of any laws; not so the now defunct Trump Foundation and its carnival of vanity and corruption. New York's Attorney General describes the state's 2018 lawsuit against Trump Foundation as driven by "a shocking pattern of illegality […] including unlawful coordination with the Trump presidential campaign, repeated and willful self-dealing, and much more" (Letitia James New York Attorney General, 2018, para. 5).

References

Campbell, R. (2003). *Media and culture*. Boston: Bedford/St. Martin's.
Clark, R. (1992). *The fire this time*. New York: Thunder's Mouth Press.
Curran, J., Fenton, N., & Freedman, D. (2016). *Misunderstanding the internet*. London: Routledge.
Dallison, P. (2018). Cambridge Analytica Suspends CEO Alexander Nix. *Politico*, 22 March. Retrieved from www.politico.eu/article/cambridge-analytica-boss-boasts-about-role-in-trump-campaign/.

DeCosta-Klipa, N. (2016). Michael Dukakis is here to remind you why to stop overreacting to the recent election polls. *Boston Globe*, 1 June. Retrieved from www.boston.com/news/politics/2016/06/01/michael-dukakis-remind-stop-overreacting-recent-election-polls.

Eagleton, T. (1991). *Ideology: An introduction*. London: Verso.

Edwards, J. (2017). British security services are vastly outgunned by the Russian counterintelligence threat. *Business Insider*, 3 December. Retrieved from www.businessinsider.com/british-security-services-vs-russian-counterintelligence-threat-2017-12?IR=T.

Faris, D. (2018). *It's time to fight dirty*. New York: Melville House Publishing.

Fenton, N. (2010). *New media, old news*. Los Angeles: Sage.

Flew, T. (2007). *Understanding global media*. London: Palgrave MacMillan.

Flynn, D.J., Nyhan, B., & Reifler, J. (2017). The nature and origins of misperceptions. *Political Psychology*, 38(S1), 127–150.

Frankfort, H. (2005). *On bullshit*. Princeton, NJ: Princeton University Press.

Gordon, J. (1999). Sanctions as siege warfare. *The Nation*, 4 March. Retrieved from www.thenation.com/article/sanctions-siege-warfare/.

Goss, B.M. (2002). "Deeply concerned about the welfare of the Iraqi people": The sanctions regime against Iraq in *The New York Times* (1996–98). *Journalism Studies*, 3(1), 83–99.

Goss, B.M. (2009). "The left-media's stranglehold": Flak and accuracy in media reports (2007–08). *Journalism Studies*, 10(4), 455–473.

Goss, B.M. (2013). *Rebooting the Herman and Chomsky propaganda model in the twenty-first century*. New York: Peter Lang.

Guardian News and Media Press Office. (2018). Carole Cadwalladr wins Reporters without Borders L'Esprit de RSF prize for Cambridge Analytica reporting, 9 November. Retrieved from www.theguardian.com/gnm-press-office/2018/nov/09/carole-cadwalladr-wins-reporters-without-borders-lesprit-de-rsf-prize-for-cambridge-analytica-reporting.

Harding, L. (2017). *Collusion*. New York: Vintage Books.

Herman, E., & Chomsky, N. (1988). *Manufacturing consent*. New York: Pantheon.

Intelligence Community Assessment. (2017). *Assessing Russian activities and intentions in recent U.S. elections*. Washington, DC: Office of the Director of National Intelligence.

Jamieson, K.H. (1992). *Dirty politics*. Oxford, UK: Oxford University Press.

Jamieson, K.H. (2018). *Cyberwar*. Oxford, UK: Oxford University Press.

Jordan, E. (2018). I've worked in Republican politics; the party's voter suppression in the midterms has been a disgrace. *Time*, 15 November. Retrieved from news.yahoo.com/ve-worked-republican-politics-party-142624012.html.

Kavanagh, J., & Rich, M.D. (2018). *Truth decay*. Santa Monica, CA: RAND Corporation.

Lazarsfeld, P.F., Berelson, B., & Gaudet, H. (1969). *How the voter makes up his mind in a presidential campaign*. New York: Columbia University Press.

Letitia James New York Attorney General. (2018). A.G. Underwood announces stipulation dissolving Trump Foundation under judicial supervision, with AG review of recipient charities, 18 December. Retrieved from ag.ny.gov/press-release/ag-underwood-announces-stipulation-dissolving-trump-foundation-under-judicial.

Loftus, E.F., & Loftus, G.R. (1980). On the permanence of stored information in the human brain. *American Psychologist*, 35(5), 409–420.

MacArthur, J.R. (1993). *Second front*. Berkeley, CA: University of California Press.
Mayer, J. (2018). How Russia helped swing the election for Trump. *New Yorker*, 24 September. Retrieved from www.newyorker.com/magazine/2018/10/01/how-russia-helped-to-swing-the-election-for-trump.
Morozov, E. (2011). *The net delusion*. London: Allen Lane.
Mueller, R.S. III. (2018). *United States of America versus Viktor Borisovich Netyksho, et al.* Washington, DC: United States District Court.
Mueller, R.S. III. (2019). *United States of America versus Roger Jason Stone, Jr.* Washington, DC: United States District Court.
Peters, C., & Broersma, M. (2013). *Rethinking journalism*. London: Routledge.
Pilkington, E. (2019). Trapped in a hoax. *The Guardian*, 24 January. Retrieved from www.theguardian.com/technology/2019/jan/23/conspiracy-theories-internet-survivors-truth.
Snyder, T. (2018). *The road to unfreedom*. New York: Tim Duggan Books.

· 2 ·

"BOW THE KNEE TO THIS NEW DICTATORSHIP": THE MANY FACES OF FLAK

Introduction: Collateral Flak Damage

Before elaborating a theory of flak, I will begin by considering the impact on a person's life to be implicated in a mediatized flak storm.

As is widely known, President William J. Clinton was impeached by the U.S. House of Representatives, then acquitted by the Senate in 1998–99. The series of events was a spin-off from an affair that he had with an intern that, in turn, was a spin-off of a special counsel's investigation of an unrelated matter. I posit this tawdry series of episodes that clotted the U.S. political stage during most of the 1990s as flak in search of a real scandal. The investigation originated with the contrived Whitewater investigations of a resort development deal in Arkansas in the late 1970s. Bill and Hillary Clinton lost money as the deal collapsed, in part due to an unscrupulous and erratic business partner (Conason & Lyons, 2000). In turn, their partner James B. MacDougal was later convicted of 18 felonies around his stewardship of a savings and loan institution.

Fast-forwarding to the 1990s, Whitewater hypertrophied into "at least four separate but overlapping federal probes" into the Clintons, at a cost of $50 million (Qui, 2015). And the outcome of the high-powered investigatory efforts, contrived by the Republican Party opposition? While the drumbeat of flak insinuation echoed across news cycles for six years, the series of special counsels scrutinizing the Clintons came up empty handed on Whitewater—albeit, not for lack of time and effort. The special counsel's final report in 2000 "concluded that there was insufficient evidence to show that either President Clinton or his wife, Hillary Rodham Clinton, had committed any crimes in connection with the Arkansas real estate venture that vexed his presidency through two terms" (Lewis, 2000, para. 1). Indeed, fifteen prosecutions occurred around MacDougal's savings and loan—against grifters such as MacDougal himself and Clinton accuser/opportunist David Hale—as part of the 1980s deregulation-enabled crime wave in the savings and loan industry (Pizzo, Fricker, & Muolo, 1989); a wave on which the Clintons were not riding, but that crashed on them via the later political flak storm.

The special counsel's null finding in 2000 against the Clintons was no surprise. By 1996, the Senate's Special Committee to Investigate Whitewater Development Corporation and Related Matters had "deposed 274 witnesses and held 60 days of public hearings, during which 136 witnesses testified" (Special Committee to Investigate Whitewater Development Corporation and Related Matters, 1996, p. 1). Under the direction of Chair Alfonse M. D'Amato, Republican of New York, the Committee parsed approximately one million pages of documents submitted by the Clintons, the White House, federal agencies and witnesses. What did this massive sleuthing effort uncover? In a word, nothing: page 466 of the Special Committee's Final Report pithily concludes, "The evidence demonstrated that no improprieties occurred in connection with any of these areas of inquiry" as concerned Whitewater and the Clintons.[1]

Investigations into Whitewater and related phantom scandals limped on for several more years after D'Amato's committee came up with nil. Flaking to pretend a scandal is in motion can almost be as good as the real item; that is, when the charade generates news coverage that flags a "problem" with *something* as concerns the flak target. Scrutiny into Clinton was a matter of investigating a person to find a wrongdoing—in contrast with the normal procedure of investigating a wrongdoing to find the person (or people) who did it. In any event, the Whitewater pantomimes finally tripped onto the peepshow optics of sex scandal in which the sitting president had inappropriate relations.

In 2017, following the death of Roger Ailes, Monica Lewinsky described having been dragooned into the 1990s Clinton flak wars. Ailes was the head of the (at the time, fledgling) Fox News network when the scandal exploded in 1998—and he "made certain his anchors hammered" at the sex scandal, "ceaselessly, 24 hours a day" (Lewinsky, 2017, para. 2). At least one Fox executive posits that coverage of whether Lewinsky was a "tramp" heralded the tabloid circus that propelled the network from curiosity to powerhouse (Lewinsky, 2017, para. 8).

Lewinsky, 24-years old when the scandal erupted, recalls that, "My character, my looks, and my life were picked apart mercilessly. Truth and fiction mixed at random"—but not in a college campus dining hall, but for the whole world and "in the service of higher ratings" (2017, para. 5). "No rumor was too unsubstantiated, no innuendo too vile" for Fox as it torched Clinton with Lewinsky as tertiary target (2017, para. 6). Lewinsky was concerned about being indicted and could not readily leave her house for fear of being pursued by a news media scrum. Not surprisingly, the young woman entertained thoughts of suicide. Lewinsky also observes that an online platform, Drudge Report, broke the news of the affair that then cascaded onto more mainstream platforms—a pattern still evident in which flak campaigns often originate under the radar. While the now-middle aged Lewinsky has gone on to a productive life, an extraordinary testimony to her character, what she experienced when flak against Clinton graduated into scandal presents a bracing vision of how devastating a harassment campaign can be.

A Road Map

Having briefly considered the phenomenal experience of being caught in a flak-to-scandal campaign, I will attempt a more fine-grained account of what flak is. This chapter's efforts at fleshed-out definition will implicate flak's relation to scandal; its scale; the contrast between flak-in-discourse and flak-in-action; the taxonomy of targets toward which flak is directed; and what flak is not (fake news, conspiracy theory, activism). At the same time, while this investigation is not a media effects study, flak's mediated dimensions necessarily implicate audiences. Thus, the discussion begs the question of how audiences decode texts—as well as the question of how audiences are constituted in the twenty-first century in ways that dovetail with flak. A brisk history of post-World War II concepts of the audience, an indispensable element of a flak campaign, initiates the discussion.

Re-Inventing the Audience

The State project of unlocking the secrets of the audience was present at the establishment of communication as an academic discipline within the Cold War environment (Simpson, 1994). Human cognition and behavior is embedded within embodied experience and an infinite regress of social contexts within social contexts; and, for this reason, the project of predicting and controlling audience behavior has long been a conundrum. During the Cold War, Bernard Berelson and collaborators acknowledged they came up short in ascertaining what moved the needle for an audience: "Some kinds of communication [...] on some kinds of issues, brought to some kinds of people under some kinds of conditions, have some kinds of effects" (Berelson et al., quoted in Franklin, 2004, p. 207).

In the same era, Paul Lazarsfeld and colleagues venture a more definite account of the audience through their concept of reinforcement effect (Lazarsfeld, Berelson, & Gaudet, 1969). They report that, during an election campaign, audience members seek out messages that confirm pre-standing predilections that "close the deal" for their vote. At the same time, the researchers conclude that audience members construct figurative walls to thwart discordant messages. In this manner, Lazarsfeld and colleagues posit audiences as actively parsing messages as well as being conditioned by social influences (e.g., co-workers respected for knowledge) situated between an audience member and the text.

With the advent of Cultural Studies after the 1960s, audiences were endowed with further powers by academic observers of them. For cultural studies scholars, audience members were generally envisioned as active decoders in partly or globally rejecting mediated premises as, for example, primers for celebration of classism (Hall, 1993). Decoding models developed in the mid-twentieth were nonetheless grounded in a media environment with far fewer broadcast platforms. In the 1970s, audiences in the United States essentially had three television networks (NBC, CBS, and ABC) from which to forage for their nightly programming. As a result, researchers could assume heterogeneous audiences to the era's dominant television medium that were exposed to similar content. When everyone—from school children to grandmas, from all regions and social classes—saw similar programming, it was easy to begin with the premise that different audience members decode *Laverne and Shirley* very differently.

Beginning with the dissemination of cable television in the 1980s, mass broadcast audiences began to splinter, driven by the marriage of new technology to capitalist logics of audience segmentation into more striated market niches. Segmentation enables far more precise advertising appeals tailored to audience demographics and psychographics, beginning with the audience's class characteristics (Hesmondhalgh, 2010, pp. 288–289).

Theorizations of media power that Des Freedman (2014) dubs "control models" assume strong media effects (audience moved this way and that, as if by joystick)—and they have long been marginal in media studies. Indeed, by the twenty-first century, investigators gleefully turned control models on their heads; audiences were not controlled by mass media, in this view, but had become increasingly important producers of discourse. Dan Gillmor's *We the media* (2004) and Clay Shirky's *Here comes everybody* (2008) insist on utopian hopes come true on new media platforms. The global brain's crowd wisdom was posited as plugged in and the so-called ex-audience had commandeered the printing presses. In *Bloggers on the bus*, Eric Boehlert (2009) envisions news media's monopoly on insider-oriented news as broken, to the benefit of independent journalism and a better-informed public. Sophisticated blogs, such as Glenn Greenwald's *Unclaimed territory*, could and did attract audiences of hundreds-of-thousands in startlingly short intervals (Boehlert, 2009, pp. 179–192), a democratization of the printing press not previously observed.

As is now more widely appreciated, new media has also unleashed a regime of fine print (Sterne, 2012), appropriation by illiberal regimes (Morozov, 2011) and *Stasi*-plus surveillance (Goodman, 2015). Moreover, after a couple of decades of shakeout, new media has replicated many of the features (concentration of wealth, power and audiences) of the dinosaur media that it ostensibly supplanted (Fuchs, 2014). Twentieth-century media was *mass* media and it attempted to synchronize a collective heartbeat for society through shared mediated experience that reached most all of society—a Sisyphean task, for reasons given. However, in a neoliberal era of pervasive audience surveillance and mass customization/market segmentation (Andrejevic, 2004), there is no logic to even support an effort to convene the whole nation together. Instead, "killer facts" and narratives effectively seek out their audience niches. On social media, unwanted or jarring messages can be shunted off by the silent work of the algorithmic filter bubble that is, in turn, fueled by data mining toward finely-grained audience segmentation. As Delia Dumitrica observes, the tailoring of messages on Facebook is relentless and creates an apparently seamless ecosystem glossed as one's preferred, "natural" habitat: "My identity, my friends, my world: the Facebook mediated global imaginary rests upon (the illusion of) choice. Today, choice is the epitome of agency, as well as a core neoliberal value" (Dumitrica, 2016, p. 199).

In turn, audience surveillance for purposes of prediction and control has achieved very high levels of sophistication. Facebook "Likes" furnish a powerful psychographic portrait of a person to whom well-tailored messages can be directed. Marcel Kosinski and colleagues explain the state of the science by 2013: "Facebook Likes, can be used to automatically and accurately predict a range of highly sensitive personal attributes including: sexual orientation, ethnicity, religious and political views, personality traits, intelligence, happiness, use of addictive substances, parental separation, age, and gender" (Kosinski, Stillwell, & Graepel, 2013, p. 5802). Kosinski and colleagues' conclusions are grounded in a massive sample "of over 58,000 volunteers who provided their Facebook Likes, detailed demographic profiles, and the results of several psychometric tests" (2013, p. 5802). After extracting out which "likes" cluster together and correlate with what traits from the psychometric tests, Kosinski and colleagues constructed models that can make accurate inferences about Facebook users. In turn, these inferences lend themselves to well-tailored, psychographics-informed messaging.

In follow-up studies, the efficacy of Facebook data for tailored messaging has been empirically confirmed across very large populations using "ecologically-valid" (non-laboratory) methods. Kosinski and colleagues report that inferences from even a small number of Facebook likes powerfully heightens the impact of targeted messages on observable behaviors: "In three field experiments that reached over 3.5 million individuals with psychologically tailored advertising, we find that matching the content of persuasive appeals to individuals' psychological characteristics significantly altered their behavior as measured by clicks and purchases" (Matz, Kosinski, Nave, & Stillwell, 2017, p. 12714). Facebook likes enable inferences into personality, for example, tendencies toward introversion/extraversion and open/closed postures toward new experience. Utilizing these inferences to tailor messages shows notable effects across large audiences: "Persuasive appeals that were matched to people's extraversion or openness-to-experience level resulted in up to 40-percent more clicks and up to 50-percent more purchases" as compared with control groups (2017, p. 12714). Messages that are 40- or 50-percent more likely to elicit the messenger's desired response can be said to have gone an appreciable distance toward prediction and control over audience response.

Fast-forwarding to the heat of the 2016 presidential campaign, Alexander Nix (2016) of Cambridge Analytica discusses the use of psychographics in political advertising. In particular, the model that Nix endorses as powerful captures an audience member's openness to experience, conscientiousness, extraversion, agreeableness, and neuroticism (acronymized as OCEAN). Informed by data-driven precision, a pro-gun ad can be designed on the assumption that distinctly different, psychographics-rooted motivations can stimulate a person's support for guns. Pro-gun ads can thusly be designed for framing around safety (e.g., "your home invaded")—or, alternatively, around tradition that appeals to arms passed "from father to son," in a traditional androgenic lineage (Nix, 2016). In other words, psychographic approaches assay to take the pulse of motivations and the internal lives of specific audience members—and do so for instrumental purposes of blasting impactful messages directed at a particular person's psychological makeup.

In this environment that draws on detailed portraits of audience members, the producers of messages encounter far less guesswork and risk of having their messages ignored. Messages can be designed to more readily push a given person's idiosyncratic buttons than the billboard by the highway that radiates the same message to all who pass it. Control model visions of "hypodermic needle" messaging injected directly into the audience may never be realized. Nevertheless, psychographics-informed messaging can plausibly take significant steps toward heightened prediction and control of audience reactions when applied on a mass scale.

The implications for flak are straightforward as concerns crafting messages that will reach an audience member's wheelhouse, wherever it may be. Moreover, flak memes more readily gain legs under them by making a debut before what could be called "a pre-existing hostile audience" that is inclined to seize on the negativism of flak toward a disfavored entity (Katherine Cross, quoted in Jeong, 2018, p. 25); it is also the type of like-minded audience that is also far easier to convene in a segmented media environment.

Two phenomena of further interest to the study of flak gain impetus in the new millennium's new media environment: directional motivation and illusory truth. As concerns the former, D.J. Flynn and colleague's recent review of the literature suggests movement full circle back to Lazarsfeld: "Directionally motivated reasoning leads people to seek out information that reinforces their preferences (i.e., confirmation bias), counterargue information that contradicts their preferences (i.e., disconfirmation bias), and view proattitudinal information as more convincing than counterattitudinal information" (2017, p. 132). Flynn and colleagues are not optimistic about how, within an avalanche of messages, audiences resolve the tension between sorting out the truth and finding reinforcement: "Facts are always at least potentially vulnerable to directional motivated reasoning, especially when they are politicized by elites." As a result, contemporary political conflict is not simply arguing over the narrower matters of "issues and public policy, *but over reality itself*" (emphasis added; Flynn, Nyhan, & Reifler, 2017, p. 144). When a concept of shared reality itself becomes increasingly contested, flak correspondingly thrives in the hot-house of ideologically-driven niches.

The concept of illusory truth also furnishes impetus for making outlandish claims in service of flak to influence audiences. Gordon Pennycook and colleagues (2018) report a series of experiments in which subjects appraise demonstrated-to-be-false headlines as significantly more plausible for having previously seen them only one time. The effect of even one prior exposure on plausibility measurably endures for at least a week. Wholly implausible control condition statements get no such boost for familiarity (e.g., positing the Earth is square), while true statements still rate higher than false ones. Nonetheless, the study underlines the incentive to move the needle of opinion via repeated tendentious statements, since the feeling of familiarity in having "heard this one before" is readily conflated with plausibility.

Indeed, the audience may not even be the flesh-and-blood audience anymore—at least not completely. The strategic use of bots and cyborg social media accounts can be managed to move the needle of opinion, in part, by circumventing the need to influence the minds of real persons. Molly K. McKew (2018) of the New Media Frontier details one such campaign in 2018. The campaign pushed Congressperson Devin Nunes' so-called "intelligence memo" that flaked Foreign Intelligence Surveillance Act (FISA) courts to Trumpian specifications. Deliberate coordination and amplification of tweets by right-wing activists and Russian cyber-agents across 11 days pushed the "release the memo" topic into a trending one—and did so with a boost from "audience members" who were not anyone's friends and neighbors, but tweet-amplifying-through-retweeting bots. A simulated audience performed for a real one to push the hashtag. Phenomena along these lines have become prevalent enough that it has a name—computational propaganda—and a unit at Oxford University dedicated to its study.

In other words, the contemporary moment has realized the long-held dream of at least partly interrupting the monologues of the media oligopolies of the twentieth century. At the same time, new media platforms have, by the advent of the third decade of the millennium, exhibited characteristics (rigorous segmenting of the audience, deployment of surveillance and psychographics) that lend themselves to an intensifying flak regime.

Having considered the audience, a necessary element to a flak campaign, I will now orient to basic dimensions of understanding flak; to begin, what is the scale of what I am defining as flak?

Definition: What Is/Is Not Flak?

In the previous chapter, I defined flak as tactics and strategies toward political harassment. To reiterate, flak is permeated with power, it is purposefully employed toward sociopolitical goals, and weaponized to disparage, delegitimize, and disable people and organizations. Below, I will endeavor to make the term less abstracted and ascribe more concrete characteristics to it. I will also delineate flak subtypes, in part through pertinent case studies. The stakes of this discussion are that flak often arises from the shadows to menace its targets with sadistic, bad faith scrutiny and delegitimization. In constructing a detailed account of flak, naming it and its sub-types, flak itself becomes the unwilling object of scrutiny—albeit, with demands for accuracy and dispassion that do not perturb flak discourses.

Flak: How Big?

There are situations that are too serious to merit description as flak; murder, for example. Flak-mongers seek to kill a reputation rather than a person, as cashiering someone's good name is sufficient for flak purposes. Similarly, physical assault is beyond flak for its literal bare-knuckled quality.

Flak should also not be construed as identity-based prejudice that is embedded in structural (often legalized, officially-sanctioned) forms of harassment to beat down subaltern populations. Examples of prejudice embedded in institutional practices include the terrors of Jim Crow in the United States. The more recent "hostile environment" program in the United Kingdom is also more than flak as it was the platform for undifferentiated harassment of immigrants in their regular encounters with the State (e.g., in the hospital, at school, with police officers in the streets). I posit that these chauvinistic practices are more serious than flak in their society-wide scale and diffusion into some of the everyday details of the victims' lives. That said, systemic abuses surely have smaller flak episodes embedded within them—but are distinct from flak campaigns in being systemized by deeply inscribed custom and law in the first place. By contrast with diffuse systematic abuses, flak that is directed at and focused on a specific person or organization toward clear political objectives presents flak's most evident and damaging form.

Some phenomena are too big to be called flak while others are too limited in scope. Schoolyard bullying and malicious neighborhood gossip do not qualify, serious as they are within their own environments, for lacking wider impact. Similarly, episodes of trolling are traumatic and cause depthless pain for the victims. However grotesque and even criminal when it exceeds protected speech as credible death threats, trolling is not flak, as I am defining it. Trolling lacks a clear political dimension when wholly constituted by personal abuse; caveats to follow.

Before I offer those caveats, consider the example of the South Korean "Dog Poop Girl" (hereafter, DPG). In 2005, DPG refused to clean the fecal matter that her dog deposited on a metro train floor, despite exhortations from others on the train. After observers recorded and disseminated the episode, DPG was the target of furious rebuke and eventually retreated from her university studies (Detel, 2013). Harassment of DPG was wildly out of proportion with her admittedly gross transgression—but it does not rise to the level of flak as there was no tangible sociopolitical goal implicated in the invective.

By contrast, in 2013 in the United Kingdom, Caroline Criado Perez successfully campaigned for a woman to be featured on a British banknote. One may call this campaign feminist or female-friendly and it led to Jane Austen replacing Charles Darwin on the "tenner." It also led to "50 tweets an hour being hurled toward her, including rape threats" (Jeong, 2018, p. 13). Sarah Jeong cites several more cases of women being abused online with a clearly gendered dimension that is, in effect, meant to harass all women. In the case of Zoë Quinn's "Gamergate" ordeal, Jeong posits her former paramour Eron Gjoni as having "managed to crowdsource domestic abuse" (2018, p. 17). Moreover, Jeong observes that internet bots with female names are subject to "25 more times 'malicious private messages" than male-named bots (2018, p. 20); chauvinism toward real people is, apparently, easy to project on to non-existent people.

The upshot is that trolling of a person may be salted with sociopolitical issues that indicate a campaign to intimidate and harass broader social groups. Online furies may thereby cross an unmarked frontier into the domain of flak when the abuse is more than trolling a convenient target with personal antipathy. In these instances, flaksters bring on board a palpable sociopolitical dimension that is, nonetheless, far less structural and lacking in the formal authority of Jim Crow or the "hostile environment." I will return to this point with further examples later in discussing issue-oriented as well as "ambient," meta-ideological flak.

Scandal—and Its Evil Twin

What flak is and is not is at the heart of its relation to scandal.

Published near the dawn of the Internet age, John B. Thompson's *Political Scandal* parsimoniously identifies three temporal phases of his book's titular subject (2000, p. 24). Thompson posits that scandal consists, first, of a transgression of consequence, coupled with an effort to hide the misbehavior. In the second phase, information leaks despite efforts to suppress it and hints of wrongdoing enter circulation. Third and finally, at an unmarked tipping point, the scandal becomes a full-blown story with the attendant disapprobation and further scrutiny.

Thompson posits that, in recent centuries, scandals have become heavily mediated events. In this view, media narratives are not "secondary or incidental" but "partly constitutive" of scandal (2000, p. 61). As journalistic and/or State investigation into the scandal ramps up, the public can become absorbed in the drip-by-drip developments. As Thompson observes, the scandal narrative plays out like "a good novel" as audiences "assess the veracity of the protagonists, to figure out the plot and to predict its resolution" (2000, p. 73). After scandal has gone into motion, investigation commences with an opportunity to clean up the political sphere. In Thompson's words, this is a public good since "scandals have highlighted hidden activities which were of questionable propriety and have helped to stimulate important debates about the conduct and accountability of those who exercise power" (2000, p. 263). In this view, scandals animate the cleansing rigors of search for the truth.

Scandal and Flak: What's the Difference?

Like scandal, flak depends upon mediatization and it also lends itself to being narrativized as an absorbing story. However, I posit several irreducible differences between flak and Thompson's account of scandal.

To start, Thompson does not address flak—which is not surprising since scandal remains a far more recognized term. However, for largely eliding strategically weaponized discourses, Thompson effectively collapses flak into scandal. The cover of his book features Clinton with head-bowed as the poster-boy of political scandal. In the text inside the cover, Thompson also amalgamates the many discourses and investigations around Clinton as scandal. In other words, Thompson does not differentiate the flak fishing expeditions around Clinton—notably the insipid nothing-burger of Whitewater—from the eventual sex scandal that years of flak yielded. This example underscores the need to tease flak from scandal and to identify what distinguishes them.

Thompson construes scandal as concerned with investigating and determining whether wrongdoing has occurred—or, importantly, has not occurred. However, flak does not conform to the same model or its logics. If political agents want to launch episodes of flak, an actual transgression or reasons to believe one has occurred (the first phase in Thompson's schematic) *are not needed to commence the mediated discourse about wrongdoings*. In terms of Thompson's schematic, a flak discourse goes directly to the third phase of disapprobation along with stepped-up (State and/or media) scrutiny. Simply acting as if there has been a transgression and proceeding from there will suffice for flak purposes! Furthermore, unlike the processes around scandal, flak-mongers are uninterested in whether there is an underlying truth to accusations. Stirring up a flak storm with its attendant scrutiny and passions *is the objective in itself*; and the lack of resolution around flak claims can mean that the flak narrative continues indefinitely. In these respects, flak is the evil twin of scandal that it mimics.

Consider the hideous, years-long campaign against Barack H. Obama as to his nation of birth, meant to impugn his basic qualifications for the presidency. While this flak discourse did not achieve mainstream play, it lingered like a low-level outbreak of dysentery in swampier districts of opinion. Nonetheless, the Hawaii State Health Department felt compelled to address the "birther" flak spasms by producing the scanned version of Obama's long form birth certificate—thereby setting off a new flak round of specious denunciations of the birth certificate as a forgery (Mikkelson, 2011). The "birther" flak campaign went straight to disapprobation, in Thompson's schematic of scandal—and *then* lurched onward, indifferent to resolution via evidence, enacting an infinite loop of accusation and disapprobation, all in contrast with a genuine scandal.

Thompson's magisterial work on scandal nonetheless anticipates what I am describing as flak, even if he does not further explore it. Thompson warns of the "roving searchlight" and avers that the essential functions of investigation into scandal must be "insulated from partisan interests" through "a clear remit and a well-defined focus" (2000, p. 269). Although he does not discuss flak, Thompson is also cognizant that a media environment characterized by untrammeled accusation becomes "conflictual, uncooperative and non-participatory"; the kind of social order riven with bilious cynicism that has come into clear view as flak has risen like a toxic plume over the political landscape. All societies have deeply inscribed divisions within them. Cynicism channeled into flak presents an instrument for exacerbating these fractures by keeping people at each other's throats while elites hover above the fray unscathed, a phenomena that has gone global and can happen anywhere.

Flak Versus Scandal Case Study: Dissing Dilma

In 2016, Dilma Rousseff was impeached and then removed from the presidency of Brazil. The series of events presented a steep fall for the twice-elected president and her *Partido dos Trabalhadores* (PT, or Worker's Party) that had ruled Brazil since 2003. The series of events also illustrates that flak and scandal can be differentiated from each other—as indeed they need to be when contentious, contrived flak poses as sober scandal.

PT's era in government registered significant successes in the decade of the 2000s. The government introduced "large scale social programs such as *Bolsa Familia*, which provided subsidies to poor families to buy food and other necessities," while riding "an upswing in economic fortunes" (Arnaudo, 2017, p. 7). The resolutely un-radical World Bank enthused that, "Brazil's socioeconomic progress has been remarkable and internationally noted," for "innovative and effective policies to reduce poverty and ensure the inclusion of previously excluded groups"; the results "lifted millions of people out of poverty" (quoted in Chomsky, 2018, para. 24).

However, by 2016, impeachment was greeted with wide public approval due to Brazil's faltering economy and antipathy toward across-the-board corruption. The proximal trigger to the impeachment was alleged accountancy crimes, including the timing of the government's payment of a loan to the Bank of Brazil. Not only were Rousseff's ostensible crimes scarcely discussed during her Senate trial, their status as crimes was itself a stretch. Stephen Mothe (2016) explains that, in Brazil,

> The president can only sign a decree once it has gone through an extensive process, which includes technical and legal analyses within the Ministry of Planning and

other organs. At the time in which the three decrees reached Rousseff's desk, there was no explicit understanding that they contravened any legal norms, but rather an implicit endorsement of their compatibility with the law, dispelling any possibility of malice or willful misconduct on the part of the president. [...] It was only through a posterior decision, reached under questionable circumstances, that the Audit Court found the decrees irregular, and applied this understanding retroactively. (2016, para. 7)

Once impeachment was in motion, Mothe claims that Brazil's senators shifted ground and transformed questions about a bureaucratic procedure into a full-blown political trial. In this view, there was no scandal to speak of; but there was abundant flak-in-action.

As Brazil's 61 senators cast their impeachment ballots, 20 of them were implicated in the sprawling *lava jato* (car wash) anti-corruption investigations that Dilma had enabled to go forward (Arnaudo, 2017; Caudros, 2016; *Democracy Now!*, 2016). Michel Temer replaced Rousseff as president—a lofty perch to reach when he had been barred from running for office for eight years due to an election fraud conviction. In a stark departure from his PT's predecessors' policy package and without an electoral mandate, Temer's administration rapidly implemented a deep austerity regime that was loathed by Brazilians. Austerity, along with Temer's recorded participation in bribery, drove his administration's approval rating in polls into single digits (Caudros, 2016)—scandal that Temer managed to weather as he hung on for two years until the end of what had been Dilma's elected term. Along with sandbagging the *lava jato* anti-corruption investigations, the flak campaign against her presidency signals restoration of traditional class hierarchy in Brazil to cancel PT's efforts toward more widely spread prosperity.

Impeachment was flak-in-action enacted by a small circle of elites. However, the campaign against Dilma also had its vox pop (or bottom-up) dimensions, implicating large numbers of Brazilians. New media was a key conscript against Dilma's government. During election season in 2014, candidates employed online computational propaganda, a large share of which was bot-driven. Following Dilma's reelection, the opposition's online apparatus was not rolled up and, instead, mobilized as a permanent flak caravan (Arnaudo, 2017). Groups such as *Revoltados ON LINE* and *Vem Para Rua* ("Go to the Street") had 16 and four million members respectively and their messaging reached many more (an estimated 80 million people). In Dan Arnaudo's appraisal, the online outrage was "boosted by botnets" and "helped lay the groundwork for the impeachment campaign" (2017, p. 15). Flak memes ricocheted through Brazil. Through sheer repetition, around half of Brazilians came to believe that PT had ushered illegal Haitian immigrants into Brazil for the 2014 election and that an armed drug gang was a PT affiliate. The delegitimizing flak tall-tales lubricated support for Dilma's impeachment (Arnaudo, 2017, p. 18).

Dilma was a prisoner of Brazil's military dictatorship, subjected to torture as a young woman at the start of the 1970s. Impeachment is a "soft" tactic by way of comparison. At the same time, if they are not confronted, the "civilized" procedures of flak may prove more destructive of governance for gutting it from inside its own system of checks and balances; in this case, by repurposing impeachment from a question of scandal to an instrument of flak.

A Survey of Sub-Categories of Flak

Having considered what flak is not—namely, scandal—I will pivot to subtypes of flak, beginning with a basic distinction between flak-in-action and flak-in-discourse. Herman and Chomsky's original characterization of flak emphasizes its manifestations in actions; to wit, letters, phone calls, or more drastic, law suits directed at flak targets. Throughout this volume, however, I will dwell more on what I am calling flak-in-discourse than on flak-in-action by mainly analyzing texts. At the same time, I readily acknowledge an often-intimate link between discourse and action; indeed, speech can be readily regarded as at once discourse *and* action.

In sharper definition, what then is flak-in-discourse? It is not garden-variety talk or writing; rather, it presents weaponized forms of discourse that at some point in the chain of its production is backed with power. The authors of flak-in-discourse do not seek to inform or educate the public as an end in itself. Rather, the flakster's objective is to inflict damage on a target. It follows that flak-in-discourse is not simply a negative review made in good faith. In this view, assessing the Los Angeles-based rock band Warpaint's most recent recording as below-standard is not in itself flak, regardless of whether the criticisms are crude or couched in sophisticated musical analysis. Good faith criticism's project is not to derail the musical career of Warpaint as an end in itself or to otherwise complicate the lives of the band members; and even if it was, a lone crank's review will not have the clout to halt the band's trajectory. In contrast with a flak campaign, a lone crank's review is similarly unlikely to incite concrete action such as a boycott of Warpaint or a committed movement devoted to hindering the band from playing. Finally, criticism of Warpaint does not in itself rise to the level of a sociopolitical issue, thus has too faint a signature to be construed as flak.

A case study of climate change denier Christopher Monckton follows to further concretize the differences between flak-in-discourse and flak-in-action—as well as discourse and action's proximity to and synergies with each other. In the case study, I will also introduce further terminology for flak targets (personalized/issue-oriented/meta-ideological) and flak modalities (boutique versus vox pop).

Flak-in-Action/Flak-in-Discourse Case Study: Lord of Flak

Christopher Monckton is a climate change denialist brand-name who has made presentations across the world, including in the U.S. Congress—a presentation that prompted a 48-page rebuttal from climate scientists (Hickman, 2010). In politics, Monckton was an adviser in the Conservative Party in the 1980s but has since careered further right in having been a (losing) parliamentary candidate for and deputy leader of the anti-Europe and anti-immigrant United Kingdom Independence Party. As concerns political activity, Monckton has asserted himself to be a member of the House of Lords—an imaginative claim for which the British State has repeatedly chastised him in writing (Beamish, 2011, para. 4). He inherited the title of Lord when his father passed away but is not a member of the House of Lords entitled to vote with the parliamentary body. Monckton has also, inexplicably, claimed to have been awarded the Nobel Prize and to have formulated an elixir that is effective against AIDS, multiple sclerosis, and the common cold (Bickmore, 2010). Notice that this brief survey of documented claims by Monckton about his CV constitutes description with implicit criticism—not flak!

As concerns discourses on climate change, Monckton has made public power point presentations in which he purports to demolish the pillars of climate science. One of Monckton's performances in 2009 was hosted by the Minnesota Free Market Institute on the Bethel University campus. Climate researcher John Abraham of University of Saint Thomas in Minneapolis attended the event. In response, Abraham crafted a university class-session length power point slide show with voice-over that he posted on his campus' server. Abraham's response adhered closely to the scientific issues and characterized Monckton as an engaging presenter—if decisively wrong on substance, hence the need for rebuttal.

Barry Bickmore, a self-described "Republican scientist [who] advocates sane energy policies" at Brigham Young University, described Abraham's slide show as "an exceptionally mild-mannered, careful critique of one of Monckton's presentations" (2010, para. 75). Monckton's response to the academically-grounded power point presentation exemplifies flak-in-discourse. He took his campaign against Abraham to Alex Jones' *InfoWars* program. To wit, "Monckton described Abraham as 'this wretched little man' who 'only belongs to this half-assed Christian Bible college'" (quoted in Winterer, 2012, para. 15). Saint Thomas is, in point of fact, a Catholic university. Continuing, "Monckton described Abraham's response as 'complete fabrication' and 'lie after lie after lie after lie'" (Winterer, 2012, para. 15). Monckton also referred to Saint Thomas' president as a "creep." On the *InfoWars* platform, Monckton executed a pivot from belittling flak-in-discourse to flak-in-action. Alongside the heated claims to delegitimize Abraham, Monckton appealed for listeners to contact the university's president/creep and agitate for discipline of Abraham for his ostensible lack of professional legitimacy; flak that extended beyond words into appeals for mass action (writing emails) with the expectation of further action internal to Saint Thomas (professional reprimand).

Monckton doubled down with further discourse to seed flak-in-action, lobbed from Anthony Watts' climate change denial flak mill, *Watts up with that?*:

> May I ask your kind readers once more for their help? Would as many of you as possible do what some of you have already been good enough to do? Please contact Father Dennis J. Dease, President of St. Thomas University, djdease@stthomas.edu, and invite him—even at this eleventh hour—to take down Abraham's talk altogether from the University's servers, and to instigate a disciplinary inquiry into the Professor's unprofessional conduct, particularly in the matter of his lies to third parties about what I had said in my talk at Bethel University eight months ago? That would be a real help. (The Viscount Monckton of Brenchley, 2010, para. 7)

In an academic environment, it is laughable that a presentation such as Abraham's that pivots almost entirely on dry scientific literature on topics such as mean ground temperatures would occasion hair-on-fire demands for a "disciplinary inquiry"; and demands for such discourse to be suppressed reek of dreaded, 200-proof political correctness. In any event, outside the academy, Monckton's 678-word flak-in-discourse accusations on *Watts up with that?* triggered more than 350 comments—or, 180 pages of responses when printed, as flak-in-discourse begat further flak-in-discourse. Moreover, Monckton again crosses from flak-in-discourse intended to harm Abraham's reputation to making an audience appeal for flak-in-action through concerted email writing to Father Dease. Numerous readers/commentators, in turn, averred that they had sent Father Dease a letter (e.g., "PJB," SimonH," "jaypan," "Billy Blofeld") as the clarion call of flak-in-action was heeded.

One reader/commentator brings added understanding of the flak technique of flooding-the-zone through flak-in-action emails by openly yearning for a deluge into Father Dease's inbox ("Robin", 2010). In turn, a professional organization is usually obligated to a respond to inquiries composed with a reasonable facsimile of pertinence and literacy. In this manner, a flak-in-action campaign can drain at least some time and resources of its target. The flak-in-action in this case also bids to position *Abraham* as the nuisance and to cultivate the idea that life on the campus would be easier without the faculty member and his slides shows. As the paroxysms of flak played out, University of Saint Thomas stood resolutely beside its faculty member. Nonetheless, Abraham acknowledges, "From the very beginning, though, I have always been concerned about the impact this might have on the University of St. Thomas. I didn't want my actions to have a negative effect on the university" (quoted in Winterer, 2012, para. 26).

Monckton's 678-word post on the *Watts up with that?* website engages with flak-in-action in another sense beyond whistling for "winged monkeys" on the internet to send emails. To wit, Monckton makes ten references to libel in his post, an unmissable attempt to play to his grandstand and to simultaneously threaten and intimidate the flak target via the prospect of legalistic flak-in-action. The not-so-veiled threats also channel a desire to criminalize academically-grounded criticism of an unfortunate venture into a field about which Monckton has militantly-held views, but no training. Moreover, Monckton's flak-in-action threats are not an aberration. Bickmore lists, for example, seven professors against whom "Monckton has threatened to instigate academic misconduct investigations and/or libel suits" for scrutiny of his work. "Before the verdict was in" on one of the investigations he had demanded of a university, "Monckton threatened to sic the police on the university" (2010, paras. 31–32).

Where Monckton's threats of lawsuits are concerned, two points are of further interest to a theory of flak. The first is that the threat of a lawsuit from someone backed by a movement with cash to burn (particularly if burning cash will grow the planetary carbon footprint), is anxiety-laden for the target and obviously detracts from the conduct of one's work and life. Second, wittingly or otherwise, Monckton's escapades also illustrate the concept of faux flak (that, in similarly alliterative terms, can be called phantom flak).

In this vein, Bickmore writes that Monckton "keeps claiming (to others) on the Internet that he is going to sic his lawyers on me for 'Lord Monckton's Rap Sheet', but miraculously, I haven't been contacted by his lawyers, either" (2010, para. 32). That is, Monckton's huffing reads as tactical flak bluff that postures as incipient flak-in-action for the grandstand. Merely *threatening* the lawsuit is enough to impugn one's target to an extent—but without the actual hassle of going to (and near certainty of losing in) a court of law. To bluff in faux flak style is to pretend that, for example, this threatened lawsuit or that tranche of hacked emails are explosively damaging to their target. Act and talk like they are in fact damaging and perhaps the grandstand will believe the faux flak—particularly if the claims are repeated often enough to achieve illusory truth status.

Personalized/Issue-Oriented/Meta-Ideological Flak

As noted, Monckton's performances illustrate a distinction between flak-in-discourse and flak-in-action; two terms that share a permeable boundary as flak-in-discourse often aspires to produce action, such as provoking an employer's disciplinary measures. Monckton's performances also illustrate further subtypes of flak. In particular, flak can be personalized at a given target (or, in a variation on personalization, a particular organization). Flak may also orient, more diffusely, to a sociopolitical issue. Finally, flak may be still more "ambient" and pitched toward broad meta-ideological postures that usually implicate the left-right political split. Where personalized flak is concerned, Monckton's attacks on Abraham have been cited as examples above and bear no repeating.

As for issue-oriented flak, in Abraham's case, Monckton's target leads back to climate science. At the same time, the distinction between the person and the issue is also a permeable one. One quick example will suffice for illustration. *Watts up with that?* reader/commentator "Kirk Myers" oscillates between personalized and issues-oriented flak in the course of his or her 87-word rally to Monckton:

> I was stunned by the level of *scientific incompetence* and the *unscholarly tone* exhibited by *"professor"* Abraham. Lord Christopher Monckton thoroughly eviscerated Abraham's presentation, question by question and point by point. Abraham's *amateurish "hit job," probably orchestrated with* the assistance and acquiescence of other AGW [Anthropogenic Global Warming] supporters, once again demonstrates the mean-spirited arrogance of many in the *AGW movement*, whose final line of defense of a now indefensible theory is the use of lies, distortions and ad hominem attacks. Such is the fallen state of *"mainstream climate science."* (emphasis added; 2010, para. 1)

Kirk Myers' canned speech bears no more resemblance to Abraham's slide presentation than it does to the plot of *Casablanca,* or a recipe for paella, or any other artifact one could select at random—but we will put that aside. Of interest is that Kirk Myers' barrage of non-sequiturs assail Abraham the individual for professional conduct that is ostensibly beyond the pale—and then quickly pirouette to the issue of climate science ("AGW" in his or her shorthand) to construct Abraham as synecdoche for the larger flak target. In other words, Kirk Myers weathervanes between flaking at the person and the issue.

Ambient or meta-ideological flak goes to further levels of abstraction beyond persons (or organizations) and issues. Meta-ideological flak is evident in discourses that gesture toward connections with larger political programs; and, as noted, these programs tend toward flaking or shoring up "right" or "left" political positions. On the meta-ideological flak front, Monckton delivers again in 2014 address in Australia:

> This [environmental treaty] process has nothing to do with the weather. It has nothing to do with man's impact on the weather. *It has everything to do with establishing the socialist international at the heart of the UN and making every nation bow the knee to this new dictatorship*, and the climate is merely a fig leaf to cover what they are trying to do. (emphasis added; quoted in Smith & Jalsevac, 2015, para. 7)

The *Life Site* reporters solemnly aver that Monckton has—apparently by the sheer force of rhetoric—discovered a "concealed push for a one-world government" that is further asserted to be proceeding to hard-left specifications. To summarize, a person (e.g., Abraham), an issue (climate change), or a meta-ideology (right-wing ideology opposed to regulated capitalism and multilateral climate amelioration) may all stack up on each other in different levels of the same flak discourse.

Flak from the Boutique/Flak from the Street Corner

The Monckton discourse also illustrates a distinction between what I am naming as boutique flak and vox pop flak. Boutique flak is conceptualized as flak that presents the look and feel of discourse that is high-brow, scholarly, supported with evidence, fashioned by credentialed and seasoned experts, backed by prestige institutions dedicated to quality control of their products. Monckton's response to Abraham is ensconced in an aura of pomp and gravity on the *Watts up with that?* website as a glossy, if wince-inducing pamphlet (Watts, 2010). Vox pop flak, by contrast, emanates from the grass roots, or the internet equivalent of the street corner, and speaks in the vernacular. By its nature, vox pop flak can be more plentiful. It may animate, for example, mass letter-writing via email, trending Twitter campaigns, or high-volume comment threads on web pages.

Having offered a distinction between boutique and vox pop flak, I will now complicate it. To begin, boutique flak is effectively an oxymoron. Flak does not readily lend itself to high-quality research given that it serves instrumental purposes in sociopolitical conflicts. To finesse this problem and generate information that is locked-and-loaded to be weaponized but that looks smart, think tanks of dubious-to-abysmal quality have long been concocted by elite backers (Soley, 1995). When flak disguised as scholarship is the core mission of such an organization it may be called a flak mill or, equivalently, a flak factory. In this vein, I have previously discussed think tank discourse that frequently lacks recognizable methodology or external review of its ideologically-loaded products that unambiguously reason backwards from tendentious conclusions (Goss, 2006).

However, boutique and vox pop flak can be construed as co-dependent. Boutique flak's project is to furnish the guy on the street—or the guy up all night in stained pajamas in the flickering aura of his laptop—with putatively wise factoids and phrases in which to express flak talking points. Vox pop flak's foot soldiers can thusly proceed with confidence that they have "prestige" backing, as they descend upon the comment section.

In this vein, in the *Watts up with that?* comment section discourse, vox pop participants rally to Monckton—and he is enabled to have it both ways. Monckton is constructed as the erudite answer man who furnishes exhaustive one-stop shopping for factoids, couched in "intellectual authority" to which vox pop flaksters defer; *and* Monckton is simultaneously construed as pure of university affiliation, a man of "the peeps" notwithstanding the elitist class background about which he ostentatiously reminds all. Ideological alchemy collapses the paradoxes of boutique and vox pop flak toward climate science.

What Flak Is Not

Having sketched out what characterizes flak and its subtypes, I will now return to differentiating it from other (better-known) terms; to wit, fake news, conspiracy theory, and activism.

The term "fake news" has spiked in usage in recent years and is up first for consideration. Throughout this volume I will eschew use of this term since its usefulness has been placed into doubt by its sheer vagueness. In July 2018, the United Kingdom's House of Commons Digital, Culture, Media and Sport Committee published *Disinformation and Fake News*. The committee reached what seems at first blush to be a surprising conclusion about the report's titular topic. Specifically, the Committee concluded that, "There is no agreed definition of the term 'fake news'" (2018, p. 7). Fake news can implicate satire and parody such as *The Onion* or *Colbert Report* that—in irreducible contrast to flak—often make laudable contributions to public discourse. In turn, fake news may also signify accurate stories with misleading click-bite titles—or it may point to entirely fabricated content. In the light of these and other forms of "news" discourse that could be called fake, the Committee concludes, "we cannot start thinking about regulation and we cannot start talking about interventions, if we are not clear about what we mean" (2018, p. 7). The Committee advises "that the Government rejects the term 'fake news' and instead puts forward an agreed definition of 'misinformation' and 'disinformation,'" that are generally understood to signify, respectively, deliberately or inadvertently wrong information (2018, p. 8).

Flak may also be taken as making contact with conspiracy theory. My posture toward conspiracies takes them as far less exotic and edgy than is often posited in discourses on them. At the same time, I concede that dedicated flak audiences may behave like the conspiracy-minded in adopting an infinite regress of suspicion toward evidence that proves their assumptions wrong (Bratich, 2008). That said, I am assaying to take conspiracy out of the grassy knoll and make it mundane in positing there is nothing "special" about conspiracy. It is, after all, a legal term that is vital in describing some forms of crime. In Robert Mueller's indictment of 12 Russian intelligence operators (Mueller, 2018), the term "conspirators" is employed throughout the text to collectively describe the 12 defendants. *Conspiracies exist*: ergo, let us get over it. In this view, a conspiracy theory is like, any other theory, subject to empirical support that (in some lesser or greater measure) provides convincing evidence or not. That (some, many, most) theories of conspiracy can be proven wrong makes them like other theories. Moreover, I am assuming a structuralist approach, such as that which Herman and Chomsky bring to the propaganda model. In this view, analysis of deep structures, such as the dynamics of capitalism, illuminates more of how the social order functions than even an empirically proven conspiracy. For this reason, I am constructing flak as structurally-grounded concept with origins in the propaganda model, with scant further reference to conspiracies or conspiracy theory.

Doing the Right Thing: Flak Versus Activism

I have been arguing that flak serves the public badly. At the same time, one may quite reasonably wonder what to make of citizens who have composed letters of complaint, or convened demonstrations, or boycotts for pro-social ends. In this vein, Amnesty International innovated methods of confronting authority via mass letter-writing campaigns, an advancement for human rights advocacy that was awarded the Nobel Peace Prize in 1977. Among other examples, Amnesty's principle method of inspiring mass letter-writing begs the question of whether it is a flak mill and whether flak may present pro-social functions. The short answer is: emphatically no. I am defining "pro-social flak" as an oxymoron. Instead, I advocate the term activism to signify pro-social actions against powerful interests and to differentiate it from flak.

Whether enacted against people who hold authority (e.g., Clinton or Dilma) or against people who demonstrably do not, a defining feature of flak is that it emanates from a position backed with substantial power. Activism, by contrast, presents guerilla-style tactics of necessity for weaker parties against stronger ones in order to leverage whatever advantage they can. Citizen numbers present that advantage where letter-writing, boycotts, or demonstrations are concerned.

Flak has on occasion been genetically modified in order to assume the veneer of activism. Campaigns for elite interests can be camouflaged as activism in what have been called AstroTurf (fake grassroots) campaigns. When AstroTurfing, industries shepherd citizens into front groups to act (even unwittingly) as their public face. For example, "smokers' rights campaigns" have enshrouded corporate interests in smoke (Stauber & Rampton, 1995, pp. 14, 30). Flak is doused with power—and so it may necessitate the concealment of that power. Moreover, convening front groups is now easier than ever with the rise of computational propaganda. Bots may not be as loud and colorful as a crowd of citizens; but they can be tirelessly enlisted in unlimited numbers to flood the zone of online discourse as needed.

Case Study: Activist Students in a Flak Storm

It is heart-wrenching to repeat the facts: on February 14, 2018, Marjory Stoneman Douglas High School in Parkland, Florida was the site of the most lethal mass shooting yet at a U.S. high school. The massacre claimed the lives of 17 students and injured 17 more. Following other shootings of staggering scale, the Parkland students commandeered the public discourse toward advocacy for stronger gun laws. A month later in the District of Columbia, Parkland students led the March for Our Lives, a name too chillingly literal in the light of the ongoing cascade of school shootings.

The students' actions readily qualify as activism, regardless of whether their families are affluent. As teens yet to graduate high school, they control no appreciable assets of their own beyond assuming the high moral ground. Moreover, the students' actions can be called activism when compared with the resources at the disposal of the gun industry and its aggressive lobby. Although the activist encounter was asymmetric in power terms, the Parkland students' registered material victories. Notably, a gun-friendly Florida governor signed restrictions into law in short order (Drobnic Holan & Sherman, 2018).

The students' articulate, uncontrived passion overwhelming impressed observers; just not all observers as the students were also subject to shockingly crass flak. *InfoWars*, *Gateway Pundit*, *Breitbart*, Russia-linked Twitter accounts, as well as Republican Party congressperson Steve King reported for flak duty against the students (Drobnic Holan & Sherman, 2018; Lopez, 2018). Trump-pardoned felon Dinesh D'Souza merits special mention for his rapid efforts to dismiss the students by cuing deranged flak mood music. D'Souza tweeted a photo of the shell-shocked victims in the immediate aftermath of the massacre with the caption: "Worst news since their parents told them to get summer jobs" (quoted in Nakamuta, para. 2).

Then, the flak got uglier. As noted, flak-in-discourse often takes the form of delegitimization in part through denigration and belittlement. The students' authenticity as students was demeaned, as they were accused of being "crisis actors" and deep-state plants reading an anti-gun script. The flak memes lingered even at the epicenter of the massacre. One Parkland teacher told *Politifact*, "I had legitimate friends asking if [student activist] David Hogg is a real person—it was crazy" (quoted in Drobnic Holan & Sherman, 2018, para. 33).

Flak at the teenagers got personalized indeed. Emma Gonzalez was derided by a Republican Party candidate for Maine's State House as a "skinhead lesbian" (Bremmer, 2018). Her Cuban heritage was problematized as well as (in "damned if you do/do not" terms) whether she speaks Spanish. In the weeks after her school was attacked with bullets, she was also attacked anew with comparisons to Hitler Youth (Lopez, 2018).

The aforementioned David Hogg was mocked by Fox News performer Laura Ingraham for not being admitted to college; he has since been accepted at Harvard. Hogg's response to these cheap, demeaning jabs once again rallied to the register of activism against the millionaire Fox News factotum and the globalist conglomerate that employs her. Going activist with success, Hogg invited his Twitter audience to pressure top advertising accounts that supported Ingraham's program to decamp from it. Further stabs at delegitimization were arrayed against Hogg. Other persons who shared his name—such as a mug-shotted 26-year old with a criminal record in South Carolina and no resemblance to the Parkland student—were asserted to be the "real" David Hogg (Garcia, 2018). In what may be a flak rite of passage, Hogg was also accused of Nazi affinities. More chilling, Hogg's residence was "swatted." In swatting, an armed Special Weapons and Tactics team is summoned by an anonymous phone "tip" alleging a situation (e.g., hostages taken) in order to trigger quasi-military intervention. People have in fact been killed in swatting incidents by innocently opening the front door (Ohlheiser, 2018).

Alongside emphatic praise for their activism, the tasteless vehemence of the flak efforts to discredit the students returns to the power asymmetries that characterize flak; in this specific case, issues-oriented flak on gun control that was cross-hatched with personalized flak at particular Parkland students. The pre-standing power symmetries that tilted against the students signified that they made difficult-to-fathom sacrifices of personal security and peace-of-mind to engage with gun control activism.

Keep Activism on the High Road

#MeToo may also be construed as activism. The movement presents dispersed activism that has blasted through millennia of male power and impunity protected by silence. Previously unassailable figures, most notably in politics and the entertainment industry, have been brought to heel by #MeToo's methods. However, it must also be noted that a figure like the heinous Bill Cosby was not sentenced to prison by a series of tweets. Cosby met justice in a courtroom, with the full protections of a presumption of innocence and vigorous advocacy, before being judged as guilty of the crimes of which he was accused.

As much as figures such as Cosby demand comeuppance with justice for the victims, it must be noted that a world run on #MeToo logics radiates the distinct possibility of being bent from activism to flak. While it is unequivocally laudable that powerful men's patterns of abuses have been confronted, tweets are not a substitute for due process. In this view, accusation that collapses into conviction is a decisive step backwards from liberal, Enlightenment concepts of justice and toward a stepped-up flak regime. Twitter is not a justice machine—no technology is—and the public must be vigilant that accusations do not become coterminous with conviction in ways that can readily converge with flak.

Conclusion: On Methods and Assumptions

Before proceeding further in this book's discussion of flak, some words on the methods by which I know what I claim to know are in order. Along with the debt to the propaganda model, this volumes' method adapts thematic analysis, as discussed by the Glasgow Media Group's Greg Philo and Mike Berry (2004). Thematic analysis presents a parsimonious method with common-sense grounding that stresses evidence over a theoretical apparatus. Its objective is to flush out the sociopolitical realities from the inundation of mediatized words and images.

Thematic analysis is broadly compatible with the propaganda model in assuming that systematic structures condition sociopolitical discourse. Moreover, thematic analysis assumes the power of mediated messages in shaping the audience's conceptions of the local and global sociopolitical environment to which those audiences have limited or no direct or exhaustive access (and thus depend upon mediation for understanding). Mediation inevitably scrambles the egg-white of reality with the egg-yolk of distortions via interest-driven representation of that same reality.

As Berry and Philo observe, the scrambling of reality and distortion occurs in large measure through the perspectivism that permeates sociopolitical discourse. In this view, where one sits—in the servants' quarters or on the veranda—goes some way toward explaining where one stands. Perspectivism is grounded in prevailing power relations and material interests that shape discourse, down to what issues are discussed and who or what are constructed as villains and problems. While perspectivism may readily warp perceptions, just as wearing the wrong pair of prescription spectacles warps one's sight, it need not annul the apprehension of agreed outlines of reality that can be obtained by collating sources. By contrast, flak campaigns can and do take steps toward annulling agreed realities, depending instead upon sheer repetition for their truth effects along with the thrills of spectacle.

In sorting out the competing claims that purport to account for reality, I adapt thematic analysis to the present investigation by

(1) drilling down into illustrative case studies in the analyses that constitute most of this book. The case studies are, by definition, elaborations of specific instances of organizations and issues implicated in flak discourses, but also meant to reveal more general patterns;
(2) endowing each case study with elaborated context prior to unpacking its flak dimensions, most notably as concerns flak-in-discourse implicated in the case study;
(3) noting the claims, explanations, justifications, and bids to define reality that animate the flak discourses; and then measuring claims against a broader sampling of evidence from scholarly books and articles, as well as methodologically rigorous reports from governments, nongovernmental organizations, and practitioners of quality journalism.

A bedrock assumption of this investigation is that some lines of explanation and evidence have a greater claim on reality than others. While difficult to apprehend, the truth is not simply up for grabs or unknowable. Stronger and weaker lines of evidence can be differentiated and stitched together to arrive at truth—that, to give away the conclusions of this volume's analysis, bend decisively away from the flaksters.

As for the structure of this volume, Part II will take up case studies of two ideologically radioactive flak mills whose function, on a full-time basis, is to generate flak behind brazenly diaphanous veneers of investigatory professionalism. The two case studies will be Heartland Institute that nominates itself as the progenitor of the "best" in research (Chapter 3) and Project Veritas that self-characterizes as a courageous investigative journalism unit (Chapter 4). Part III of the volume turns to issues that have become ensconced in flak campaigns; to wit, contention over the conduct of elections that are basic infrastructure of a democratic social order (Chapter 5) and universities that are necessary, but not in themselves sufficient, as infrastructure toward a just and prosperous society (Chapter 6).

Note

1. To be clear, I did not vote for Clinton when I had the chance in 1992 and 1996. Moreover, my early academic investigations cross-examined Clintonian neoliberalism (Goss, 2001, 2000) and the heinous sanctions siege warfare on civilian life in Iraq during the 1990s

(Goss, 2002). Although Clinton's administration was clearly competent, Clinton's practice of "triangulation" made his administration into the archetype of DemoRepublican governance. In this passage, I am focusing on the out-of-all-proportion reactions to Clinton's administration in the 1990s that prefaced the surging hysteria of the U.S. right (cf., Lofgren, 2011).

References

Andrejevic, M. (2004). *Reality TV*. Lanham, MD: Rowman and Littlefield.
Arnaudo, D. (2017). *Computational propaganda in Brazil* (Computational Propaganda Research Project Working Paper 2017:8). Oxford University. Retrieved from blogs.oii.ox.ac.uk/politicalbots/wp-content/uploads/sites/89/2017/06/Comprop-Brazil-1.pdf.
Beamish, D. (2011). A letter to Viscount Monckton of Brenchley from the Clerk of the Parliaments. *UK Parliament website*, 18 July. Retrieved from www.parliament.uk/business/news/2011/july/letter-to-viscount-monckton/.
Bickmore, B. (2010). Lord Monckton's rap sheet. *Climate Asylum*, 26 July. Retrieved from bbickmore.wordpress.com/lord-moncktons-rap-sheet/.
Boehlert, E. (2009). *Bloggers on the bus*. New York: Free Press.
Bratich, J. Z. (2008). *Conspiracy panics*. Albany:State University of New York Press.
Bremmer, J.P. (2018). Skinhead lesbian. *ABC News*, 13 March. Retrieved from www.nbcnews.com/feature/nbc-out/skinhead-lesbian-gop-candidate-attacks-parkland-teen-emma-gonzalez-n856311.
Caudros, A. (2016). Brazil after Dilma Rousseff. *New Yorker*, 1 September. A Retrieved from http://www.newyorker.com/news/news-desk/brazil-after-dilma-rousseff.
Chomsky, N. (2018). I just visited Lula, the world's most prominent political prisoner. *The Intercept*, 2 October. Retrieved from theintercept.com/2018/10/02/lula-brazil-election-noam-chomsky/.
Conason, J., & Lyons. G. (2000). *The hunting of the president*. New York: Saint Martin's Press.
Democracy Now! (2016). Complete reversal of democracy: Glenn Greenwald on Brazilian president Dilma Rousseff's impeachment. 29 August. Retrieved from https://www.democracynow.org/2016/8/29/complete_reversal_of_democracy_glenn_greenwald.
Detel, H. (2013). Disclosure and public shaming in the age of new visibility. In J. Petley (Ed.), *Media and public shaming* (pp. 77–96). London: I.B. Tauras.
Drobnic Holan, A., & Sherman, A. (2018). *PolitiFact*'s lie of the year. *PolitiFact*, 11 December. Retrieved from www.politifact.com/truth-o-meter/article/2018/dec/11/politifacts-lie-year-parkland-student-conspiracies/.
Dumitrica, D. (2016). Facebook's global imaginary. In B.M. Goss, M.R. Gould, & J. Pedro Carañana (Eds.), *Talking back to globalization: Texts & performances* (pp. 193–214). New York: Peter Lang.
Flynn, D.J., Nyhan, B., & Reifler, J. (2017). The nature and origins of misperceptions. *Political Psychology*, 38(S1), 127–150.
Franklin, B. (2004). *Packaging politics*. London: Bloomsbury.

Freedman, D. (2014). *The contradictions of media power*. London: Bloomsbury.

Fuchs, C. (2014). *Social media*. Los Angeles: Sage.

Garcia, A. (2018). Far right blogs, conspiracy theorists attack Parkland mass shooting survivor. *Snopes*, 20 February. Retrieved from www.snopes.com/news/2018/02/20/right-wing-media-david-hogg/.

Gillmor, D. (2004). *We the Media*. Sebastopol, CA: O'Rielly Media.

Goodman, M. (2015). *Future crimes*. New York: Doubleday.

Goss, B.M. (2000). Hail to the subject: The durability (for the Moment) of neo-liberalism. *Cultural Studies: A Research Annual*, 5(1), 363–393.

Goss, B.M. (2001). "All our kids get better jobs tomorrow": The North American Free Trade Agreement in *The New York Times* (1993). *Journalism and Communication Monographs*, 3(1), 5–47.

Goss, B.M. (2002). "Deeply concerned about the welfare of the Iraqi people": The sanctions regime against Iraq in *The New York Times* (1996–98). *Journalism Studies*, 3(1), 83–99.

Goss, B.M. (2006). Sex education fantasies: Ideology and right-wing science. *Southern Review*, 39(1), 8–24.

Hall, S. (1993). Encoding/decoding. In S. During (Ed.), *The cultural studies reader* (pp. 90–103). London: Routledge.

Hesmondhalgh, D. (2010). *The cultural industries* (2nd ed.). London: Sage.

Hickman, L. (2010). Chemical nonsense. *The Guardian*, 21 September. Retrieved from www.theguardian.com/environment/2010/sep/21/climate-scientists-christopher-monckton.

House of Commons Digital, Culture, Media and Sport Committee. (2018). *Disinformation and fake news: Interim Report*. 24 July. Retrieved from publications.parliament.uk/pa/cm201719/cmselect/cmcumeds/363/363.pdf.

Jeong, S. (2018). *Internet of garbage*. New York: Vox Media Incorporated.

"Kirk Myers". (2010). I was stunned […]. *Watts up with that?* 14 July. Accessed February 15, 2019, from https://wattsupwiththat.com/2010/07/14/abraham-climbs-down/.

Kosinski, M., Stillwell, D., & Graepel, T. (2013). Private traits and attributes are predictable from digital records of human behavior. *Proceedings of the National Academy of Sciences of the United States of America*, 110(15), 5802–5805.

Lazarsfeld, P.F., Berelson, B., & Gaudet, H. (1969). *How the voter makes up his mind in a presidential campaign*. New York: Columbia University Press.

Lewinsky, M. (2017). Roger Ailes's dream was my nightmare. *New York Times*, 22 May. Retrieved from www.nytimes.com/2017/05/22/opinion/monica-lewinsky-roger-ailess-dream-was-my-nightmare.html.

Lewis, N.A. (2000). Whitewater inquiry ends. *New York Times*, 21 September. Retrieved from www.nytimes.com/2000/09/21/us/whitewater-inquiry-ends-a-lack-of-evidence-is-cited-in-case-involving-clintons.html.

Lofgren, M. (2011). Goodbye to all that. *Truthout*, 3 September. Retrieved from truthout.org/articles/goodbye-to-all-that-reflections-of-a-gop-operative-who-left-the-cult/.

Lopez, G. (2018). Conservative attacks on March for Our Lives leaders are getting very personal. *Vox*, 29 March. Retrieved from www.vox.com/policy-and-politics/2018/3/29/17176174/laura-ingraham-boycott-david-hogg-guns.

Matz, S.C, Kosinski, M., Nave, G., & Stillwell, D.J. (2017). Digital targeting as an effective approach to digital mass marketing. *Proceedings of the National Academy of Sciences of the United States of America, 114*(48), 12714–12719.

McKew, M.K. (2018). How twitter bots and Trump fans made #ReleaseTheMemo go viral. *Politico*, Retrieved from https://www.politico.com/magazine/story/2018/02/04/trump-twitter-russians-release-the-memo-216935.

Mikkelson, D. (2011). Is Barack Obama's birth certificate fake? *Snopes*, 27 August. Retrieved from https://www.snopes.com/fact-check/birth-certificate/.

Morozov, E. (2011). *The net delusion*. London: Allen Lane.

Mothe, S. (2016). Was Brazil's impeachment of Dilma Rouseff in fact a coup? *OpenCanada*, 8 September. Retrieved from www.opencanada.org/features/was-brazils-impeachment-dilma-rousseff-fact-coup/.

Mueller, R.S. III. (2018). *United States of America versus Viktor Borisovich Netyksho, et al.* Washington, DC: United States District Court.

Nakamura, R. (2018). Even conservatives denounce Dinesh D'Souza after he mocks Parkland school shooting survivors. *The Wrap*, 20 February. Retrieved from www.thewrap.com/even-conservatives-denounce-dinesh-dsouza-mocks-parkland-school-shooting-survivors.

Nix, A. (2016). Cambridge Analytica: The power of big data and psychographics. *YouTube*, 27 September. Retrieved from www.youtube.com/watch?v=n8Dd5aVXLCc.

Ohlheiser, A. (2018). Someone 'swatted' Parkland survivor Hogg's family home. *Mercury News*, 6 June. Retrieved from www.mercurynews.com/2018/06/05/someone-swatted-parkland-survivor-hoggs-family-home/.

Pennycook, G., Cannon, T.D., & Rand, D.G. (2018). Prior exposure increases perceived accuracy of fake news. *Journal of Experimental Psychology: General, 147*(12), 1865–1880.

Philo, G., & Berry, M. (2004). *Bad news from Israel*. London: Pluto Press.

Pizzo, S., Fricker, M., & Muolo, P. (1989). *Inside job*. New York: Open Road.

Qui, L. (2015). Bill Clinton Says Hillary was 'completely exonerated' in Whitewater. *Politifact*, 23 June. Retrieved from www.politifact.com/truth-o-meter/statements/2015/jun/23/bill-clinton/bill-clinton-says-hillary-was-completely-exonerate/.

"Robin". (2010). I've just written […]. *Watts up with that?* 14 July. Retrieved from wattsupwiththat.com/2010/07/14/abraham-climbs-down/.

Shirky, C. (2008). *Here comes everybody*. London: Penguin Books.

Simpson, C. (1994). *Science of coercion*. Oxford, UK: Oxford University Press.

Smith, A., & Jalsevac, S. (2015). Monckton: Harper defeat in Canada election will allow "World Government" win at UN Paris Climate Meet." *Life Site*, 18 October. Retrieved from web.archive.org/web/20151116184831/https://www.lifesitenews.com/news/monckton-harper-defeat-in-canada-election-will-cause-world-government-win-a.

Soley, L.C. (1995). *Leasing the ivory tower*. Boston: South End Press.

Special Committee to Investigate Whitewater Development Corporation and Related Matters. (1996). *Investigation of Whitewater Development Corporation and Related Matters—Final Report*. Washington, DC: United States Government Printing Office.

Stauber, J., & Rampton, S. (1995). *Toxic sludge is good for you*. Monroe, Maine: Common Courage Press.

Sterne, J. (2012). What if interactivity is the new passivity? *FlowTV*, 9 April. Retrieved from http://www.flowjournal.org/2012/04/the-new-passivity/.

Thompson, J.B. (2000). *Political scandal*. Cambridge, UK: Polity Press.

Van Dijk, T. (1998). *Ideology*. London: Sage.

Viscount Monckton of Brenchley, The. (2010). Abraham climbs down. *Watts up with that?* 14 July. Retrieved from wattsupwiththat.com/2010/07/14/abraham-climbs-down/.

Watts, A. (2010). Condensed Monckton. *Watts Up With That?* 14 July. Retrieved from wattsupwiththat.com/2010/07/14/condensed-monckton/.

Winterer, J. (2012). John Abraham takes a stand. *University of Saint Thomas Newsroom*, 1 March. Retrieved from news.stthomas.edu/john-abraham-takes-a-stand/.

Part II
FLAK MILLS

· 3 ·

"WE ARE THOSE EXPERTS": HEARTLAND INSTITUTE AND THE THINK TANK AS FLAK MILL

> Of course, not all global warming alarmists are murderers or tyrants […]
> —Heartland Institute (2012, quoted in Hickman, paras. 6–7)

Introduction: A Hot News Story

The two-minute news segment from 2014 looks like many other ostensibly balanced news reports (Heartland Institute, 2014). Specifically, the Fox News segment recites the climate change paradigm in voice-over, backed by a montage of shots of forest fires and droughts. The narration then pirouettes to the arrival of good news; to wit, a report that suggests more carbon in the air is not at all bad and, in any event, human activity has a negligible impact on ground temperatures. After describing these claims as the work of a scientific panel convened by Heartland Institute, the segment executes a sound bridge to a bearded man, earnestly proffering the sweeping conclusions of a hip new wisdom: "corrupted" academic journals cannot be believed on climate change due, he claims, to what he diagnoses as their ethical failings around alleged financial and peer pressures.

The bearded man and ostensible arbiter of scientific truth is Joseph Bast, then president of Heartland Institute. The message of the Fox News segment message in which Bast prominently features is chimerical indeed; while there is little climate change to speak of, the segment suggests, Bast simultaneously posits a heat-driven boon for agriculture that is feeding "billions" of people who otherwise would go hungry. In this view, it is high time to scale-up one's carbon footprint—*call it a donation to the poor and hungry*—and perhaps to pray for massive flooding, since plants like water as well as heat. In the news segment, Bast is staged for the camera as a figure of gravity, laboring at an imposing desk behind a phalanx of books, displaying monk-like focus as he makes notations by hand on scrolls of research.

The segment dramatically places the cover of Heartland Institute's climate change denialist report in front of a billowing U.S. flag—semiotics too obvious for comment. The "good news on climate" narrative is momentarily interrupted by a clip of a University of Illinois professor sputtering about Heartland, claims that are answered by the Fox reporter's stolid insistence on the bullet-proof rigor of Heartland's Nongovernmental International Panel on Climate Change.

In many respects, Fox's item is not so different from a significant share of news coverage on climate change over a long period of time. It features a "balanced" presentation of claims. In Fox's hands, the formal balance is nonetheless tilted toward Bast, a college drop-out (Tollefson, 2011), as scientific "go-to answer man" in contrast with the academic community that he derides.

Contrived attempts to engineer balance have long been a defect of U.S. news. In the case of climate change coverage, the rituals of balance are particularly questionable. In this vein, the administrator of the United States National Oceanic and Atmospheric Administration concluded by 1997 that "there's a better scientific consensus" on climate change "than any issue I know—except maybe Newton's second law of dynamics" (quoted in Boykoff & Boykoff, 2004, p. 125). Maxwell T. Boykoff and Jules M. Boykoff have used the term "balance as bias" around climate news as it presents an essentially settled question as a matter of substantial contest. In this view, climate "balance" is the photo-negative homologue to convening a "two sides" debate on astrology in which supporters and skeptics are subject to exquisitely balanced presentation of their views. More recently, Aaron Huertas and Rachel Kreigsman (2014) present evidence that U.S. cable news stations—with the exception of Fox News—have become wiser about ritualistic procedures of balance that are in themselves a form of skew away from the state of knowledge where climate reporting is concerned.

A further implication of the Fox News segment is that Heartland's activities are deemed as consequential enough to merit respectful news coverage. The coverage, in turn, synergizes with the release of one of Heartland's products. What then is Heartland? And what, more broadly, are think tanks and flak mills?

From Think Tank to Flak Mill

Arlington, Illinois-based Heartland Institute was founded in 1984 by David Padden and the previously mentioned Bast who was the organization's longtime president and is still an active presence. As of 2018, Heartland's landing page rallies around its slogans: "Freedom rising" and, more expansively, "*Our Mission:* to discover, develop, and promote free-market solutions to social and economic problems." In the words of its 2018 annual report, Heartland is "a national non-profit research and education organization devoted to improving our world using positive, pro-liberty ideas. We discover, develop and promote free-market solutions to social and economic problems" (Heartland Institute, 2018a, p. 2).

Heartland calls itself a think tank. The feel-good self-characterizations notwithstanding, I am positing Heartland as a flak mill. Think tank is a neutral descriptor that simultaneously trades on positive connotations. By contrast, as I argued in the introductory chapters, to call something flak is a criticism in itself. It follows that a flak mill is a producer of regularly or systematically defective discourses toward flak ends of political combat. That said, while the signification of the terms "think tank" and "flak mill" seem unambiguously distinct, the difference in practice may be not be as dramatic as it seems at first blush.

The term "think tank" first appeared in the dictionary in the mid-1960s—and, after a notable proliferation in the 1970s, the United States had more than 1,000 think tanks by the start of the 1990s (Smith, 1991, p. xiv). In terms of what they are presumed to do, think tanks have been idealized as the "university without students" where cardigan-clad scholars "hold weighty and leisurely discussions around the coffee maker" (Jacobson, 1995, p. 1768). David Ricci's buys in on this trope and maintains that think tanks realize The Enlightenment project of "growth of knowledge," shepherded by "wise people" toward a "*great conversation*" that is "largely commendable" (original emphasis, 1993, pp. 17, 19, 24). At the very least, think tanks have been productive in getting their word out. The US' oldest and perhaps most venerable think tank, the centrist Brookings Institution, produces books at a level comparable with a major research university.

However, a newer wave of smaller, often single-issue think tanks after the 1970s have oriented toward producing concise and targeted advocacy, as opposed to channeling considered, Solomonic wisdom on society and governance. New wave think tanks have sought to register impact in the political arena by, for example, swaying legislators votes on bills—or by giving legislators cover for unpopular votes by furnishing ostensibly sagacious intellectual backing via reports and briefing papers. The rarefied connotations of the term notwithstanding, many think tanks are dedicated to hyperactive marketing of ideologically-driven policies (Goss, 2000, pp. 105–122). Even some well-known think tanks are staffed with woefully underqualified personnel; and the resultant research products are further vexed by a lack of external peer-review procedures as quality control between a think tank's ostensibly scholarly "report" and its trajectory to the think tank web site (Goss, 2006).

Think tank founders corroborate this seemingly harsh view of the think tank as carnival barker. Fred L. Smith, founder of the Competitive Enterprise Institute, describes the think tank's job as "creating public policy ideas and marketing the hell out of them" (quoted in Jacobson, 1995, p. 1767). Edwin Feulner, founder of Heritage Foundation, construes think tanks as institutions to "popularize and propagandize an idea" (1985, p. 22). Feulner goes further in characterizing think tanks as promoting political ideas through methods redolent of commercial campaigns to market toothpaste. In turn, by the 1990s, critical scholarship on think tanks posited them as "Howdy Doody-like" puppets for their funders (Soley, 1995, p. 94). In turn, funders may include whole industries, such as restaurants with a bottom-line interest in finding ostensibly considered justifications for keeping wages low. As I have previously argued, "think tanks are not dispassionate, commenting like a Greek chorus on the action from which they are otherwise detached"; rather, think tanks are "an important node in the vertically integrated circuit" of informational and ideological production (Goss, 2000, p. 122). Toward these ends, think tanks are "participating in the policy process, exerting influence on Congresspersons and media while recruiting and training new [ideologically-driven] cadres for the future" (Goss, 2000, p. 122).

While think tanks are often compromised, the rise of flak mills extend these logics still further. A flak mill (or flak factory) is dedicated to the production of harassment that belittles, derides and delegitimizes ideological opponents while feigning professional status as a quality source of information and original research. While Heartland self-characterizes as a think tank, in this chapter, I describe the priority of flak over recognizably good faith, rigorous research in its products. As a large share of Heartland's discourses have had implications for questions around the scientific endeavor, it is also of moment to consider what science is.

Science and What Is at Stake

In the popular imagination, scientific inquiry may appear to be an uninterrupted march from one certitude or useful invention to the next; after all, one hears about the breakthroughs and not the dead ends. The view from the laboratory bench looks different. *The Independent Climate Change Email Review* (widely known as the Russell Review) observes that, "Scientific hypotheses and theories are presumed to be provisional: they can be refuted by testing but they cannot be verified as correct or true in an absolute sense." However, if experimental evidence "can be repeated, and produce the same results," the underlying theories "are said to be validated"—until they are not (Russell, Boulton, Clarke, Eyton, & Norton, 2010, p. 36). Given the essential role of doubt in the scientific endeavor, bad faith actors may readily corrupt scientific understanding in the public arena of policy, with sophistic games redolent of belligerent lawyering.

Enter flak campaigns to stimulate climate change skepticism.

By the late 1980s, the tipping point in climate science workers' findings about human-forced climate change brought about the formation of the Intergovernmental Panel on Climate Change. In short order, in the 1990s, efforts to pushback against the crystallizing climate consensus were in motion. Naomi Oreskes and Erik M. Conway (2010, pp. 1–35) posit that carbon industries took inspiration from the cigarette interests' decades-long campaign to put off regulatory reckoning. The cigarette industry aggressively contested findings on the dangers of smoke by mobilizing its own stable of seemingly independent investigators (boutique flak) while also stimulating front groups of citizens to act on the industry's behalf (i.e., vox pop flak).

There are, nevertheless, important differences between cigarettes and carbon-based commodities. While cigarettes are a significant industry, many people have never smoked. Moreover, tobacco is not an essential element of an industrial economy. By contrast, carbon products are at the foundation of the modern industrial order. Carbon impacts on most every other commodity through, at least, transport to market. The CEO of Royal Dutch Shell, Peter Voser, estimates five-percent of U.S. employment is implicated in the petro industry and accounts for an estimated eight-percent of the US' GDP (Patel & Moore, 2018, p. 178). If and when carbon is finally phased out in favor of renewables, it will happen gradually if steadily to avoid sudden impacts; but, if climate science is even partly correct, the renewable-powered train has to start rolling.

While Heartland Institute glibly dismisses climate science as a species of "political correctness" (*Left exposed*, 2017, para. 19), the Pentagon is one hard-nosed institution that has taken a keen interest in climate change. U.S. Secretary of Defense Chuck Hagel devoted a 2014 speech to what he calls "environmental security" in the event of runaway climate chaos. Hagel posits, that "Climate change is a 'threat multiplier.'" This is because climate change

> has the potential to exacerbate many of the challenges we already confront today—from infectious disease to armed insurgencies—and to produce new challenges in the future. The loss of glaciers will strain water supplies in several areas of our hemisphere. Destruction and devastation from hurricanes can sow the seeds for instability. Droughts and crop failures can leave millions of people without any lifeline, and trigger waves of mass migration. (Hagel, 2014, paras. 13–15)

Along with questions of security and order, unmitigated climate change augers a devastating impact on the quotidian, material basis of life as transacted through the economy. By 2006, the Stern Review concluded that "if we don't act, the overall costs and risks of climate change will be equivalent to losing at least five-percent of global GDP each year, now and forever." A five-percent decline presents a staggering wallop and it is, in turn, a conservative estimate: "If a wider range of risks is taken into account, the estimates of damage could rise to 20-percent of GDP or more" (Stern, 2006, p. vi). In this view, climate change convulsions are comparable to the world wars and depression of the 1910s–1940s period—except those conflagrations ended relatively quickly, whereas galloping climate change would be an ongoing, open-ended disaster.

Those are some of the stakes. At the same time, given how much more powerful carbon commodities are vis-à-vis tobacco, carbon industries are fiercely resisting the renewable future. Moreover, as these appraisals suggest, climate change presents a plausible scenario for putting state power on steroids in response to civilizational breakdown. Indeed, as cultural psychologist

Michele Gelfand (2018) argues on the basis of a massive raft of research, crisis always prompts tighter mores and less liberty in human societies. In this view, "libertarian" talking points that flak climate science as an alibi for stepped-up state power and *un*freedom are deeply wrong-headed or disingenuous. Only enhanced state authority would present the reach and resources to manage unprecedented climate change chaos (to the limited extent it could be managed) ushered in by "business-as-usual" inaction on climate. The flak campaigns to gut regulation of carbon industries as well as to hobble support for sunrise renewable industries (via tax breaks, research and development) present the fast track to putting the State on steroids.

Polls as of summer 2018 suggest that 71-percent of U.S. respondents accept climate science warnings, a number that ticked upward for the concatenation of extreme events in that year (Dewan, 2018). While that seems to be robust support for climate science, it also suggests that public acceptance lags behind the degree of consensus in the scientific community. Years of flak against climate science that plays to the grandstand has fomented doubt, even if skepticism has not been able to win the argument. In the opening page of her 2016 "Foreword" to a signature Heartland publication devoted to climate skepticism, Marita Noon gloats that the public's concern on climate "peaked in 2000 and today, people are no more worried about it than they were 26 years ago" (2016, p. xi). Noon betrays the extent to which public perceptions (and the management of them) are a central stake in Heartland's work.

In the balance of this chapter, I will examine Heartland as think tank *cum* flak mill, beginning with its own characterizations of its work. I will then analyze signature Heartland publications on climate change and its attention to what it calls "Climategate" as flak campaigns. Finally, I will make a comparison between Heartland's flak discourses around a prominent climate scientist and its vigorous promotion of a scientist who has been a rare voice of climate skepticism. Throughout the discussion, the question of how a self-proclaimed think tank at once feigns analysis of pressing problems while radiating flak is a matter of central importance.

Freedom Risible: Overview of Heartland Institute

Heartland's 2018 annual report, *Freedom Rising*, presents the organization's ideal self as it cues feel-good mood music. The report constructs the organization as polished, professional, and effective as a political player. Good vibes begin with the cover photo of children carrying balloons toward a sun-drenched horizon. As for Heartland's organizational contours, *Freedom Rising* reports a full-time staff of 39—"plus approximately 500 policy advisors, 25 senior fellows, and more than 250 elected officials in Heartland's Legislative Forum" (2018a, p. 2). The organization's current president, Tim Huelskamp, is a former legislator in the United States House of Representatives from Kansas (2011–2017). While in congress, Huelskamp aligned with the rightward wing of the Republican Party (House Freedom and Liberty Caucuses, Tea Party Caucus).

As of 2018, Heartland positions itself as advising "Trump and thousands of free-market-minded state legislators [who] need help formulating and then articulating a free market agenda. They need the advice of experts who have studied the issues closely." Immodestly, Heartland proclaims, "We are those experts" (2018a, p. 2). Heartland maintains that, "We effectively market the best work of other free market think tanks, not just our own" (2018a, p. 3). Heartland repeats the claim that it sponsors "the best research" on the following page of the annual report with another echo on page nine. A flak mission is, in this manner, expressly disavowed in favor of something more rarified.

Heartland bids for mainstream trappings and respectability. Thus, the annual report flags staff members that possess doctorates and utilizes titles such as "Director of Government Relations" and "Research Fellow" to credential them with professional status; in constructing this self-perpetuating semiotic loop, Heartland staff are professionally titled because Heartland is a putatively professionalized organization. "Key personnel" side-box biographies pepper the annual report and demonstrate that the staff has been overwhelmingly incubated within a network of right-wing institutions. Heartland staff have gained their professional experience in vehicles of the right-wing movement such as the American Legislative Exchange Council, Hudson Institute, Heritage Foundation, Cato Institute, *The Blaze*, *Townhall*.com, and *The Washington Times*. The pattern demonstrates that movement right-wing funders have assiduously developed a network of organizations to advance right-wing politics (McLean, 2017; Mayer, 2016); and in doing so, the network of organizations trains and advances the career trajectories of ideologically-aligned prospects who can staff that network.

Despite its insistence on maverick-like independence that is above partisan politics, Heartland exhibits submissiveness toward the right-wing social-economic program and its variants in Trumpism. The opening of the annual report celebrates what it calls "truly a second chance for freedom to rise" via a Trump administration that is "good news for freedom lovers"—language that pins Heartland's deeply inscribed ideology to the mast while conjuring religious connotations of a "second coming" around a far right-wing administration (Heartland Institute, 2018a, p. 2).

A Messaging Mission

Notwithstanding boasts about its research prowess, Heartland is at base a communications-based enterprise. *Freedom Rising* claims, "We reach more elected officials, more often, than any other think tank in the United States" (Heartland Institute, 2018a, p. 3). In this respect, Heartland does what think tanks have long attempted to do in impacting legislators (Goss, 2000, p. 121). On its website, Heartland elaborates that it is "an 'action tank' as well as a 'think tank'" that calibrates its "success by the impact we have in the real world" (2018b, para. 7). In particular, Heartland maintains that 82-percent of elected officials at the state level have read its publications and that 45-percent report having been influenced by these products. The report claims that, in 2017, "Heartland contacted elected officials nearly a million times"—or, a shade less than 4,000 times every Monday through Friday work day during the calendar year (2018a, p. 6). More than research is in play.

An organizational mission that is grounded in communication also squares with the project of a flak factory. Rather than the production of original and credible research, Heartland's center of gravity can be found in "The Heartland Institute's Marketing and Communication Teams." They "produce a steady stream of news releases, op-eds, and letters to the editor, blog posts, podcasts, live-streamed events, radio and TV interviews, videos and speaking engagements" (Heartland Institute, 2018a, p. 8). Indeed, Heartland's annual report states that the largest share of its budget—32-percent, or one of every three dollars—is devoted to the "Communications/Marketing" category (2018a, p. 14).

Although Heartland is perhaps most known for its posture on climate change, its annual report does not discuss new facilities that would be salient to original investigation in this or any other pertinent domain. Rather, "In 2017, Heartland built a TV studio in its building in Arlington Heights"—a "professional setup" that enables Heartland staff to readily appear in international programming for messaging purposes (2018a, p. 8). In the register of communication, the annual report also emphasizes Heartland as a family of web sites domiciled on its landing page. The family of sites is, in turn, organized around ideologically-flagged themes such as *American exceptionalism*, the *Freedom pub* blog, and *Left exposed*. For the purposes of the ensuing analysis of its discourses, Heartland has the full ownership over what it characterizes as its family of websites featured on its landing page.

If Heartland is principally a messaging enterprise, what, more specifically, does it communicate? Heartland nominates itself as part of what it calls "the freedom movement" (2018b, para. 7). The 2018 annual report asserts, "*We believe ideas matter, and the most important idea in human history is freedom*" (original emphasis, 2018a, p. 15). In this light, one may ask what concept(s) of freedom animate Heartland. Franklin Delano Roosevelt gave his government's answer to the question when he famously characterized freedom in the 1941 State of the Union address. Roosevelt (n.d.) posited freedom as supported on the pillars of the universal writ of civil liberties (freedom of speech, freedom of worship), material and economic freedom (freedom from want), and human rights to liberate the whole person in a milieu of peace (freedom from fear). On the Rooseveltian view, a chronically hungry or homeless person is not free from fundamental wants, ergo, is not free.

Heartlandian freedom presents as more nebulous, but does implicate the liberation of commercial activity. This freedom train is driven toward de-regulation, de-taxation, and de-unionization as its final destination; a society exposed to the full force of liberated markets without the breaks, traffic lights, or seat belts of regulatory intervention. Guns are among the products that Heartland unswervingly supports against regulation as a baseline matter of "freedom" (Bast & Publius, 2018). Heartland first gained attention for its support for cigarettes and has later downplayed the impact of secondhand smoke and the need for regulation around it. With deregulatory zeal, Heartland honcho Bast "is among the last public defenders of smoking and has argued that concerns about second-hand smoke are as bogus as those surrounding greenhouse gases" (Tollefson, 2011, para. 9). In pondering on liberationist causes, Heartland also champions "energy freedom" (2018a, p. 11) that collapses into unconditional support for established players in carbon industries.

Heartland strives to be taken as serious, sagacious and scholarly—yet, glib anti-intellectualism and boorish blogging for flak purposes constitute a large share of Heartland's website discourse. Heartland seeks to have it both ways; to wit, marketing itself as professional and scholarly, while frequently marshaling ideologically top-heavy discourses in the service of right-wing flak. As Timothy Snyder phrases it, this type of performance transmits "both the thrill of transgression *and* a sense of legitimacy"—even as those performances may be constituted by neither in substance (emphasis added, 2018, p. 248). Heartlandian flak oscillates awkwardly between its reaches for transgression and legitimacy.

More specifically, Heartland wagers on presenting itself as professionally trustworthy and as a fount of quality research in publications such as *Why scientists disagree about global warming* (Idso, Carter, & Singer, 2016). A few clicks away from simulations of boutique atmospherics, Heartland indulges discourses redolent of "wise-ass" vulgarity. In this vein, the *Left exposed* blog is a Heartland product that links from Heartland's landing page. As the name suggests, the blog is supposed to confront and denude Heartland's ideological opposition. *Left exposed*'s blog-post punditry drops many of the pretenses of boutique flak discourse as the political id runs riot. For example, one entry rants, "The left's ideas are awful," the left is "fraudulent," and emits "claptrap"—although Seton Motely has notable difficulty identifying what the left is (2018, paras. 2–4). In turn, Motely is characterized by Heartland as a "policy adviser" and "One of America's leading authorities on technology and telecom policy" (2019, para. 2). His insight as a leading authority consists of "free market" bromides and dehumanizing language as he conjures "hominoid absurdities who infest Hollywood" and "hominoid absurdities who infest the Silicon Valley." These same people could, of course, be called exceptionally successful capitalists. In any event, the glib, disgusting discourse does not illuminate reality—but it does correspond with the crapulous quality of other right-wing flak discourses that read as most concerned with outdoing each other in grotesque caricature. These and other screeds on Heartland's website reside in close proximity to the organization's self-proclaimed status as imagined fount of "the best research."

Answering the Critics

Heartland has been implicated in a number of fiascos. In 2012, for example, Heartland-sponsored billboards equated environmentalists with the murderers' row of the Unabomber, Charles Manson, and Osama bin Laden. The berserk messaging led to almost one million dollars in lost donations as well as 100 cancellations from Heartland's climate change denialism conference (*The Economist*, 2012). However, Heartland has assayed to recycle criticism of its previous flak campaigns into a belching fuel for further flak emissions. In this vein, Heartland's "Reply to Critics" is extensive, consisting of 14 "Frequently Asked Questions" sections as of July 2018 (about 30 pages when opened simultaneously from the menu and printed). "Reply to Critics" is augmented by links to 50 letters that Heartland has composed to critics of its work between 2001 and 2017.

As of July 2018, Heartland's "Reply to Critics" opens by positing itself as the victim of "of misinformation and even outright lies […] from left-wing advocates who object to our principled stand in defense of liberty and limited government" (2018b, para. 1). The "Reply" discourse marshals legalistic threats from a source identified as "Legal Counsel, The Heartland Institute":

> "There have been numerous false and malicious claims that The Heartland Institute is a front for the energy industry and is funded by 'the Koch brothers.' These statements are often made with full knowledge they are untrue; in some cases they are made without such knowledge. With this notice, the reader is informed he/she will have no defense of 'innocent mistake' made because of lack of knowledge and may have legal liability for defamation." (2018b, para. 5)

Putting aside the passage's shameless "political correctness" around speech rights, Heartland acknowledges that it *does not reveal its donors*. To wit, "people who disagree with our views sought to smear and defame us by selectively disclosing the names of donors they thought were especially unpopular" (2018b, para. 9). It stands to reason that revealing the donors would halt questions as to who they are (and are not). Furthermore, to do so would in itself enact the independence from its donors for which Heartland praises itself (!).

It can also be safely inferred that Heartland's staff members do not need to be bribed by funders since, as already noted and to all appearances, they long ago internalized right-wing politics as part of their career trajectories. However, the quantity of funding does make an important difference in Heartland's appearance of professionalism as a well-kitted organization. For example, Heartland boasts an "Andrew Breitbart Freedom Center"—actual name—at which it convenes events "almost every week" (2018a, p. 8). The scale of its funding endows Heartland with a more attractive, seemingly professionalized stage on which to perform its flak song-and-dance over a driving neoliberal ("free market") beat.

Going on Offense

When Heartland pivots from responding to critics to going on offense, it makes aggressive efforts to flak its ideological opponents as presenting grade-zero professional standing. For example, academic researcher Robert Brulle is waved off via unsourced personalized flak assertions: "his work is inaccurate and has been thoroughly debunked," apparently by a secret tribunal, as no source is cited (2018b, para. 35). Heartland announces that Brulle is "just another liberal activist pretending to be a 'social scientist'" (2018b, para. 35). Particularly in contrast with Heartland's often histrionic products, Brulle's published work reads as dry and measured statistical modelling (e.g., Carmichael & Brulle, 2017).

Along with flak toward specific individuals, Heartland flaks the Union of Concerned Scientists (UCS). Heartland denounces UCS as "far-left" (2018b, para. 61) and repeatedly criminalizes its activities through litigious language. While marshaling a paucity of evidence, Heartland contends that UCS engages in "slandering," is "inaccurate and libelous" (2018b, para. 61), and makes "absolutely false, malicious and libelous" claims (2018b, para. 64). Although Heartland rarely conducts what could be called original research (e.g., gathering and/or interpreting datasets), it further asserts research superiority over UCS. In examining UCS' products—to wit, content analysis of cable news coverage of climate change—one finds that UCS' reports include detailed methods sections, literature reviews, prose to academic specifications, consideration of contradictory findings, flagging of ambiguities, as well as transparency around funding (Huertas & Adler, 2012; Huertas & Kreigsman, 2014). Practices such as detailed methods sections are standard within academic investigation, but alien to the corner-cutting of the flak factory. While these professional practices do not guarantee sound results, they are part-and-parcel to good faith effort to make a contribution to knowledge.

Some Like It Hot: Flaking Climate Science

Heartland promotes itself as "a think tank devoted to finding and speaking the truth" (2018b, para. 31). As concerns its climate science posture, Heartland praises itself as supported by "official state climatologists, professors from prestige universities all over the world (including Harvard, Yale, and MIT) and officials at the Department of Energy and the Department of the Interior" (2018b, para. 93). Heartland asserts that its finger is firmly on the pulse of climate science:

> In fact, the positions on global warming expressed by spokespersons for the Heartland Institute are closer to where most scientists and economists stand [...]. The Heartland

Institute is firmly within the 'mainstream' of expert opinion on global warming. Its spokespersons are credible and respected in the national and international debate. (2018b, paras. 96–97)

If these particular claims were even moderately accurate, it would be sufficient to negate characterizations of Heartland as behaving as a flak mill on this issue. However, despite the confident statements, Heartland's claims are untenable when confronted with evidence.

Heartland forces its conclusion that the preponderance of climate researchers find no evidence either for climate change or for human drivers of it, in part by asserting that many or most climate investigators are falsely conscious about their own findings. This bizarre assumption drove Heartland's publication of "The List of 500 Scientists with Documented Doubts of Man [sic] Made Global Warming Scares" (Avery, 2007)—doubts that, according to Heartland, these scientists did not know themselves to be experiencing. More than ten years after the publication of the list, Heartland continues to insist that, "the published work of many scientists, even those who publicly support the alarmist position in the global warming debate, supports the view that most or all of the modern warming is due to natural causes." For Heartland, "This is simply a fact" (2018b, para. 44).

When *DeSmogBlog* contacted scientists on the lists whose work was being re-purposed as fodder for climate skepticism, responses were scathing. For example, Dr. Ming Cai of Florida State University stated,

> I am very shocked to see my name in the list of "500 Scientists with Documented Doubts of Man-Made Global Warming Scares." Because none of my research publications has ever indicated that the global warming is not as a consequence of anthropogenic greenhouse gases, I view that the inclusion of my name in such list without my permission or consensus has damaged my professional reputation as an atmospheric scientist. (quoted in Grandia, 2008, para. 5)

Similarly livid, Dr. Paul F. Schuster of the U.S. Geological Survey, comments, "They have taken our ice core research in Wyoming and twisted it to meet their own agenda. This is not science" (quoted in Grandia, 2008, para. 8).

R-E-S-P-E-C-T

As noted above, Heartland claims to be discharging "credible and respected" messengers on climate change to the public arena. In the world beyond web site boasts, Heartland's team generally presents a striking lack of salient academic and professional qualifications on the topic. One example will suffice for the moment.

Steve Goreham is listed as a "policy advisor" on Heartland's web site. He and has carved out a niche as a climate skeptic—although Heartland's web site (2018c) characterizes his graduate training as implicating a Master of Business Administration. Goreham's polemically titled volume, *The mad, mad, mad world of climatism*, can be called a signature Heartland product. In particular, Heartland mailed 100,000 copies of Goreham's tome, unsolicited, to "educators, business and civic leaders, judges, environmental journalists, and elected officials across the country" (Heartland Institute, 2013, p. 1).

John Abraham (2013) of University of Saint Thomas University in Minnesota begins his appraisal of *Mad, mad, mad* by cross-examining the characterization of Goreham as researcher. Abraham finds no entries in peer-reviewed literature by Goreham, a fact corroborated by email when Abraham asked Goreham about his credentials. By contrast, Abraham's profile on the University of Saint Thomas website (n.d.) logs almost 200 books, book chapters and journal articles by the time he was in his early 40s, along with ten patents granted or pending; phenomenal output, particularly for a professor appointed at a medium-size university.

Abraham (2013) finds no sources cited at the end of Goreham's book, a stunning lack in what presents itself as a learned volume. He did find passages of what, following the "500" list precedent, might be called "heartlanding." To wit, Goreham draws conclusions about research reports that contradict what the author of the report posits. Suspected heartlandings were confirmed when Abraham personally asked Goreham-cited researchers for the correct interpretation of their published work vis-à-vis climate change.

Abraham (2013) flags several claims in *Mad, mad, mad* as flatly incorrect, based on the pertinent literature. For example, Goreham asserts that scientists have neglected solar activity as principally driving warming. Elsewhere, Abraham flags at least 11 studies that include wide literature reviews that have posited solar variation as very unlikely to be driving climate change (Abraham n.d., slides 98–108). Abraham's summary appraisal posits Goreham's work as a riot of "errors, misinterpretations and misguided comments" framed within a "glossy-covered book" (2013, para. 16). Respect and credulousness toward Heartland's product are conspicuously absent, notwithstanding Heartland's claims about the esteem in which it is regarded. However, *Mad, mad, mad*'s intended audience is the grandstand from which internet winged monkeys may be recruited and where climate change consensus can still be polemicized into non-existence.

Did Someone Just Say Climate Change Consensus?

Perhaps Heartland's boldest flak-in-discourse move is its insistence that there is no scientific consensus around the fundamentals of human-forced climate change. In this manner, Heartland can be taken as targeting its opponents' demonstrable strengths. While that may appear counterintuitive, it is a strategy that has worked in other contexts. For instance, New England Patriots *ur*-coach Bill Belichick went at strength in 2002's Super Bowl XXXVI by harassing and slowing down the heart of Saint Louis' vaunted offense, Marshall Faulk. The go-at-strength strategy concedes there is a formidable obstacle that cannot be avoided—but that can perhaps be problematized or diminished by flooding-the-zone with irritants.

Going at strength, Heartland boldly demands that its opponents "document the existence of the alleged 'consensus' in favor of their alarmist views" (Heartland Institute, 2018b, para. 97). Heartland wagers that the demand to document will be read by its followers as prompting a panic for those who assume climate change consensus—even as it is a losing wager on Heartland's part since the consensus among researchers is robust. The target audience for this phantom flak bluff is not the research-informed but Heartland's true-believer core audience subject to the illusory truth of repeated assertions.

In answer to the bluff, here goes with some documenting. On June 28, 2016, the American Association for the Advancement of Science (AAAS) sent a letter to the U.S. Congress that opens in neon-obvious language:

> We, as leaders of major scientific organizations, write to remind you of the consensus scientific view of climate change. Observations throughout the world make it clear that climate change is occurring, and rigorous scientific research concludes that the greenhouse gases emitted by human activities are the primary driver. This conclusion is based on multiple independent lines of evidence and the vast body of peer-reviewed science. (American Association for the Advancement of Science, 2016, p. 1)

The letter was signed by 31 professional organizations (e.g., American Institute of Biological Sciences, American Society of Naturalists, Association of Ecosystem Research Centers, Society of Systematic Biologists). The letter, in turn, references the Intergovernmental Panel on Climate Change, itself informed by thousands of studies. Some organizations that signed the AAAS statement had already issued their own statements on climate change. In this vein, the American Geophysical Union opens its statement with another thunderbolt of clarity: "Human activities are changing the Earth's climate" (2013, p. 1).

Another entry to the climate discourse, the U.S. Global Change Research Program (USGCRP), coordinates climate-related knowledge across a wide swath of agencies that include the National Science Foundation as well as the Departments of State, Interior, Commerce and Agriculture. Following its remit, USGCRP pulls together what has been observed across disparate research groups. It concludes that, *"Thousands of studies conducted by researchers around the globe have documented changes in surface, atmospheric and oceanic temperatures; melting glaciers, diminishing snow cover, shrinking sea ice; rising sea levels, ocean acidification; and increasing atmospheric water vapor"* (original emphasis, 2017, para. 4). Each of these developments is predicted by climate change models as a concomitant of spiking greenhouse gas accumulation. Moreover, in recent years, the ensemble efforts of climate research indicate "stronger evidence […] for continuing, human-caused warming of the global atmosphere and ocean" (2017, para. 14). The USGCRP report reiterates that "it is *extremely likely* that human influence has been the dominant cause of the observed warming since the mid-twentieth century" (original emphasis, 2017, para. 20). "No convincing alternative explanations," such as rising solar output or other natural variations (e.g., El Niño) account for the many dimensions of the observed data, in USGCRP's appraisal (2017, para. 20). In turn, USGCRP posits potentially unspeakable consequences from climate change for the basic civilizational infrastructure of agriculture, water supplies, human health, and ecosystems.

More consensus: the Geological Society of America (GSA) concurs with the massive thrust of published research "that global climate has warmed in response to increasing concentrations of carbon dioxide (CO_2) and other greenhouse gases" (Geographical Society of America, 2015, p. 1). Notice that the GSA, founded in 1888, claims more than 25,000 members spread across more than 100 countries (2015, p. 4). And so on, with regard to statements by scientific organizations (e.g., Commonwealth Academies of Science, 2018) and survey data from individually-polled climate science workers that I will address later (Bray and von Storch, 2016). On the evidence, Heartland's demands for proof around consensus presents phantom flak—a bold, misleading and substantially vacuous bid to bluff the reader into assuming that

Heartland would never ask the question unless cocksure about an answer affirmative to its contentions.

One public statement of interest does challenge the climate consensus: a 2018 letter to Trump with 21 signatories that follow Heartland President Tim Huelskamp's lead signature (Huelskamp, 2018). The other signatories may present even less connection to original climate investigation than Heartland—for example, the Media Research Center (discussed in Goss, 2013, pp. 141–166), a flak mill supposedly devoted to studying mass media. On examining the evidence, Heartland's claim that climate scientists reject climate change conclusions collapses on factual grounds. Nevertheless, by flak logics, Heartland's claims serve the purpose of impugning climate science, even if on the weak reed of bluffing, toward the flak objective of delegitimizing moves toward sunrise energy technologies.

Why Scientists Disagree as Flak Performance

Heartland aggressively promoted a product entitled *Why scientists disagree about global warming* (hereafter, *WSDAGW*) by Craig D. Idso, Robert M. Carter and S. Fred Singer (2016). Outdoing the mailing for Goreham's *Mad, mad, mad*, Heartland sent the 110-page tract to approximately 300,000 kindergarten-through-twelfth grade science teachers in the United States during the spring of 2017. One could say that when the denialism battle is decisively lost in the university or government laboratory, it is a cue to change venue to the middle school teachers' lounge or third grade science lesson.

WSDAGW's "Foreword" keynotes the volume's flak premises against climate science. Although it is axiomatic for Heartland that climate science is saturated with ideology, its publications constantly reframe science matters in manifestly political terms. Marita Noon's "Foreword" radiates politicization as it opens by assailing the Obama administration's attention to climate. Her bid to change the subject begins with her first sentence that invokes ISIS "beheading innocent people" (2016, p. xi). Ideology takes full command of the discourse as climate issues are reduced to "individual liberty and protecting our way of life"—both of which are recent human inventions that are sure to be abolished if climate projections are even partly correct (2016, p. xii). Noon charges that (unnamed) "leaders of the global warming movement [...] know most scientists do not endorse their simplistic and alarmist narrative of a complex scientific question" (2016, p. xii)—an empirical matter, addressed earlier. Citing no evidence, Noon attributes the climate change discourse to "the most extensive and most expensive public relations campaign in the history of the world," enacted by a "small politically connected cabal" with a penchant for "transfers of wealth" (2016, p. xi). Transfer of wealth is indeed in play—just not in the way that Heartland suggests. According to the Environmental Law Institute (2009), fossil fuel firms were pampered by champaign socialism to the tune of over US$70 billion in government subsidy across seven recent years, a sum that dwarfs subsidy for renewables.

Noon proclaims that, "the voices of real scientists need to be heard" (2016, p. xiii). Indeed: Noon's bionote characterizes her as "a columnist for *Breitbart.com*" among other right-wing affiliations. Moreover, Heartland states, "Prior to her work in energy, Noon was a known as a motivational speaker and author" (2016, p. xiv). Despite Heartland's consistent flak-in-discourse line that a clear majority of science workers think as it does, a "Foreword" for one of its signature products by someone with a background in right-wing activism and opinion indirectly reveals the contours of consensus among active science workers.

Majority Silenced

As prefigured in Noon's "Foreword," the main text of WSDAGW pushes the flak premise of giving voice to an aggrieved silent majority of climate scientists, ostensibly sulking in their laboratories and victimized by the "green giant." Idso, Carter and Singer contend on page one of WSDAGW that the often-cited "97 percent" consensus figure among scientists on anthropogenic warming is "false," "either false or meaningless," and "an insult to science." WSDAGW quickly turns to aggressive lawyering. Idso, Carter and Singer criminalize negative appraisals of climate skepticism performances such as theirs as—*somehow*—"libeling scientists" for whom they position themselves as gallant protectors (2016, p. 8). After ducking, weaving, moon-walking, and double- and triple-talking around the studies that they survey, Idso, Carter and Singer circle back to the pre-ordained conclusion from which they begin and end: "There is no scientific consensus on global warming" (2016, p. 29).

More specifically, Idso, Carter and Singer dismiss one study of the degree of climate consensus in part through name-calling (personalized flak) at the author, "a socialist historian named Naomi Oreskes" (2016, p. 10). Snide, personalized flak notwithstanding, Oreskes is appointed in the History of Science Department at Harvard University. WSDAGW also takes up mind-reading exercises that posit that, "Bray and von Storch [...] have succumbed to the very cognitive dissonance that they once described" (2016, p. 23).

Rather than depend on *WSDAGW*'s hopelessly vague account, let us take a look at the data that Dennis Bray and Hans von Storch (2016) actually report. Bray and von Storch's survey of 640 scientists presents powerful documentation of consensus on climate change science, around which Idso, Carter and Singer shuffle, shimmy—and finally spin on their heads in a full-blown "up is *really* down" ideological break dance. To wit, in answer to the question, "How convinced are you that climate change, whether natural or anthropogenic, is occurring now?," Bray and von Storch report that 91-percent of the polled scientists rated their confidence as a "6" or "7" on a 1–7 scale. Moreover, Bray and von Storch report that four out of five (79-percent) climate scientists opted for "7" on the seven-point scale of certainty as to whether climate change is now in motion. By contrast, a combined 0.3-percent of the polled climate scientists (two out of 640) rated their confidence at the other end of the scale as "1" or "2" (i.e., little or no confidence that climate is changing). Given the scientific method's grounding in uncertainty, the degree of confidence expressed in these figures is stunning.

As for the key question, "How convinced are you that most of recent or near future climate change is, or will be, the result of anthropogenic causes?," agreement is also very high—albeit, not as high since causation is more vexed than observation. To wit, 73-percent of surveyed climate scientists gave answers of "6" or "7" in agreement with the anthropogenic climate change thesis. By contrast, four-percent rated their confidence in human-forced climate change as "1" or "2." Notice that the figures indicate an *18 to one* ratio of climate workers positing high certainty of human-caused climate perturbations (i.e., "6" or "7" out of 7) versus low confidence ("1" or "2" out of 7) (Bray and von Storch, 2016, pp. 10–11).

"Cognitive dissonance," indeed: in cross-checking Idso, Carter and Singer's claims with their sources, the Heartland authors present as yelling over the straightforward findings of the sources whom they cite. By the data, the question is how solid is the ensemble of scientists' consensus that has consolidated around climate change. There is nonetheless a logic, however tenuous, behind Idso, Carter and Singer's brazen brand of flak at climate science. To wit, the skepticism project has already decisively lost the argument among dedicated climate investigators; and because that battle is lost, the way to salvage something is by relitigating the matter all over again, on flak terms before a different audience in the grandstand.

Meanwhile, investigators project dire outcomes in the difference between 1.5°C rise in global mean temperatures on the Earth's surface (that appears to be locked-in by already accumulated greenhouse emission) versus a 2°C rise (Schleussner et al., 2016). The World Bank observes that a rise in global mean temperature of 4°C would place the world's ecosystems "into a state unknown in human experience" as concerns food production, normalization of extreme climate events, and disruptions of infrastructure and supply lines, with the attendant disruptions of social order (2012, p. xvi). The World Bank suggests that the Russian heatwave of 2010 presents a troubling preview of what is in store if what is now exceptional is dialed up to the norm: "Preliminary estimates" around Russia's heatwave "put the death toll at 55,000, annual crop failure at 25 percent, burned areas at more than one million hectares and economic losses at about US$15 billion (one percent of Gross Domestic Product [GDP])" (World Bank, 2012, p. xiv).

If climate science is even partly prescient, the stakes for humanity are unfathomably high in changing course to renewables. Heartland's flak campaign talks around these stakes, angering about "libels" and banging on over an abstracted "freedom"—even as human liberty would be eviscerated in a state of ongoing climate emergency and Malthusian crisis.

Saviors of Science: Flaking at the IPCC

One stream of Heartland's flak-in-discourse activity takes shots at the IPCC reports that are regarded as the gold-standard compilation of climate science. At the same time, Heartland promotes its own "alternative," the Nongovernmental International Panel on Climate Change (NIPCC). The similarity in the names reads as an attempt to hijack the prestige of the IPCC that was awarded a Nobel Peace Prize in 2007 and to trade on the positive connotations of nongovernmental organizations (NGOs). The similarity of Heartland's name for its project also reads as a bid to confuse the public with semiotic games around "who is who" and "what is what" in climate science. Beyond the nomenclature, Heartland's Manichean construction of its flak narratives are as simplistic as "IPCC *equals* unvarnished bad!" and, as concerns its own creation, "NIPCC *equals* quintessential good!" Within a self-perpetuating rhetorical loop, Heartland constructs itself as the foil to what it flaks, thereby justifying its existence as a flak mill (then, repeat cycle).

While Heartland evidently seeks to confuse matters, I will sort them out. Founded in 1988, IPCC's remit is to collate and assess "the scientific, technical, and socioeconomic information relevant for the understanding of human-induced climate change" (quoted in Union of Concerned Scientists, 2017, para. 6). IPCC has produced five comprehensive reports, in 1990, 1996, 2001, 2007, and 2013. The colossal five-to-six year effort to produce reports involves science workers from 80 countries, shepherded to completion by 830 lead authors, 1,000 contributors and 2,000 reviewers knowledgeable in topical areas (Union of Concerned Scientists, 2017, para. 4).

Heartland's flak-in-discourse posture presents itself as coming to the rescue of beleaguered scientists, in the face of IPPC oppression. According to Heartland, IPCC is "designed to put political leaders and bureaucrats rather than scientists in control of the research project" who go so far as to "revise and rewrite the reports after the scientists have concluded their work" (2017a, para. 7). In Heartland's judgement, the IPPCC "*is* government-sponsored [and] politically motivated" (original emphasis, 2017b, para. 3), thus alienated from scientific practice.

The Union of Concerned Scientists (UCS) is a bona fide organization of professional scientists that includes Nobel Prize winners. On the topic of IPCC processes, UCS observes that "Government representatives are not permitted to edit these book-length [IPCC] reports" and science-credentialed authors "bear the sole responsibility for the content of their chapters" (Union of Concerned Scientists, 2017, para. 24). UCS notes that government representatives, in fact, take part in composing shorter summaries for policymakers. However, "The [IPCC] chapters that underpin all the documents"—source material for the summaries—"are written by and under the control of scientists" (Union of Concerned Scientists, 2017, para. 38).

Governments indeed try to influence IPCC's work—albeit, not in the ways that Heartland insinuates. Saudi Arabia and Kuwait, nations entirely beholden to fossil fuels for the functioning of their economies, have attempted to intervene in IPCC reports to suit their short-term national interests (Oreskes & Conway, 2010, pp. 204–205). In contrast with Heartland's insinuations, the effect of back-seat-driving by governments has likely been to make climate change claims *weaker* where possible on climate change than they would otherwise be.[1]

The sourcing of Heartland's assertions about the IPCC as politically-driven and anti-science are meagre, further demonstrating the organization's commitment to flak-in-discourse over science. Specifically, Heartland's IPCC page cites an Australian journal of right-wing opinion (*Quadrant*) and editorially right-leaning business press (*Forbes, Wall Street Journal*). Heartland also cites a tome from the CreateSpace Independent Publishing Platform—a self-publication mill to serve the vanity of the author who may otherwise take up the quill in vain.

When Heartland assays sourcing with an academic imprimatur, it mangles the source's unambiguous message to align with flak ends. Heartland asserts that the editorial board of *Nature* calls for "the IPCC to be dismantled and for its Fifth Assessment to be its last" (2017a, para. 12). The clear implication is that a prestige scientific journal is decamping from climate change science. In fact, the *Nature* editorial states unequivocally that, "Most importantly, the [IPCC] panel has increased its confidence in the underlying message—that greenhouse gases are altering Earth's climate. No serious politician on the planet can now dispute that" (2013, para. 2). Following the massive effort behind the voluminous IPCC reports that reinforce climate change consensus, *Nature* posits that the science is clearly settled. *Nature* recommends that the IPCC should retool toward devoting itself to "smaller and more rapid assessment of more pressing questions that have a particular political interest and for which science is evolving quickly" (2013, para. 8). In other words, Heartland misuses the editorial's title ("The Final Assessment") to dragoon *Nature* into its flak narrative and to misrepresent the publication's robust support of climate science findings as its opposite.

Nuts about NIPCC

Alongside its flak to undermine IPCC, Heartland offers a correspondingly glowing account of its own creation NIPCC. While numbers are not the truth in themselves, they complicate Heartland's efforts to extol its own product. As noted earlier, thousands of scientists from around the globe participated in the most recent IPCC report. By contrast, NIPCC lists nine contributing authors, most of whom (in the now predictable pattern) have no evident connection to climate science; three are appointed to university faculties in business or economics (Heartland, 2017c). The roster of "Chapter Reviewers" presents a larger if still thin roster at 69. Alongside figures with government or university appointments, the reviewer roster is larded with self-described "consultants," "physicians" and "meteorologists"—despite Heartland's insistence that it has summoned pertinent expertise. In stacking the deck for skepticism in its NIPCC report, Heartland claims repeatedly and without evidence, that climate sceptics are politically barred from peer-reviewed publication. As remedy, Heartland notes that non-reviewed products are considered for inclusion in its report despite (or, *because of*) the lack of independent vetting for quality.

Practicing scientists have been far less impressed with the NIPCC than its Heartland sponsor. A 2011 editorial in *Nature* states: "Despite criticizing climate scientists for being overconfident about their data, models and theories, the Heartland Institute proclaims a conspicuous confidence in single studies and grand interpretations." The editorial concludes, "Many climate sceptics seem to review scientific data and studies not as scientists but as attorneys, magnifying doubts and treating incomplete explanations as falsehoods rather than signs of progress towards the truth" (*Nature*, 2011, para. 5).

In a bid for prestige around NIPCC in 2013, Heartland boasted about the publication of a translated, abridged version of the NIPCC text by a division of the Chinese Academy of Sciences (CAS). Heartland's June 12, 2013 announcement claims that the translation is "a landmark event that puts enormous scientific heft" behind climate change denial, given what Heartland profusely characterizes as the high global prestige of the CAS (Lakely, 2013a, para. 3). As of April 2019, Heartland's assertion of CAS' strongly implied support for denialism remains on different parts of its web site, including Jim Lakely's afore-cited news item. Problem: the translation quickly became a full-blown fiasco for Heartland. To wit, within days of Heartland having trumpeted CAS' "support" to the world in June 2013, CAS used strong language to characterize itself as dragooned into Heartland's bid for denialist self-promotion. CAS' smoking slap down of Heartland's reads in part:

> [...] the Heartland Institute published the news titled "Chinese Academy of Sciences publishes Heartland Institute research skeptical of Global Warming" in a strongly misleading way on its website, implying that the Chinese Academy of Sciences (CAS) supports their views, in contrary to what is clearly stated in the Translators' Note in the Chinese translation.
>
> *The claim of the Heartland Institute about CAS' endorsement of its report is completely false.*

CAS itemizes some of what it objected to in Heartland's attempts to pimp the Academy's prestige to boost its own:

(1) The translation and publication of the Chinese version of the NIPCC report, and the related workshop, are purely non-official academic activities the group of translators. They do not represent, nor have they ever claimed to represent, CAS or any of CAS institutes. [...]

(2) The above fact was made very clear in the Translators' Note in the book, and was known to the NIPCC report authors and the Heartland

Institute before the translation started. The false claim by the Heartland Institute was made public without any knowledge of the translator group.

(3) Since there is absolutely no ground for the so-called CAS endorsement of the report, and the actions by the Heartland Institute went way beyond acceptable academic integrity [...] (emphasis added; Chinese Academy of Sciences Scientific Information Center for Resources and Environment, 2013, paras. 1–5)

The response from CAS should not be taken as a surprise given China's participation in IPCC, its efforts to mitigate its immense industrial pollution problems, and the country's eagerness to invest in sunrise renewable industries that may rule the future. What may be a surprise is that Heartland audaciously continues, albeit in vague phrasing, to cite the translation debacle as a sign of high regard for its NIPCC product and the denialist cause (Heartland, 2017b, para. 7).

Revisiting "Climategate"—or, Hack-and-Flak-"Gate"

The Climate Research Unit (CRU) is a research center domiciled at the University of East Anglia University in United Kingdom. Following its establishment in 1972, CRU achieved a high profile in academic circles. It did so despite its diminutive size of three full-time and one part-time academic appointment, along with a dozen research associates, graduate students and support staff (Oxburgh, Davies, Emanuel, Graumlich, Hand, Huppert, and Kelly, 2010, p. 1). This small research unit became the center of a jumbo-sized flak storm at the end of 2009 that has raged (in phantom form) ever since. The flak storm originating around CRU has become a central trope in the efforts to disable confidence in climate science—and Heartland has been a zealous participant in this discourse.

More specifically, a set of 1,073 emails composed by climate scientists were stolen by hack from a back-up server at East Anglia University. On November 17, 2009, a month prior to the highly anticipated December 2009 United Nations Climate Change Conference (or, "Copenhagen Summit") the emails were document-dumped onto a Russian website, from which they quickly spread across the globe. The hacked set emails were accompanied by an anonymous note that stated,

> We feel that climate science is, in the current situation, too important to be kept under wraps. We hereby release a random selection of correspondence, code and documents. Hopefully, it will give some insights into the science and the people behind it. (quoted in House of Commons Science and Technology Committee, 2010, p. 6)

The hacked emails were composed across more than 13 years, from March 7, 1996 to November 12, 2009, a mass of material that lends itself to cherry-picking, rather than the randomness flagged in the hackers' note.

Heartland asserts that the emails were released by a white-hat "whistle-blower inside" the CRU (*Left exposed*, 2017, para. 27); a story that is not plausible on its face, given the diminutive size of the unit that would make the identity of a so-called whistle-blower obvious. By contrast, the UK's Science and Technology Committee of the House of Commons describes the events as the work of hackers (2010, p. 6), noting that the breach "was the subject of a police inquiry" by the Norfolk Constabulary (2010, p. 8).

In Heartland's semiotics, the crime of hack-and-flak against CRU is known as "Climategate"—and the criminals are the climate science workers. Placing the term "Climategate" in Heartland's web site search function in March 2019 yields 266 hits with articles from as recently as 2018, nine years after the hacked material was released. In defiance of all evidence, Heartland continues to assert that "a small cabal of climate scientists" had corrupted the whole field; "that this was a real conspiracy is beyond argument" (John Costella, quoted in *Left exposed*, 2017, para. 29). In Heartland's narration, CRU's emails index "one of the most serious scientific frauds in the history of Western science" (*Left exposed*, 2017, para. 32). The claim dissolves into sheer nonsense toward flak ends of delegitimization of climate science, given the climate consensus (discussed earlier) and in the light of multiple investigations into the CRU emails (discussed below).[2]

From Flak-in-Discourse to Flak-in-Action

Returning to November 2009, as the pilfered emails begin to circulate, outraged right-wing discourse demanded punitive action. In the case of Pennsylvania State University, where CRU collaborator Michael E. Mann is employed, Sarah M. Assman et al. (2010), pick up the narrative:

> On and about November 22, 2009, The Pennsylvania State University began to receive numerous communications (emails, phone calls and letters) accusing Dr. Michael E, Mann of having engaged in acts, beginning in approximately 1998,

that included manipulating data, destroying records and colluding to hamper the progress of scientific discourse around the issue of anthropogenic global warming, These accusations were based on perceptions of the content of the emails stolen from a server at the Climatic Research Unit of the University of East Anglia in Great Britain. (Assmann, Castleman, Irwin, Jablonski, and Vondracek, 2010, para. 1)

Assman et al. write that, "Given the sheer volume of the communications to Penn State" that asserted wrongdoing, an investigation into Mann was deemed necessary by university administration (2010, para. 2). Thus, far from University of East Anglia, formal investigation of Mann went set into motion almost immediately around his communications with CRU. Flak-in-discourse begat flak-in-action investigation in short order. Given the timing of the hack-and-flak, the hacked emails hung like smog over the long-anticipated Copenhagen Summit.

While insinuating criminality—on the scientists' part, not the hacker(s)—Heartland maintains disciplined silence around the exoneration of CRU and its collaborators by at least six entities with high professional standing. The investigations were conducted by The House of Commons Science and Technology Committee (2010), the Oxburgh Panel (Oxburgh et al., 2010), the Russell Review (Russell, Boulton, Clarke, Eyton, & Norton, 2010), the US' Environmental Protection Agency (2010), National Oceanic and Atmospheric Administration (2011) and Pennsylvania State University (Assmann, Castleman, Irwin, Jablonski, & Vondracek, 2010). I will address some of the details of the investigations' findings below, as they come to bear on an analysis of Heartlandian flak.

As concerns University of East Anglia, within weeks, the university convened two inquiries into CRU (i.e., the aforementioned Oxburgh panel and Russell Review). East Anglia has an academic reputation to uphold in a competitive milieu in order to attract quality students and faculty—as well as a commitment to ascertain truth as a baseline academic objective. Nonetheless, the university was boxed-in once the flak trap had been sprung. On one hand, there would be a cloud over its staff during a tense, time-and-resource-draining process of investigation. In turn, as often happens in a flak episode, the 2009 hack was a far bigger news splash than the eventual 2010 exonerations.

By contrast, an organization such as Heartland has no similar concerns or obligations. An organization in the harassment racket is incentivized to continue to spray flak like drunks with pop-guns since, once in a while, its scatter-shot efforts may transcend reputational vandalism, hit a target and provoke an actual scandal; and, if not, phantom flak can be summoned around the mere fact that an investigation had been convened *as if* a scandal occurred.

The Verdicts

As noted, the results of the raft of investigations around the CRU hack strongly supported the scientists. The *Report by the Lord Oxburgh's Independent Panel* concluded that the CRU researchers "represented an honest and scientifically justified interpretation of the data" (2010, p. 1). Following on-site interviews and close reading of the unit's academic papers, Oxburgh and colleagues posit that CRU's research has "been carried out with integrity." Oxburgh and colleagues conclude that the flak-driven assertions about manipulating data "are not valid" (2010, p. 3) and that the CRU researchers display the scientific virtues of being "objective and dispassionate in their view of their data and results" (2010, p. 4). The Oxburgh Panel also reports good scientific practice as CRU's "published work also contains many cautions about the limitations of their data and their interpretation" (2010, p. 2) along with "appropriate caveats" (2010, p. 4)—as scientists are trained to do, in contrast with flak agents seeking to make flak-in-discourse go viral.

As the hacked emails ricocheted around the world, they also become the bases of petitions of complaint about climate research to the US's Environmental Protection Agency (EPA). The EPA's conclusions are unequivocal: "After months of serious consideration of the petitions and of the state of climate change science, the EPA has found no evidence to support these claims. [...] its review shows that climate science is credible, compelling, and growing" (Environmental Protection Agency, 2010, para. 4). Although the agency found the petitions to present "no evidence," months were nevertheless devoted to parsing all of the hacked emails, as a matter of professional due diligence. Once again, to divert a consequential organization from its core mission—in this case, EPA's mandate to assess and protect the environment—is a cardinal flak strategy.

CRU and its collaborators such as Mann were placed in the dock through the hacked-and-flaked emails. Nonetheless, following lengthy investigation of the petitioners' complaints against the conduct of climate science, the EPA offered some observations about the accusers:

> [The] petitioners have routinely misunderstood or mischaracterized the scientific issues, drawn faulty scientific conclusions, resorted to hyperbole, impugned the ethics of climate scientists in general, characterized actions as "falsifications" and

"manipulation" with no basis for support, and placed an inordinate reliance on blogs, news stories, and literature that is often neither peer reviewed nor accurately summarized in their petitions. (Environmental Protection Agency, 2010, para. 5)

The Russell Review also vindicated the CRU researchers in its findings:

On the specific allegations made against the behavior of CRU scientists, *we find that their rigor and honesty as scientists are not in doubt*. In addition, we do not find that their behavior has prejudiced the balance of advice given to policy makers. In particular, *we did not find any evidence of behavior that might undermine the conclusions of the IPCC assessments*. (original emphasis, Russell, Boulton, Clarke, Eyton, & Norton, 2010, p. 20)

In one of the most devastating passages of the report, Russell et al. use already available raw (unadjusted) temperature data sets to test the pattern of recent rises of global temperatures. In short order, they replicate the "hockey stick" pattern of spiking ground temperatures in recent decades (2010, pp. 44–51). If CRU had improperly manipulated raw data in order to manufacture their preferred results, as flak narratives insist, Russell et al. would not have obtained the same pattern of results as CRU—to say nothing of Russell et al.'s convergence with the results of other researchers' "hockey stick" findings (2010, pp. 44, 49). The Russell Review further observes that, in contrast with a persistent flak talking point, "Any independent researcher may freely obtain the primary station data. It is impossible for a third party to withhold access to the data. It is impossible for a third party to tamper improperly with the data" (2010, p. 48).

Despite the clearly stated affirmation that the Russell Review presents for the integrity of CRU's work, the review also deals out some dings. These arise around CRU's defensiveness toward skeptics making inquiries. In the Russell Review's prose, exoneration of CRU tends to be phrased as an absence of guilt; for example, "the allegations cannot be upheld" (2010, p. 13). In this manner, the hack-and-flak gambit pays off as the reader is constantly reminded that CRU was in the dock.

Despite the repeated vindications of CRU around the hack-and-flak, Heartland's hair-on-fire flak narratives continued throughout the 2010s with the same discredited tropes first launched in 2009. When Heartland has acknowledged the exoneration around the CRU scientists, the exonerations are crudely dismissed and subjected to further flak in an effort toward denigration and delegitimization. In response to Penn State having cleared Mann, Heartland's James Taylor (2010) pushes evidence-free belittlement of the investigation as the work of "ayatollahs"—begging the question of in what country Taylor understands himself to reside. Rather than acknowledge that its claims around the hack-and-flak have been subject to extensive, rigorous investigation and found to be lacking, Heartland has doubled down. Indeed, by 2011, Heartland flogs what it calls "Climategate 2" for flak purposes via the same debunked tropes (Taylor, 2011). Heartland's perseveration and lack of correction in its discourse demonstrate that flak does not have to be remotely true, it does not even have to make sense; it merely has to reach the far lower standard of keeping the pressure on the flak target and echoing other flak discourses on the topic.

The vox pop flak around the CRU hack has also been ugly. In the case of Phil Jones, CRU's longtime director at the time of the hack-and-flak, reactions from internet winged monkeys were abusive and included death threats abetted by with doxxing. In turn, Jones reports having contemplated suicide, lost 10 kilos (22 pounds), and resorted to a regime of beta blockers and sleeping pills while waiting out the conclusion of East Anglia's two investigations (Hickman, 2010). While vox pop reactions cannot be pinned squarely on Heartland, the organization's prominent position within climate skepticism places it within the frame of discussion about vox pop flaksters inspired to further harass targets of flak campaigns.

Super Mann, Global Leviathan

Along with discourse on "the left" (meta-ideological flak) and climate science (issue-oriented flak), Heartland also engages in personalized flak that spotlights one figure as synecdoche for "the left" and/or its brigades of putative climate science Dr. Frankensteins. Even as Heartland has assembled a rogue's gallery of villains on its website, the organization can be said to have a special fetish around the previously mentioned climate researcher Michael E. Mann. The search function on Heartland's web site returns over 200 results on Mann as of 2018. Heartland's Mann-dedicated 3,600 word page flaks him as a "catastrophe advocate" and "militant" (*Left exposed*, 2017, para. 1) who produces "one-sided" research—a contrast, one is supposed to assume, with Heartland's panoramic offerings (2017, para. 10). Mann is "self-aggrandizing" (2017, para. 2), "arrogant, intolerant and vengeful" (2017, para. 3), as well as "very thin skinned" (2017, para. 15). Mann "demands that everyone obey his wishes" (2017, para. 16); and is driven to "silence disagreement"—presumably, across all the world's universities and research units (2017, para. 17).

The Kim dynasty-style "Maximum Leader" Mann is imagined as "gaining control of science journals" so that he can "destroy the careers and publications of perceived opponents" (*Left exposed*, 2017, para. 18). With no irony, dedicated flak mill Heartland diagnoses a culture of "bullying and intimidation that prevails in climate science"—and it must, necessarily, lead back to Mann (2017, para. 45). While Mann rides roughshod over the world, the globally-dispersed community of scientists is implied to cower in fear at the figure Heartland calls an "autocrat" (2017, para. 14). Heartland insists that Mann's work, notably the "hockey stick" temperature graph, has also been "discredited" (repeated twice in *Left exposed*, 2017, para. 1)—a further nonsensical assertion, given Mann's putative dictation of doctrine to the scientific community. In substantive fact, the hockey stick ground temperature pattern has also been corroborated repeatedly, as previously pegged in the discussion of the Russell Review.

Mann, Mann and more Mann: nonetheless, there are some matters around him on which Heartland is, nevertheless, silent for the purposes of preserving its personalized flak narrative. In the aftermath of having had his emails stolen as part of 2009's hack-and-flak, Mann was the target of abuse and death threats including a mailed envelope containing white powder. "Fearing anthrax, he called the campus police," Jane Mayer writes. "Soon the FBI quarantined his office behind crime tape, disrupting the whole department," in a chilling scene (2016, p. 356). While death threats are far more than flak, they can nonetheless be inspired by campaigns of flak.

In a more traditional flak range, Mann has been the repeated target of legal action for his work on climate change that is otherwise regarded as exemplary among scientific peers. Virginia Attorney General Kenneth T. Cuccinelli sued for access to Mann's emails from his former employer, University of Virginia. Cuccinelli contended that Mann committed fraud in his work on global temperatures. The legal confrontation went on for two years, while Cuccinelli was also gearing up for a run for the higher office of governor of Virginia (that Cuccinelli subsequently lost). In the court case's endgame, Virginia's Supreme Court dismissed Cuccinelli's suit "with prejudice"—a final judgement slap down, in other words, that prohibits the case from being refiled (Basken, 2012). However, a loss can be a perverse form of "triumph" to flak specifications for the two years of time-and-effort-draining harassment of Mann as a personalized target of legalistic flak-in-action.

For his part, Mann has pushed back at the flak campaigns. Pushback includes his eye-opening book-length account of being subjected to personalized flak-in-discourse and flak-in-action (Mann, 2012). Moreover, Mann sued right-wing flakster Mark Steyn for his sickening comparison of Mann to serial pedophile Jerry Sandusky. In Heartland's at once appalling and weepy judgement, the series of events constitute *Steyn* as an aggrieved victim (*Left exposed*, 2017).

Notwithstanding Heartland's flak-driven hysteria about a climate scientist as de facto world despot, one suspects that if climate scientists elected to rent their brains to the fossil fuel industries and/or a flak factory, (1) the scientists' compensation would be higher and (2) the harassment they experienced would be infinitely lower. Claim (2) at least is not merely a thought experiment, as I will discuss next.

Heartland's No-Mann

No repulsive statements in the service of flak-in-discourse is beyond the pale for Heartland if the target is Michael E. Mann. However, there is an almost symmetrical anti-Mann in Heartland's discourse: Wei-Hock "Willie" Soon, an unpaid part-time researcher at the Harvard-Smithsonian Center for Astrophysics. Soon posits that variation in solar activity substantially accounts for Earth's surface temperature variation—and not, following the rise of the carbonized industrial economy, human activity. In contrast with Heartland's usual parade of blog-grade discourse, Soon has a doctorate and is an academically published scientific investigator. Whether some of his research should have been in print has been an issue, as editors and editorial board members have resigned over publication of his work that was deemed deeply flawed (cf., *Science*, 2003).

Soon's probity and transparency were in question when it was reported that he had published research in journals without disclosing sources of funding. The funding sources could readily be construed as broadly having a stake in Soon's research program as they were fossil fuel interests. Soon absorbed approximately US$1.2 million in grant monies from carbon firms from 2001 to 2012 (Mulvey & Shulman, 2015, p. 6). One of his papers was billed to a fossil fuel interest, Southern Company, as a "deliverable" (Malakoff, 2015) as was congressional testimony that Soon gave without disclosing his funding (Mulvey & Shulman, 2015, p. 6). While funding disclosures have not always been compulsory, it has tended to be routine—and, indeed, Soon's earlier papers from the 1990s and into the 2000s acknowledged funding from fossil fuel interests (Abraham, n.d., slides 110–114). Moreover, in a startling retreat from investigator independence, "the Smithsonian Institution entered into funding agreements that gave Soon's funders the right to review his scientific studies before they were published" (Mulvey & Shulman, 2015, p. 6).

Soon has been confronted with flak about his work and secrecy around the funding streams of it. Climate Truth orchestrated a petition directed at Smithsonian that called for Soon to be sacked, citing some of the episodes reviewed above. Climate Truth's petition may be construed as an effort toward flak-in-action. While there may be good reason to sack Soon, the petition extends beyond criticism by exerting outside pressure against an organization toward forcing a specific outcome against an employee.

At the same time, much of the criticism toward Soon is just that: criticism. For example, at an event at University of Wisconsin in 2013, Soon is recorded in front of an audience as he loses his cool when asked about the funding matters (Climate Slate, 2017). While the questioners were persistent with Soon in a Q&A context, the incident does not rise to flak as it involved inquiries that an academic investigator should be able to answer, convincingly and without acting hysterical. Placing the discourse around Soon side-by-side with the gutter-grade abuse, law suits, death threats, etc., directed at Mann and other climate workers, presents an unmissable contrast as concerns flak against climate science.

In turn, Heartland dons the Kevlar and goes to considerable lengths to present Soon as a climate martyr and to promote his work. As of July 2018, Heartland's "Who We Are" page on Soon extends to 17 printed pages (Heartland Institute, 2018d). The text vibrates with indignation: "Willie Soon debunks lies of the generously funded environmental left's attacks on an honest climate scientist" (2018d, para. 1). Bast adopts the schoolyard idiom in rallying to Soon: "His critics are all ethically challenged and mental midgets" (Heartland Institute, 2018d, para. 3). On *Breitbart*.com, Bast goes further still and compares Soon to Christ via the bonkers (and Christianity-trivializing) headline, "The crucifixion of Dr. Wei-Hock Soon" (Bast & Morris, 2015). While Heartland is adamant in its support of illegally hacking emails—provided the victims of the hacking crime are climate researchers—it is similarly vehement in defending Soon against legally-channeled Freedom of Information Act requests for his emails. The requests were, in turn, set up by his (wholly avoidable) selective transparency around funding.

Heartland's list of "Articles defending Dr. Soon" extends for five printed pages and assays to "flood the zone" with support from all corners. However, the Soon-shielders are notable for their ideological-in-the-first-instance affiliations, with a concomitant paucity of scientists taking up the cause. One exception: Massachusetts Institute of Technology climate change sceptic Richard Lindzen—and his defense of Soon was published in *Wall Street Journal*. *Breitbart* published ten of the articles that make the list, *Washington Times* published three articles, *NewsMax* published two, among other titans of the non-scientific, right-wing community. Heartland also rallies to Soon with five of its own articles included on the list that it compiled.

Conclusion: Politicizing Science on a Galactic Scale

As of July 2018, Heartland prominently featured a 20-page interview with Soon on its landing page that was originally published as a glossy PDF pamphlet by Calgary, Canada-based Friends of Science. Heartland's use of the material demonstrates the synergy between right-wing flak mills that package themselves as progenitors of boutique discourses.

Under the vainglorious title *Science, philosophy and inquiry on a galactic scale*, Soon self-characterizes as driven by a "humble but sincere premise." To wit, "No religious, social, political or philosophical convictions must be allowed to confuse, corrupt or deny the inherent beauty and purity and truth that subsist in the scientific method" (Friends of Science, 2018, p. 18). Windy self-promotion notwithstanding, Soon channels inaccurate information as well as thunderously politicized judgements on science during the same interview.

Where inaccuracy is concerned, Soon claims that, "the High Court in London condemned [*An Inconvenient Truth* narrator Al] Gore for his false statements about polar bears" (Friends of Science, p. 3). Far from having "condemned" the documentary, Judge Michael Burton ruled that Gore's *Inconvenient Truth* documentary should be exhibited in *all* British schools, albeit with corrections on a couple of subsidiary claims; that is how it works in institutions devoted to accuracy and not to flak. Burton's decision posits that Gore's documentary, "is substantially founded upon scientific research and fact" that is upheld "by the great majority of the world's climate scientists" (Burton, 2007, para. 17). On consulting the original source of Soon's claims, it is a *Twilight Zone* plotline to conscript Burton's decision as favorable toward climate skepticism, although Burton's decision has previously been rhetorically kidnapped by other sceptics (Goss, 2013, pp. 158–159).

Soon insists without skipping a beat that, "I do not do politics, as the environmentalist socialists do. I do science. […] Science is my be-all and end-all" (2018, p. 18). In almost the same breath, Soon expressly posits the reigns of terror of Mussolini, Hitler, Lenin, Stalin and Mao as rehearsals for contemporary environmentalism. His words:

> Each of these monsters, whatever they may have preached about the importance of science, showed the same propensity to interfere with it, to politicize it, and to wrench it into conformity with some dull but dangerous, ingenious but ignorant, marketable but murderous party line as environmentalist international socialism does today. (Friends of Science, 2018, p. 17)

It is not a momentary verbal glitch. Soon doubles down and transmits the politicization of his understanding of science with unashamed clarity: "And it should never be forgotten that modern environmentalist socialism was invented by Hitler in *Mein Kampf* as a method of exercising that fingertip control over every aspect of people's lives and work that all totalitarians crave" (Friends of Science, 2018, p. 18).

Case closed: Nazism pivoted on environmental regulations, the secret portal to totalitarianism, international aggression, and genocide, a point on which to ponder the next time one goose-steps to the recycling bin. Soon's statements are not simply a form of criticism, nor are they merely destitute of logic or evidence. Soon engages in flak by delegitimizing ideological opponents as having a direct line of lineage from the worst regimes, thus opponents are far beyond the pale of further consideration.

Next, Soon puts the campaign button on his lapel and rallies to Trump as champion of coal—a dying, economically uncompetitive industry in which no lucid person would want his or her children to work. On the other side of his clumsy construction of political Manicheanism from Trump, Soon impugns "totalitarian 'Democrats'" (Friends of Science, 2018, p. 18). In these moments, Soon hurtles beyond the orbit of being merely political and is screaming-through-the-bullhorn partisan. Soon's own statements have, moreover, made it unmistakable that his climate findings and his political ideology adhere to each other like a hand in a tailored glove—although, in the next evidence-free verbal paroxysm, Soon accuses *other* investigators of that very same politicized condition.

Soon and his Heartland sponsor assay to browbeat the reader so they may have it both ways: "humble but sincere" servant to science who disavows politics in one moment, awkwardly pivoting to partisan warrior in full ideological warpaint unsheathing the flak sword in the next. One position (apolitical science servant) crudely annuls the other (science politicizer). Believe in nothing—aside from one's license for roaring double-standard for flak purposes, in support of elite authority—and all ideologically serviceable beliefs become possible under the flak mill aegis.

Gravely flawed ideas will always hail dispersed adherents; but with the establishment of dedicated flak mills to promote and disseminate those discourses in a well-funded and message-disciplined fashion, salted with heavy doses of delegitimation toward ideological foes, flak can become a persistent nuisance or even a difference-maker.

Notes

1. Government harassment of climate science has been documented to have occurred in recent years—albeit not quite in the way that Heartland asserts. For example, the right-wing government of Stephen Harper in Canada clamped down on government climate scientists' access to the public arena as a means of suppressing dissemination of climate science (Evans Ogden, 2016).
2. An episode in 2012 demonstrates Heartland's almost comical inconsistency on the topic of the unwanted circulation of an organization's internal correspondence. Climate scientist (and MacArthur Genius Award recipient) Peter Gleick obtained and disseminated internal documents from Heartland by (falsely, unethically) claiming to be a board member who had changed his email address. Heartland's legal representation referred the matter to the US Attorney, in an unsuccessful stab at prosecution of Gleick (Lakely, 2013b).

References

Abraham, J. (n.d.). *A scientist responds to Christopher Monckton*. Minneapolis, MN: Saint Thomas University. Retrieved from static.stthomas.edu/jpabraham/?utm_source=ustredirect&utm_medium=Vanity&utm_campaign=Abraham%20Presentation.

Abraham, J. (2013). Heartland Institute wastes real scientist's time—yet again. *The Guardian*, 20 May. Retrieved from www.theguardian.com/environment/climate-consensus-97-per-cent/2013/may/20/heartland-institute-scientists.

American Association for the Advancement of Science. (2016). Dear Members of Congress […]. 28 June. Retrieved from www.aaas.org/sites/default/files/06282016.pdf.

American Geophysical Union. (2013). Human-induced climate change requires urgent action. August. Retrieved from sciencepolicy.agu.org/files/2013/07/AGU-Climate-Change-Position-Statement_August-2013.pdf.

Assmann, S.M., Castlemann, W., Irwin, M.J., Jablonski, N.G., & Vondracek, F.W. (2010). *Final investigation report involving Dr. Michael E. Mann*. State College, PA: The Pennsylvania State University.

Avery, D. (2007). 500 scientists whose research contradicts man [sic]-made global warming scares. Heartland Institute. 14 September. Retrieved from www.heartland.org/publications-resources/publications/500-scientists-whose-research-contradicts-man-made-global-warming-scares.

Basken, P. (2012). Virginia Supreme Court rejects Attorney General's demand for climate documents. *The Chronicle of Higher Education*, 2 March. Retrieved August 16, 2018 from https://www.chronicle.com/article/Virginia-Supreme-Court-Rejects/131063.

Bast, J.L. (2018). *The patriot's guide to freedom and firearms*. Arlington, IL: Heartland Institute.

Bast, J.L., & Morris, J.A. (2015). The crucifixion of Dr. Wei-Hock Soon. *Breitbart*.com, 24 February. Retrieved from https://www.breitbart.com/politics/2015/02/24/the-crucifixion-of-dr-willie-soon/.

Boykoff, M.T., & Boykoff, J.M. (2004). Balance as bias. *Global Environmental Change*, 14, 125–136.

Bray, D., & von Storch, H. (2016). *The Bray and von Storch fifth annual survey of climate scientists*. Geesthacht, Germany: Helmholtz-Zentrum Geesthacht.

Burton, M. (2007). *In the High Court of Justice, Queen's Bench Division, Administrative Court, before Mr. Justice Burton, between Stuart Dimmock and Secretary of State for Education and Skills: Judgment*. Case No.: CO/3615/2007. London: Royal Courts of Justice. Retrieved from http://www.bailii.org/cgi-bin/markup.cgi?doc=/ew/cases/EWHC/Admin/2007/2288.html&query=title+%28+dimmock+%29&method=boolean.

Carmichael, J.T., & Brulle, R.J. (2017). Elite cues, media coverage, and public concern. *Environmental Politics*, 26(2), 232–252.

Chinese Academy of Sciences Scientific Information Center for Resources and Environment. (2013). The statements on the Chinese translation of the *Climate change reconsidered—NIPCC report*. 14 June. Retrieved from english.llas.cas.cn/ns/es/201306/t20130615_104626.html.

Climate Slate. (2017). Willie Soon brought to you and funded by Exxon. *YouTube*, 23 November. Retrieved from www.youtube.com/watch?v=BxXTgcwk3jQ.

Climate Truth. (n.d.). Smithsonian: Drop Willie Soon. Retrieved from act.forecastthefacts.org/sign/willie_soon/.

Commonwealth Academies of Science. (2018). Consensus statement on climate change. 12 March. Retrieved from: https://royalsociety.org/~/media/news/2018/commonwealth-academies-consensus-statement-on-climate-change-12-march-2018.pdf.

Dewan, A. (2018). Our climate plans are in pieces as killer summer shreds records. *Cable News Network*, 5 August. Retrieved from edition.cnn.com/2018/08/04/world/climate-change-deadly-summer-wxc-intl/index.html.

Economist, The. (2012). Toxic shock. 26 May. Retrieved from www.economist.com/international/2012/05/26/toxic-shock.

Environmental Law Institute. (2009). U.S. tax breaks subsidize foreign oil production. September. Retrieved from www.eli.org/news/us-tax-breaks-subsidize-foreign-oil-production.

Environmental Protection Agency. (2010). U.S. Environmental Protection Agency dismisses allegations against CRU, 29 July. Retrieved July 20, 2018, from https://www.uea.ac.uk/about/media-room/press-release-archive/cru-statements/other-reports/epare-report.

Evans Ogden, L. (2016). Nine years of censorship. *Nature*, 3 May. Accessed from www.nature.com/news/nine-years-of-censorship-1.19842.

Friends of Science. (2018). *Science, philosophy and inquiry on a galactic scale: An interview with Dr. Willie Soon*. Calgary, Canada: Author.

Feulner, E.J. (1985). Ideas, think-tanks and governments. Quadrant, November, 22–26.

Gelfand, M. (2018). *Rule makers, rule breakers*. New York: Scribner.

Geological Society of America. (2015, April). *GSA position statement: Climate change*. Boulder, CO: Author.

Goreham, S. (2013). Revisiting climategate as climatism falters. Heartland Institute, 7 June. Retrieved from www.heartland.org/news-opinion/news/revisiting-climategate-as-climatism-falters?source=policybot.

Goss, B.M. (2000). *Teeth-gritting harmony*. Doctoral thesis, Institute of Communications Research, University of Illinois at Urbana-Champaign.

Goss, B.M. (2006). Sex education fantasies. *Southern Review*, 39(1), 8–24.

Goss, B.M. (2013). *Rebooting the Herman and Chomsky propaganda model in the twenty-first century*. New York: Peter Lang.

Goss, B.M. (2018). Veritable flak tactics. *Journalism Studies*, 19(4), 548–563.

Grandia, K. (2008). Outrage in the climate science community over the "500 Scientist" list. *DeSmogBlog*, 29 April. Retrieved from www.desmogblog.com/outrage-in-the-climate-science-community-continues-over-the-500-scientist-list.

Hagel, C. (2014). Secretary of Defense speech: Conference of Defense Ministers of the Americas. U.S. Department of Defense, 24 October. Retrieved from www.defense.gov/News/Speeches/Speech-View/Article/605617/.

Heartland Institute. (2013). Heartland Institute celebrates Earth Day with release of new book. 22 April. Retrieved from www.ucsusa.org/sites/default/files/legacy/assets/documents/global_warming/Global-Warming-Skeptic-Organizations-Source-40-Heartland.pdf.

Heartland Institute. (2014). Joe Bast on *Special Report* with Bret Baier. *YouTube*, 8 April. Retrieved from www.youtube.com/watch?v=lA6oFArNYfk.

Heartland Institute. (2017a). About the IPCC. Retrieved from http://climatechangeconsidered.org/about-the-ipcc/.

Heartland Institute. (2017b). About the NIPCC. Retrieved 20 July from climatechangeconsidered.org/about-the-nipcc/.

Heartland Institute. (2017c). NIPCC scientists. Retrieved from climatechangeconsidered.org/nipcc-scientists/.

Heartland Institute. (2018a). *Freedom rising*. Arlington Heights, IL: Heartland Institute.

Heartland Institute. (2018b). Reply to critics. Retrieved from www.heartland.org/about-us/reply-to-critics/index.html.

Heartland Institute. (2018c). Steve Goreham. Retrieved from www.heartland.org/about-us/who-we-are/steve-goreham.

Heartland Institute. (2018d). Willie Soon. Retrieved from www.heartland.org/about-us/who-we-are/willie-soon.

Heartland Institute. (2019). Seton Motely. Retrieved from www.heartland.org/about-us/who-we-are/seton-motley.

Hickman, L. (2010). Climate scientist vilified by sceptics "relieved, vindicated" and back at CRU. *The Guardian*, 7 July. Retrieved from www.theguardian.com/environment/2010/jul/07/climategate-scientist-relieved-vindicated.

Hickman, L. (2012). Heartland Institute compares belief in global warming to mass murder. *The Guardian*, 4 May. Retrieved from www.theguardian.com/environment/blog/2012/may/04/heartland-institute-global-warming-murder.

House of Commons Science and Technology Committee. (2010). *The reviews into the University of East Anglia's Climatic Research Unit's e-mails*. 11 January. London: House of Commons.

Huelskamp, T. (2018). Dear Mr. President [...]. Heartland Institute, 11 April. Retrieved from www.heartland.org/_template-assets/documents/Pruitt%20Coalition%20Letter.pdf.

Huertas, A., & Adler, D. (2012). *Is News Corp. failing science?* Cambridge, MA: Union of Concerned Scientists.

Huertas, A., & Kreigsman, R. (2014). *Science or spin?* Cambridge, MA: Union of Concerned Scientists.

Idso, C.D., Carter, R.M., & Singer, S.F. (2016). *Why scientists disagree about global warming*. Arlington Heights, IL: Heartland Institute.

Jacobson, L. (1995). Tanks on the roll. *National Journal*, 8 July, 1767–1771.

Lakely, J. (2013a). The Chinese Academy of Sciences publishes research skeptical of global warming. Heartland Institute, 12 June. Retrieved from www.heartland.org/news-opinion/news/chinese-academy-of-sciences-publishes-research-skeptical-of-global-warming.

Lakely, J. (2013b). The criminal case against Peter Gleick. Heartland Institute, 11 February. Retrieved from www.heartland.org/news-opinion/news/the-criminal-case-against-peter-gleick.

Left exposed. (2017). Michael E. Mann. Retrieved from leftexposed.org/2016/07/michael-e-mann/.

Malakoff, D. (2015). Journals investigate climate skeptic author's ties to fossil fuel firm as new allegations arise. *Science*, 10 June. Retrieved from www.sciencemag.org/news/2015/06/journals-investigate-climate-skeptic-author-s-ties-fossil-fuel-firm-new-allegations.

Mann, M.E. (2012). *The hockey stick and the climate wars*. New York: Columbia University Press.

Mayer, J. (2016). *Dark money* (large print). New York: Random House.

McLean, N. (2017). *Democracy in chains*. New York: Viking.

Motely, S. (2018). The left's copy-and-paste fake grassroots campaign. *Left exposed*, 26 January. Retrieved July 20, 2018 from leftexposed.org/2018/01/lefts-latest-copy-paste-fake-grassroots-campaign/.

Mulvey, K., & Shulman, S. (2015). *The climate deception dossiers*. Cambridge, MA: Union of Concerned Scientists.

National Oceanic and Atmospheric Administration. (2011). Inspector General's review of stolen emails confirms no evidence of wrong-doing by NOAA climate scientists. 24 February. Washington, DC: United States Department of Commerce.

Nature. (2011). Heart of the matter, 28 July. Retrieved from www.nature.com/articles/475423b.

Nature. (2013). The final Assessment. 18 September. Retrieved from www.nature.com/news/the-final-assessment-1.13757.

Noon, M. (2016). Foreword. In *Why scientist disagree about global warming* (pp. xi–xiv). Arlington Heights, IL: Heartland Institute.

Oreskes, N., & Conway, E.M. (2010). *Merchants of doubt.* New York: Bloomsbury.

Oxburgh, R., Davies, H., Emanuel, K., Graumlich, L., Hand, D., Huppert, H., & Kelly, M. (2010). *Report of the international panel set up by the University of East Anglia to examine the research of the Climatic Research Unit,* 12 April. Norwich, UK: University of East Anglia.

Patel, R., & Moore, J.W. (2018). *A history of the world in seven cheap things.* London: Verso.

Ricci, D. (1993). *The transformation of American politics.* New Haven, CT: Yale University Press.

Roosevelt, F.D. (n.d.). *State of the Union address: The four freedoms (6 January 1941).* Retrieved 17, from voicesofdemocracy.umd.edu/fdr-the-four-freedoms-speech-text/.

Russell, Sir M., Boulton, G., Clarke, P., Eyton, D., & Norton, J. (2010). *The independent climate change emails review.* Retrieved from www.cce-review.org/pdf/final%20report.pdf.

Saint Thomas, University of. (n.d.). *John P. Abraham.* Retrieved from courseweb.stthomas.edu/jpabraham/.

Schleussner, C.F., Lissner, T.K., Fischer, E.M., Wohland, J., Perrette, M., Golly, A., et al. (2016). Differential climate impacts for policy-relevant limits to global warming: The case of 1.5°C and 2°C. *Earth System Dynamics, 7,* 327–351.

Science. (2003). In the eye of the storm, 15 August, *301,* 914.

Smith, J.A. (1991). *The idea brokers.* New York: The Free Press.

Snyder, T. (2018). *The road to unfreedom.* New York: Tim Duggan Books.

Soley, L.C. (1995). *Leasing the ivory tower.* Boston: South End Press.

Stern, N. (2006). *Stern review on the economics of climate change.* London: Government of the United Kingdom/Her Majesty's Treasury.

Taylor, J.M. (2010). Ayatollahs clear Ahmadinejad—I mean Penn State clears Mann. *Heartland Institute,* 2 July. Retrieved from www.heartland.org/publications-resources/publications/ayatollahs-clear-ahmadinejad--i-mean-penn-state-clears-mann.

Taylor, J.M. (2011). Climategate 2 emails loaded with bombshells. *Heartland Institute,* 5 December. Retrieved from www.heartland.org/news-opinion/news/climategate-2-emails-loaded-with-bombshells?source=policybot.

Tollefson, J. (2011). Climate change politics. *Nature,* 27 July. Retrieved from www.nature.com/news/2011/110727/full/475440a.html.

Union of Concerned Scientists. (2017). *The IPCC.* Retrieved from www.ucsusa.org/global-warming/science-and-impacts/science/ipcc-backgrounder.html.

U.S. Global Change Research Program. (2017). *Fourth national climate assessment: Executive summary.* Washington, DC: U.S. Global Change Research Program.

World Bank. (2012). *4°: Turn down the heat.* Washington, DC: Author.

· 4 ·
"TRANSCENDENT TRUTH" IN DISGUISE: PROJECT VERITAS' FLAK TRAPS

> We're going to create an army of exposers and if you are lying or stealing or cheating, we are going to find you and make you an unwilling Internet celebrity. [...] And you can continue to say it's a joke, but people are gonna be resigning.
> —Project Veritas founder James O'Keefe (quoted in Nuzzi, 2015, para. 38)

Introduction: Hanging on the Telephone

In 2016, Jane Mayer of *The New Yorker* reported on a strange and lengthy phone message on the messaging service of Dana Geraghty of the Open Society Foundations in New York. The Open Society is an initiative of billionaire/philanthropist George Soros who has been subject to blasts of flak from the political right for decades. For her part, Geraghty directs the foundations' pro-democracy programs in Eurasia. In Mayer's narration, the lengthy phone message began as follows:

> "Hey, Dana," a voice began. The caller sounded to her like an older American male. "My name is, uh, Victor Kesh. I'm a Hungarian-American who represents a, uh, foundation that would like to get involved with you and aid what you do in fighting for, um, European values." (Mayer, 2016, para. 2)

Geraghty thought it was very curious that someone ostensibly from a foundation would call and not state *which* foundation he was with, alongside apparently *offering* rather than seeking funds. However, the episode took an even more bizarre turn. "The caller had failed to hang up," thus was "unaware that he was still being recorded, [and] seemed to be conducting a meeting about how to perpetrate an elaborate sting on Soros" (Mayer, 2016, para. 5) "Victor Kesh" turned out to be a *nom-de-guerre* of James O'Keefe, founder of Project Veritas.

Into the still open phone line, O'Keefe regaled the audience in the room on his end of the line with techniques that would be directed at Geraghty and her employer. There would be hundreds of such efforts, O'Keefe vowed, to ensnare the tentacles of Soros: money would be offered, undercover operatives would "talk the talk" (presumably of liberal gibberish, so they could better insinuate themselves), LinkedIn accounts would be penetrated. There would be more, O'Keefe's promised. An operative with "a real heavy British accent" (2016, para. 7), a putative sign of gravitas, would be mobilized to record covertly from inside Soros' foundation as its malign plots played out.

As the accidental phone message discourse indicates, Veritas is dedicated to claiming what O'Keefe calls "scalps" (quoted in Weigel, 2016, para. 4). In other words, Veritas' flak-in-discourse to trash targets' reputations is designed to stimulate action such as upending careers and organizations. In this case, the 2016 phone-fail caper did not claim the scalp of Soros and did not clip Open Society's tentacles. Open Society President Chris Stone nonetheless captures the strange chimera of Veritas' flak project: "These guys can't even figure out how to use an Internet browser, let alone conduct an undercover operation. [...] But the issues here aren't funny. There's some kind of dirty-tricks operation in play against us" (quoted in Mayer, 2016, para. 9). Despite a resume pocked with inept interludes, Project Veritas has claimed scalps. Even Inspector Clouseau will hit a shot in the dark once in a while, while causing mayhem for his mere presence.

Now consider the paradox. Highly professionalized organizations with a name to uphold in a field such as academics, journalism, business, government (and so on) harbor baseline concern with maintaining their reputations to high standards. At the same time, a flak mill's station at the bottom of the reputational totem pool becomes a weird form of advantage in dealing with people and organizations of high repute. With two perpetual black-eyes in reputational terms, a flak mill has nothing to lose; indeed, a worse reputation may be better in performing sordid work. High-functioning institutions devote years of effort toward cultivating strong reputations as their supreme assets. A good name is a garden that can be trashed across a handful of news cycles and therefore calls for vigilance if, for example, any employees are accused of unsavory activity. In the flak milieu, weakness can become strength—and vice-versa.

Splicing the Truth

Let us be more concrete and consider a stunt that played out in Washington, DC in 2011. National Public Radio (NPR) fund-raising executive Ron Schiller met for a two-hour lunch with representatives of what claimed to be the "Muslim Education Action Center" (Project Veritas, 2011a). The "action center" did not exist and its putative representatives were imposters employed by Project Veritas who clandestinely recorded the lunch meeting. Once the recording was secured, Veritas sculpted the two-hour lunch into an 11-minute video that was disseminated via internet. The video, with the authority of an ostensibly indexical relation to material reality, looked sufficiently damning as to necessitate Schiller's immediate resignation from NPR. For good measure, Schiller was terminated from the position he was about to assume at the Aspen Institute. NPR also fired Betsy Liley who was present at the lunch and CEO Vivian Schiller (no relation) who was not present.

Veritas' 2011 NPR stunt was primed for a livid right-wing reaction through the intersecting tropes of a suspect media outlet and the always-already-at-hand figure of the Muslim as alien "Other." However, the Veritas stooges' faked identities were not the only phoniness around this flak trap. In Scott Baker's analysis of the complete two-hour recording of the lunch for the right-wing publication *The Blaze*, he finds that NPR behaved credibly and professionally (2011). While Schiller exhibits moments of questionable judgement, Baker argues that Veritas edited the supposedly *cinéma vérité* video toward misleading ends.

In one of the opening moments of the edited video, Schiller apparently gives an amused response to the idea that Sharia law is on the march through the United States—a bold deception through editing as Schiller was actually responding to an unrelated moment of the lunch discourse. Moreover, Schiller's criticisms of Republicans in general and the contemporaneous "Tea Party" were also exaggerated through selective editing. In the full video, Schiller flagged his comments as re-stating criticisms that establishment Republicans and friends had made. Schiller acknowledged that he shared many of these criticisms, while also praising conservatives (for, e.g., supposed fiscal discipline).

Upon seeing Veritas' 11-minute montage of the encounter, Al Tompkins, a journalist and ethics instructor at the Poynter Institute, describes himself as having been disturbed. However, on seeing the full two-hour tape, Tompkins was struck by the impact of Veritas' selective snipping: "The message that he [Schiller] said most often—I counted six times: He told these two people that he had never met before that you cannot buy coverage [...] He says it over and over and over again." Tompkins summarizes Veritas' manipulative editing of the video by observing that, "I tell my children there are two ways to lie [...] One is to tell me something that didn't happen, and the other is not to tell me something that did happen. I think they [Veritas] employed both techniques" in the NPR video (quoted in Folkenflik, 2011). Nonetheless, against the evidence of this and other episodes, Veritas' founder O'Keefe continues to insist in 2018 that, "we do not put words in our subjects' mouths" (2018, para. 41).

Project Flak

Veritas has developed a strain of flak that pivots on staging contrived scenarios around its targets, such as the NPR lunch with the non-existent "action center." Some targets unwisely if unwittingly facilitate the flak through poor discretion in talking at length about professional matters with people whom they do not know; for example, a teachers' union lawyer discussing cases on which he has worked (Project Veritas, 2017). Overly credulous and loquacious targets notwithstanding, several secret ingredients turn these episodes into flak. In particular, the flaksters employ false identities and motives, are kitted with clandestine recording devices—and, importantly, they harbor the abundant ill-will to cause damage to their targets through manipulative editing of the recording if needed. Following a video's production and distribution, Veritas flak-in-discourse is fashioned to elicit flak-in-action—the "people are gonna be resigning" outcome, flagged in the epigram.

Even as its own actions have in some cases occurred in a legal twilight—surreptitious recording is illegal in many jurisdictions—Veritas assumes that its targets habitually engage in wrongdoing. Moreover, there is apparently no chance for the assumption to be proven wrong by evidence, thereby annulling a basic characteristic of a rigorous quest for truth. Veritas' practice of deceptive editing, often amped-up further by voice-over editorial comment, has been flagged over and again (Media Matters, 2016). Given the persistence of the pattern, Veritas' ideologically-loaded editing techniques can be called a motif in its products and not an occasional glitch.

As a result of embarrassing exposures of its deceptive practices while editing, Veritas no longer releases the full unedited videos of its flak traps (Weigel, 2016). Nevertheless, further Veritas deceptions have been exposed when suspicious targets of flak traps have made their own recordings of interaction with Veritas' imposters. In one instance, documentarian Josh Fox taped a phone call with a Veritas stooge as he sensed a suspicious offer of funding for a film in the light of the imposter's previous, shambling email approaches to him. Fox was likely deemed a flak target for having directed the anti-fracking documentary *Gasland*. In any event, Fox refused to consider the funds over a lack of concrete information about the (in reality, non-existent, invented-for-flak-purposes) funders; a polite but clear "no." Veritas' version of the encounter cuts the recording before Fox demands more information about funders as the unmet condition for signing on to any project (Project Veritas, 2014b). Veritas' editing subterfuge thereby engineers the false impression that Fox *accepted* rather than *turned down* the funding offer (Dickson, 2014). In the flak regime, "no" can and does become "yes." O'Keefe's contention about not putting words in targets mouths reads as hollow in this light.

After a video is produced, Veritas disseminates its resultant version of events for further impact. "Hollywood celebrities caught on hidden camera accepting money from 'Middle Eastern oil interests'" (Project Veritas, 2014b) that flaked at Fox and other (to their chagrin, more trusting) environmentalist documentary filmmakers was garlanded with the prestige of exhibition at the Cannes Film Festival. Along with the high-profile festival platform, the same video has also been viewed more than 300,000 times on YouTube.

Flak accusation collapses into conviction, along with another unstated premise. To wit, rampant wrongdoing is the work of the political left, as Veritas' traps are locked-and-loaded to assume. In this vein, Veritas' targets of flak tightly align with the meta-ideology and obsessions of the political right. The litany of Veritas product fixates on alleged election mischief that is always coded as Democrat (Project Veritas, 2014c, 2015b), the sieve at the US' southern border (Project Veritas, 2014a), media shamelessly pandering to Islam (2011a), craven environmental hustlers (2014b), and loveless gay marriage (Project Veritas, 2008). The circus of higher education merits notice (Project Veritas, 2015a) alongside a putatively terrifying news media-academic-activist nexus, that actually reflects Veritas' manifestly obvious "misunderstanding" of Clay Shirky's claims about *The New York Times* and Occupy Wall Street (Project Veritas, 2011b).

In the balance of this chapter, I will survey Veritas' backstory and characterizations of itself. I will then examine Veritas' flak activities as concerns a nongovernmental organization and around elections, including the implications of its spectacular flak-trap failure in the 2017 Alabama Senate contest. We begin the examination of ten years of Veritas with the organization's founder.

Founding Flakster

Veritas is the brainchild of O'Keefe, a 2006 graduate of Rutgers University where he began his career as a right-wing activist. O'Keefe gained support for his campus capers from the infrastructure developed to groom precocious rightists; notably, the Leadership Institute (parent organization of *Campus Reform*, discussed in Chapter 6) for whom O'Keefe also worked for a period after graduating. According to Zav Chafets (2011), Leadership Institute (LI) furnishes assistance to about 100 right-wing student publications around the US. With LI's support, O'Keefe founded *The Centurion* at Rutgers as an undergraduate; a battle-hardened title, with a dollop of Roman gravitas, although O'Keefe's preferred battlefield during George W. Bush's "Global War on Terror" was the editing suite.

While further preparing for right-wing meme combat as a student, O'Keefe protested the distribution of Lucky Charms cereal in Rutgers' dining halls. The ostensible reason was the cereal box's depiction of people of Irish descent. In retrospect in 2018, O'Keefe writes, "For the flak catchers at Rutgers, it was pure lose-lose" as to whether to hold the line against the "aggrieved" ethnicity, or give in to the disingenuous gambit; in other words, a double-bind that was "win-win" for the flak merchants (2018, para. 25). O'Keefe found gratification in the precocious flak trap: "We posted the video on YouTube and watched the counter go nuts. I saw immediately that video had a viral power that print simply did not have" (2018, para. 25)—perhaps because video can be edited even drastically without losing the aura of indexical authenticity. In turn, O'Keefe has graduated into flaking targets with more expansive remits than Rutgers administrators deliberating over cereal.

The Contours of "Transcendent Truth"

Despite the lowered stakes around their reputations, noted earlier, flak mills may nevertheless feign high standards and flash supposed signs of pedigree for their core audiences. In O'Keefe's narration, Veritas is an organ of muscular investigative journalism that doggedly pursues power, corruption and lies. The organization channels no small opinion of itself, as the name "Veritas" translates from Latin not as some "ordinary" sense of truth—but full-blown *transcendent truth*. He nominates himself as "an investigative journalist," possessed by visions of "a more ethical and transparent society." O'Keefe posits that, "What I do is the truest form of journalism there is. We hit the record button and show people what we found" (quoted in Mayer, 2016, para. 32). It is a less than exact account of Veritas' record, given its previously noted predilection for strategically hitting the delete button while editing.

According to O'Keefe, Veritas has mobilized "twelve fulltime journalists *risking their lives*" (emphasis added, 2016, para. 24). The quality of what O'Keefe is calling journalism will be examined later, while he does not explain the alleged mortal threats. O'Keefe maintains that Veritas "takes the filters off" and has placed its finger on the pulse of an "inarguable reality" (2018, para. 30). In this view, Veritas is driven by the uncompromising demands of its transcendent truth brand name: "The goal of Project Veritas is to show the world as closely as possible to the way the world really is," through "exposure of corruption" (2018, para. 31). O'Keefe intones that, in this quest, "We cannot afford to be wrong" (2018, para. 30). Cloying self-importance aside, Veritas has been proven wrong repeatedly—and without consequence, as it expanded the scope of its action in 2014 by initiating a political arm, Project Veritas Action, alongside the ambitions flagged in this chapter's epigram.[1]

In contrast with news workers of the mainstream whom he derides as "such corrupt scum," O'Keefe characterizes Project Veritas as soldiering on through "civil lawsuits, jail, defamation, lies, [and] slander" (2016, para. 1). O'Keefe has indeed acquired a criminal record. He was arrested and charged with a misdemeanor for posing as a phone repairperson to gain entrance to a Democratic Party Senator's Washington office in 2010. The stunt is of a piece with O'Keefe's penchant for donning costumes. However, unlike a counter-hegemonic journalist risking menacing responses in Putin's Russia, O'Keefe was not immortalized in a mugshot for seeking out truth amidst mafia-state peril. Rather, the repairperson episode generated legal problems for Veritas from whole cloth, through the amateur attempt to tap a phone on an extra-legal (literally warrantless) presumption of wrongdoing by the Senator. In contrast with creating legal peril and spectacle were there otherwise would have been none, Veritas could have simply asked informed, probing questions of the Senator's office and/or investigated by parsing documents and sources to test hypotheses against evidence. O'Keefe's wholly avoidable collision with the law may, in any event, drive his livid assertions that the U.S. legal system is "lawless" and "systematically corrupt" (2018, para. 44). A flak organization may even gain some perverse benefit from legal actions against it that can be spun for the faithful audience as evidence of being a victim (rather than an instigator) of flak.

On Script?

A sympathetic feature story on O'Keefe in 2011 in *The New York Times Magazine* suggests the degree to which Veritas may, in effect, script reality in order to endow its flak stunts with impact (Chafets, 2011). Here is part of the discussion between O'Keefe and his associates on a planned flak trap at a social services office:

> "A couple could approach a caseworker and say they're thinking of getting married, but they can't decide if they should because it might be a loss in benefits," Adeleye offered.
> "A mom and a baby daddy, and the caseworker telling them not to get married," Jean-Louis added. (quoted in Chafets, 2011, paras. 38–39)

The video flak trap would not only show the very idea of family being crushed by Statist bureaucrats, as O'Keefe and his collaborators also identify a racial angle.

> "Right," Jean-Louis. "A caseworker telling a black man not to marry."
> "A white caseworker," Adeleye said. (quoted in Chafets, 2011, paras. 41–42)

O'Keefe and his colleagues sniff out a wedge-issues around race and double down on what they want the camera to capture:

> "O.K., a white woman caseworker telling a black man not to marry a black woman. You know sisters are going to be outraged at that!"
> "Maybe we should do a comparison video," O'Keefe said, "with a white couple or a white man." (quoted in Chafets, 2011, paras. 45–46)

Along with checking the box of racial outrage, O'Keefe envisions that the video should demonstrate a big-picture certitude that, "Marriage is being challenged, made extinct" (quoted in Chafets, 2011, para. 48).

Although Veritas claims that its videos index unvarnished reality, its internal discussions before a sympathetic scribe suggest effort to stage-manage scenes to ideologically-resonant specifications. Moreover, there is no evident concern with whether the recordings capture typical happenings. In this view, Veritas' videos are more like puppet theatre than "fly-on-the-wall" recording—with deceptive editing as the final step in contriving reality. In contrast with the scientific method that is structured to set up tests in which the investigator has a fair chance to be shown to be *wrong* in his or her assumptions, Veritas appears willing to seed the battlefield beforehand in order to obtain some semblance of the findings it seeks out.

Straight-Talking Underdog?

O'Keefe's construction of Veritas' mission rests on several pillars. Along with positing itself as the fount of "transcendent truth," Veritas' discourse constructs itself as dedicated to a "populist" project that is hounded by the elite. O'Keefe (2018) further asserts Veritas to be non-ideological and even-handed in its scrutiny toward all political persuasions. I consider the claims in turn.

Despite the insistence on subaltern, underdog status, Veritas has been backed by the right-wing funding channel Donors Trust, a honey pot for movement right-wingers to obtain discretely donated funds (Mayer, 2016). Moreover, whatever "risks" O'Keefe claims to have endured have been tempered by a reported US$317,000 annual salary (Nwanevu, 2017). By 2016, O'Keefe namechecked Veritas' elite network of supporters in a speech at the "David Horowitz Freedom Center's 2016 Restoration Weekend" convened in a Palm Beach resort. For its part, the Freedom Center pulls in funds from the plutocratic right-wing foundation circuit; to wit, the Lynde and Harry Bradley, Sarah Scaife, and Olin Foundations (SourceWatch, 2018). Besides naming the deceased Andrew Breitbart as his mentor, O'Keefe's address gave shout out to supporters on lofty perches that include Fox News performer Sean Hannity and then president-elect Trump (O'Keefe, 2016).

As concerns the claim to be remote from the elite circle, the opening scene of O'Keefe's 2018 book, *American Pravda*, is similarly striking, albeit not in the ways that the narration presumably intends. In the book's opening paragraph, O'Keefe visits Trump's Manhattan office during the Obama presidency. In O'Keefe's recounting, the two men immediately hurtle into tawdry political fantasies and commiserate over "Obama's birth certificate" (2018, para. 2) as well as "that pimp and hooker thing" (i.e., Veritas' flak stunt against Association of Community Organizations for Reform Now). O'Keefe's claims of oppressed, subaltern status are complicated by the personal connection with—as well as funding from—the bile-spewing billionaire. In particular,

Veritas obtained funding from the Trump Organization of US$20,000 in 2015 (Pilkington, 2017). O'Keefe was one of Trump's invited guests at a 2016 presidential debate. Candidate Trump also approvingly cited a Veritas video during the third presidential debate in autumn 2016 for an audience of tens of millions. As president, he has posted Veritas product on Twitter accompanied by glowing appraisals. Sarah Huckabee Sanders, Trump's Press Secretary, has similarly endorsed Veritas videos from her podium (Pilkington, 2017). In other words, Veritas hurtles far outside of the subaltern orbit and is proximal to the right's power elite.

Another wobbling pillar of Veritas' account of its mission concerns O'Keefe's insistence on Veritas' innocence of any party or ideology. He claims, "We take no position on issues beyond free speech and honest government" (2018, para. 9). The latter assertion is suspect for Veritas' resolute support for the indictment-and-conviction machine known as the Trump inner circle. Moreover, Veritas' videos are unswervingly consistent in following conventional right-wing obsessions, for example, Hillary Clinton (Project Veritas, 2016). As we will see later, Veritas was also an active participant during the 2016 election cycle in releasing inflammatory election-season products—to the benefit of candidate Trump (Smith, 2016).

Citation of Veritas' alleged findings in mainstream news has prompted apologetics to the audience from figures such as CNN presenter Anderson Cooper—even as the network airs Veritas product, since "some of the things you'll hear on the tape are hard to ignore" (Cooper, quoted in O'Keefe, 2016, para. 11). It is indeed an objective of flak traps to generate eyeball-grabbing content that garners attention in mainstream coverage. In the light of Veritas' poor track record, *The Washington Post*'s David Weigel similarly observes that Veritas' October Surprise-style presidential election videos in 2016 "got a skeptical reception—at first" (2016, para. 6). Weigel then leans on the videos' content to construct his news narrative. The contradictory news media behavior in the instances cited above—disavowing Veritas, then utilizing its product—channels a paradox long evident around Veritas (Meares, 2011). Like the bobo doll that is easy to knock over, Veritas has been bouncing back up to radiate still more flak (often with mainstream media assistance) for ten years.

Flak Origins: The ACORN Ambush

O'Keefe writes, "When two of my colleagues dressed as phone repairmen to enter [Senator] Mary Landrieu's office, they were not there to repair the phones" (2017, para. 5). In other words, *the fakery was real*; ergo, *it really was deception*, thus a paradoxically "pure" truth in Veritas' self-serving if head-spinning construction of the universe of meaning and knowing. "Veritas" must be understood to (somehow) vibrate through deliberate untruths. On this score, O'Keefe consistently maintains that deception and covert methods elicit more truthful reactions from targets. Problem: The assertion is baldly untrue. It is an article of common-sense that people may maintain a poker-face or go along with someone who is aggressively annoying (e.g., asking leading questions), as a means of ridding themselves of the aggravating interlocutor more quickly than would be realized by pursuing confrontation. For example, Veritas set a flak trap for government and union officials who were supposedly entranced by contracting with a company (in reality, Veritas imposters) with an avowed practice of digging holes—and then filling them. Media Matters reports:

> The raw footage of the video revealed that the officials featured in the video did not express support for the fake company or offer to help the actors find funding at all, but rather politely questioned the actors posing as their constituents about their clearly made-up operation. The officials later clarified they had assumed at the time that the discussion "must be a scam" but had "tried to be courteous." (2016, para. 23)

It is called humoring someone to exit the encounter more gracefully and children can master it by age ten to cope with nuisances.

O'Keefe (2018) contends that deception is stock-in-trade, even sacrosanct, for journalists. The self-serving claim is not true to the spirit or letter of professional mores. The Society of Professional Journalists (SPJ) codifies the use of deception as ethically unacceptable outside of exceptional circumstances: "Avoid undercover or other surreptitious methods of gathering information unless traditional, open methods will not yield information vital to the public" (2014, p. 2). Undercover stings have long been out of fashion in the conviction that truth is the method as well as the destination. Moreover, covert recording without subjects' permission is illegal in many jurisdictions, a protection for the public that has complicated the Veritas model from its origins.[2]

Veritas' debut flak target was Association of Community Organizations for Reform Now, better known by the acronym ACORN. However well-meaning, ACORN was "a gift from heaven" for right-wing flaksters for its often sloppy work on behalf of poorer citizens alongside demonstrable corruption in the organization's upper reaches (Hasen, 2012, p. 70). Nevertheless, Veritas' accusations against low-level ACORN employees after its flak stunt did not withstand scrutiny. While critical of ACORN in his office's investigation that followed Veritas' 2009 flak trap, California Attorney General Jerry Brown found no crimes to prosecute vis-à-vis ACORN (Office of the Attorney General)—the same finding as in other jurisdictions that scrutinized ACORN after Veritas' tapes circulated (Media Matters, 2016). While ACORN met the low standard of not engaging in criminality, it was also less effective and professional for many of its constituents than it should have been. At the same time, while tasked with examining ACORN, Brown was scorching toward the veracity of accuser Veritas' product following study of it: "The evidence illustrates [...] that things are not always as partisan zealots portray them through highly selective editing of reality. Sometimes a fuller truth is found on the cutting room floor" (State of California Department of Justice, 2010, p. 2).

By the time follow-up investigations of Veritas' accusations rolled in, flak had exacted its toll. ACORN had been defunded by the U.S. government, private supporters followed suit—and the organization disbanded. Further irony: as noted, Brown could find no ACORN crimes to prosecute when called upon to do so, even as he was highly critical of the professional quality of its work (Office of the Attorney General, 2010). However, Veritas would have likely been prosecuted for violating privacy laws if it had not been immunized for turning over the full tapes of its dodgy deeds: "An application of these principles to the facts presented here strongly suggests that O'Keefe and [collaborator Hannah] Giles's violated state privacy laws and provides fair warning to them and others that this type of activity can be prosecuted in California" (Office of the Attorney General, 2010, p. 17).

As the same report from the Attorney General observes at length, O'Keefe's video accounts of interactions with ACORN were dishonest down to the costume he claims to have been wearing to the ACORN offices. Ostensibly, O'Keefe was kitted as a 1970s pimp, as if auditioning for a high-school musical revival of *Shaft*. In fact, O'Keefe wore a suit to the meetings where he was almost wholly off-camera, aside from tell-tale suitcoat cuffs that entered the video frame. O'Keefe only donned the pimp costume for the opening, framing commentaries of the video, optics that made ACORN appear at once more craven and gullible. In other words, O'Keefe pretended to be pretending to be dressed as Blaxploitation pimp while he otherwise pretended to be a pimp—an unalloyed triumph for the cause of transcendent truth.

In the longer-term aftermath of their ACORN stunt, O'Keefe and Giles agreed to a six-digit settlement for the misleading video that cost ACORN organizer Juan Carlos Vera his job (Media Matters, 2016, para. 21). Veritas' covertly recorded, then selectively-edited and distributed video constructed Vera as enabling O'Keefe and Giles' (fabricated) plan to smuggle teenage Salvadoran sex workers into California. In fact, Vera talked to O'Keefe and Giles long enough to gather information about their alarming story. Vera then dismissed them from his office—and called the San Diego police department. In other words, Veritas misrepresented Vera as willing to abet a heinous plot. Despite probity of Vera's actions, he experienced enormous disruptions of his life for the fleeting contact with the pointless, cheap-shot deceptions of flak-mongers that also puts the lie to deception as high road to truth.

As for O'Keefe's motivations for Veritas' inaugural stunt, he took to the Breitbart's *Big Government* web site to recast flak against the weak and their institutional resources in ACORN as self-defense: "ACORN has ascended. They *elect our politicians and receive billions* in tax money. Their world is a revolutionary, socialistic, atheistic world, where all means are justifiable" (emphasis added, quoted in Office of the Attorney General, 2010, p. 6). While accusing others of employing "all means" toward nefarious ends, the flak debut rehearses for Veritas' later disregard for accuracy. To wit, ACORN's national operations received US$2.5 million from the federal government in the year prior to its dissolution—a faint shadow of chump change in the government budget and also 1/400 of the "billions" that O'Keefe conjures (Office of the Attorney General, 2010, p. 4).

For years after ACORN disbanded following the flak hit, Republican Party congresspeople perseverated in their indignant demands to block funding to the already defunct ACORN. In a startling residue of the initial stunt, flak can be said to have begat more flak toward anyone who could be rhetorically linked to ACORN: "Public Policy Polling found that nearly half of Republicans believed President Obama only won re-election because of ACORN's interference—although ACORN didn't exist at the time" (Benen, 2014, p. 1). One could say that, within the flak regime, ACORN is literally the stuff of legend.

Flak on the Ballot

Veritas participates in the contemporary right-wing obsession with "voter fraud" even as the phenomenon has been found to be empirically negligible, as will be further discussed in Chapter 5. Veritas' flak campaigns around voting issues have been dire, although not for lack of effort. According to

University of California law professor Richard Hasen, "It seems like most of the fraud O'Keefe uncovers he commits himself" (quoted in Mayer, 2016, para. 19). Despite Veritas' claims about an ideologically non-aligned posture, its election-oriented activity almost always implicates traps against Democrats that would straightforwardly benefit Republican opponents.

The midterm election year of 2014 summoned Veritas flak traps against the Democratic Party and its base demographics. In Colorado, O'Keefe donned makeup, including a vintage *Brokeback Mountain* mustache, to pose as a "civics professor" named "John Miller." In turn, "Professor" "Miller" claimed to be the "faculty advisor" to the ostensible gay group "Rocky Mountain Vote Pride." In an apparent effort to link Democratic Party election campaigns with a legitimate NGO called New Era in a manner proscribed by election law, New Era staff claim that O'Keefe as "Miller" attempted to cart literature from local political campaigns into their offices. If so, it is called planting evidence. The "Professor" was rebuffed as the weird make-up and costume were in themselves suspicious. Following verbal confrontations, O'Keefe tried to force a microphone through New Era's closed door; a creepy gesture, answered by New Era's complaint to local police (Kroll, 2014).

O'Keefe's Twitter feed concurrently boasted that "this time, people may lose their jobs" (quoted in Kroll, 2014)—an exciting prospect for the self-appointed flak policeman patrolling the beat, to partisan specifications. It should be noted that it is surely difficult to steer electoral campaigns in toss-up states such as Colorado, without simultaneously maintaining vigilance for flak-mongers and their outbursts of performance art at the door. But that is a keynote purpose of flak: bend people and organizations away from their core mission to play defense, to suspect the people around them, to drain time and effort.

Bogus Battleground

Along with claims to harbor no ideology outside free speech advocacy and zero tolerance for corruption, Veritas self-characterizes as freedom-fighters, raging against the machine. O'Keefe: "Unlike *Pravda* or the [*New York*] *Times*, our truth is not protected by power. Our truth is *tested* by power" (original emphasis, 2018, para. 30). In *American Pravda*, O'Keefe posits that "our critics [...] cannot deny that we get results." In his list of "what we have been able to accomplish," he includes "criminal investigations into voter fraud in Texas" (2018, para. 51). While it is true that Veritas provoked an investigation, it is interesting that O'Keefe glosses over what the investigation concluded. Let us take a look how Veritas' "results" hold up when tested.

In its 2014 Bexar County, Texas video, entitled "Battleground Texas Illegally Copying Voter Data," Veritas (2014c) bluntly asserts criminality against the voter registration group starting with the video's title. In the video's opening minute, Veritas revives its "greatest hit" for purposes of flak synergy and claims to have uncovered a "new ACORN." More specifically, Veritas recorded a deputy registrar for the Battleground Texas voter registration group claiming that she records the phone numbers of people whom she registered. The deputy registrar speaks on tape of her plan to call the people whom she registered shortly before Election Day with a reminder to vote. This was, indeed, the Battleground Texas *modus operandi* that the deputy registrar taught to her colleagues as a means of enhancing the chances that registered voters would cast ballots at election time.

In the video, Veritas (2014c) presents calling registered voters as a skin-crawling plot, conveyed to the viewer over ominous rap beats and slurred camerawork as the "authentic" signature of fly-on-the-wall recording. Edited-in materials include title card citations of Texas statue books, staged to awe the viewer with authority and to clinch a seemingly airtight case of electoral malfeasance. Veritas further assays to trace a direct line between the Democratic Party candidate for governor, Wendy Davis, and Battleground Texas. When it seems that matters could not become more worrisome—New ACORN! Fraud! Democrat candidate for governor!—Veritas dials up further alarm with the alarming claim that "maybe even health data" had been sucked into Battleground Texas' sinister matrix.

Veritas' seven-minute video provoked indignation and calls for investigation, as it was designed to do. The video's flak-in-discourse thusly mobilized legal flak-in-action. Special prosecutors Christine Del Prado and John M. Economidy were empaneled to examine the Battleground Texas case. Once the professional investigators were on the scene, however, Veritas did not pass the test. The resultant 17-page special prosecutors' judgement is devastating in its appraisal of Veritas, even as Battleground Texas was supposed to be the object of scrutiny given the flak trap setup. In making their judgement, Del Prado and Economidy observe that it is not legal for the *county registrar* to take phone numbers from registrants. However, *deputy registrars* working on registration drives—such as the one featured in the video—are legally empowered to take down numbers. The special prosecutors' claims are backed by the interpretation of several attorneys general of Texas. It is also salient that a phone number is not codified as private information in Texas law.

Veritas' stunt reduces, in other words, to sounding noisy alarms against registering people to vote—and then the subsequent effort to see that registered voters do in fact vote. To flag the obvious, getting out the vote presents a very strange issue on which to provoke flak and white-knuckle anger within a self-proclaimed democracy.

Although they had been appointed to investigate an alleged Battleground Texas crime wave that Veritas claims to have discovered, the special prosecutors' rout of the Veritas video gets worse. Del Prado and Economidy peg a couple of moments in the seven-minute video in which Veritas fail to differentiate between recorded and staged footage. Although Veritas characterizes itself as an apostle of true journalism, this (slothful, at best) practice defies SPJ's ethical standards for journalists: "Never deliberately distort facts or context, including visual information" and, more specifically, "Clearly label illustrations and re-enactments" (2014, p. 2).

The special prosecutors are particularly blistering about Veritas' claim that Davis' campaign was poised to—*somehow*—access and use registrants' health data to the benefit of its campaign. Del Prado and Economidy conclude:

> The Veritas video was little more than a canard and political disinformation. The video was particularly unprofessional when it suggested that the actions of Battleground Texas were advocated by a Texas gubernatorial candidate and that the actions of a single volunteer deputy registrar may even involve health data, which is not involved in the voter registration process. (2014, p. 16)

The special prosecutors' use of the term "disinformation" vis-à-vis Veritas suggests their judgment of deliberate attempts to deceive, in contrast with the common understanding of the term "misinformation" that signifies an inadvertent falsehood. In the light of the evidence, it is risible for O'Keefe to claim, years later, that "while we use deception to gain access, we never deceive our audience" (2018, para. 60).

While the special prosecutors' final word on Veritas cheap stunt against Battleground Texas (and Davis' gubernatorial candidacy) is neon-clear, one may also see the flak logics in motion. To wit, the accusations against Battleground Texas quickly circulated among the public and officialdom. However, the special prosecutors' decisive slap down of those claims was relatively tortoise-like in arriving, even if it was rigorous in method. In any event, Democrat Wendy Davis was defeated by Republican Greg Abbott in Texas' 2014 gubernatorial contest, in a state in which Republicans have swept statewide elections in recent decades. The Veritas video is unlikely to have tipped the election result. Nonetheless, the Veritas video was one more episode in a long litany of right-wing efforts to push the corrosive, empirically-impoverished narrative that extensive vote fraud, all of it generated by the political left, vexes U.S. elections; a narrative with further vignettes that I take up below.

From *O! Canada!* to "Lock Her Up!"

Hillary Clinton may be the leading attractant for right-wing flak among known entities. It is therefore not surprising that when Clinton kicked off her campaign for the Democratic Party's presidential nomination at a rally in 2015, Veritas was on the scene with imposters and clandestine cameras (Project Veritas, 2015b).

The resultant stunt reveals the contours of an explosive international scandal, in Veritas' narration, aimed at the heart of the U.S. electoral system. The stunt implicated a Veritas stooge buying paraphernalia from the Clinton campaign table on behalf of an ostensible "Canadian" citizen who was asserted to have no relation to Veritas. The Canadian was (serendipitously, conveniently) on hand at that moment Veritas arrived—*and* was seized by an irresistible urge to flag her Canadian nationality for the camera. At the campaign swag table, the self-proclaimed Canadian was still unable to suppress her maple-leaf mania—and was informed by Clinton campaign workers that she could not legally purchase paraphernalia as it would constitute a foreign contribution. The fast-thinking Project Veritas stooge, stationed next to the Canadian, pleaded on behalf of someone she supposedly did not know: "She traveled all the way from Canada to support Hillary!" Veritas' stooge then sought clarification from the campaign staff: "Canadians can't buy them [campaign trinkets], but Americans can buy it for them?" Molly Barker, Clinton's National Marketing Director replied, "Not technically. You would just be making the donation" (Project, 2015b). To peg the obvious, the setup of the situation looked suspiciously staged.

The table staff was, if anything, diligent about the law when a stooge prepared for legalistic cross-examination popped out of the grass. And the only way to prevent the swag caper would have been for the campaign workers to vault over the table and prevent the handover of a tee-shirt from one person to another following the aggressive effort to push money at them. O'Keefe nevertheless conjures a relentless Clintonian machine during the video's press conference unveiling: "It's about the willingness to break the law," an assertion that contradicts the evidence of one's eyes, "and not about the amount of money" (quoted in Nuzzi, 2015, para. 26). Veritas' apostleship for the strict letter of the law notwithstanding, Olivia Nuzzi identifies illegalities around Veritas' construction of the ten buck tee-shirt flak stunt: "A close reading of the Federal Election Commission's campaign finance laws makes it clear that [...] individuals cannot 'knowingly provide substantial assistance' by 'acting as a conduit or intermediary for foreign national contributions and donations'"—as the Veritas stooge demonstrably did on behalf of "the Canadian" (2015, para. 27). Perhaps Veritas, self-proclaimed centurions for ultimate truth whose methods in practice depend upon deception, needed to break the law in order to "uphold" it. In any event, by the summer of 2015, Clinton's still coalescing campaign was already on guard, given evidence of infiltration from flak agents with Veritas ties (Miller, 2015).

At the press conference to introduce the video, O'Keefe could not identify who the mysterious Canadian at the center of this putatively hold-the-presses "scandal" was—or whether she was indeed Canadian. Nevertheless, the video dwells on nationality as a crucial datum. O'Keefe also refused to identify either the Veritas stooge standing next to the "Canadian" or the video recorder of the incident. His explanation for the lack of transparency suggests reveries of *Mission: Impossible* as he "compared his activists to Navy Seal Team Six members, explaining that identifying them would jeopardize their mission" (Payton, 2015, para. 16). For Veritas, the U.S. presidential campaign was apparently redolent of a shooting war's state of belligerence.

O'Keefe was asked whether the Clinton swag flak trap was a "joke" when it was unveiled at a press conference (Lachman, 2015). While the premise of the question is scathing, Veritas nonetheless convened a press conference that trained journalists attended. Moreover, Dave Weigel's *Washington Post* coverage of the video gave the stunt a legitimizing platform as he composed the article in the objective idiom of claim/counter-claim between Clinton's campaign and Veritas (Weigel, 2015). By contrast, Dana Millbank's article in the *Post* on the press conference is contemptuous of Veritas. At the same time, Millbank repeats the memes that Veritas was trying to channel about Clinton (e.g., "untrustworthy"), regardless of whether these memes are more, or less, true of Clinton than anyone else with a similar grade of authority (2015, para. 10). In this view, O'Keefe had reason to gloat about the swag table video "going viral [...] it's in the *Washington Post* right now" (Millbank, 2015, para. 19).

From the enhanced hindsight of a few years later, the 2015 stunt reeks even more of contrived flak. Veritas is a self-proclaimed institution of journalism that insists it performs to higher standards than more established entities. In this light, it is dazzling to observe the opportunity costs around Veritas' swag table charade. By August 2016, Paul Manafort resigned as Trump campaign manager in large part over the shadiness around his prior work in Russia and Ukraine—a matter that was widely reported at the time (by, e.g., McCaskill, Isenstadt, & Goldmacher, 2016). The smoke of scandal, in this case, led back to a blaze of crimes committed by Manafort. By 2019, he had registered ten convictions (and counting) on his rap sheet. Given a record that was already beginning to unravel during the campaign, Manafort was an extraordinary choice to lead a major party's general election campaign.

In this light, placing Clinton and Trump side-by-side presents a surreal contrast; a pattern of high-level links with a hostile foreign power that was already coming into view during the 2016 campaign (Harding, 2017), versus the pale shadow of a rumor of a hologram of a molehill. Yet, Veritas stooges donned no fake mustaches and/or wristwatch cameras for surveillance around Manafort or Trump's campaign in 2015 and 2016, in defiance of Veritas' self-promotion about seeking truths wherever they may be found. Veritas eschewed stunts that could have reflected badly on the billionaire Republican) candidate's campaign, even as it was a demonstrably target-rich environment; the same billionaire who has also donated money and extensive hype to Veritas and its founder.

Scalps

Along with stumbling fails, Veritas notched flak successes in obtaining "scalps" during the 2016 campaign. In October, the release of its "Rigging the Election" video (Project Veritas, 2016) prompted Democratic Party operative Robert Creamer to announce he was "stepping back" from work at Democracy Partners (quoted in Weigel, 2016, para. 1) while Scott Foval was discharged from his post with Americans United for Change. The news circulated further when Trump referenced these happenings during a presidential debate in the same month.

The Washington Post's Weigel characterizes Foval in the Veritas video as someone who "repeatedly ties a noose with his tongue" and who "seems to overhype his success" as a party operative (2016, para. 9). Foval demonstrates notably suspect judgement and lack of discretion in talking too much (or even at all) about his political work with people whom he did not know. In his own defense, Foval claims that many of the situations he was describing on tape were hypothetical political operative scenarios, in response to similarly hypothetical questions that were not included in Veritas' video (Potter, 2017). In this vein, Foval plausibly claims that his reference in the video to "bussing people in" refers to giving citizens transport to protests—and not, as Veritas ominously implied, ushering ineligible voters to the polls.

Veritas (2016) insinuates law-breaking in the video by operatives one step removed from Clinton's campaign. What happened next in Foval's case is of interest from a flak perspective. Subsequent investigation by Roy Korte, Wisconsin's Assistant Attorney General and head of the criminal litigation unit, reached the following conclusion: "Based on all the available facts, I do not believe there is any basis to conclude that the videos demonstrate or suggest violations of Wisconsin criminal laws" (quoted in Murphy, 2017, para. 9). In a judgement that chimes with Foval's contentions—and not Veritas' claims about the content of its surreptitious recordings—Korte judged that, "The conversations remain best described as vague and theoretical in many respects" (quoted in Murphy, 2017, para. 10). Moreover, the Assistant Attorney General infers that Veritas tampered with the ostensibly complete tapes that it submitted for the investigation since "they begin in the middle of conversations, contain gaps and include inaccurate time counters" (Murphy, 2017, para. 11).

The flak narrative took another turn when Veritas subsequently threatened the Wisconsin Attorney General Brad Schimel, a Republican, with some form of reprisal if he did not reverse course on Foval's case and indict him for *something* (Marley, 2018). Schimel reopened the case—and Foval was once again exonerated by the state's justice apparatus, following further examination of the recordings by Special Agent Dorinda Freymiller. Nonetheless, flak had exacted its toll. Foval reports harassment, having had property vandalized, and death threats, following the publication of Veritas' video (Marley, 2018). While he was not indicted of any crime, the flak trap was a direct hit. Foval has taken up residence far from Wisconsin and his career is at a dead end.

As for Creamer who was also flaked, his organization Democracy Partners is suing Veritas in U.S. federal court. In turn, Veritas' representation argued that the Veritas imposter planted inside Democracy Partners had been granted access to its operations, ergo, the case was fit to be dismissed. U.S. District Court Judge Ellen Huvelle ruled for Democracy Partners' argument that the operative, Allison Maass, lied about her name and falsified her work history as well as her motives for seeking the position at Democracy Partners. Without the deceit, she would have had no chance to work there. Democracy Partner's lawsuit against Veritas will go forward and, as of 2019, is in its discovery phase (Gerstein, 2018; Palma, 2017).

The Moore Culture War

Professional journalists can hardly run riot across the newsroom or on the air with vanity-driven showcases of their own views while reporting, even if they were inclined to do so. Besides the potential for flak, checks on journalists' professional conduct come from all directions: above (ownership, editors, advertisers who furnish revenue), below (audiences), and laterally (from colleagues) (Bennett, 2001). Unfortunately, much of the constraint on journalism can be read back to deeply inscribed elite influence that structures the news media industry in the first instance, a key premise of the propaganda model. Moreover, the industry's mania for balanced news has long been designed to leverage the commercial advantages of putting off no potential audience members or advertisers through overt embrace of ideology. At the same time, objectivity has proven sterile and stronger on facts than on truth—and, in consequence, the US' journalism system indeed needs to raise its game. In this vein, failures around the 2003 invasion of Iraq, when news organizations bowed to Bush administration messaging while operating within an objectivity paradigm, is perhaps this century's epitome of the propaganda model in motion (Goss, 2013, pp. 93–118).

In stark contrast with a structural account of news media grounded in professional and industry logics, Veritas asserts simplistic and one-dimensional caricatures of media industries. In giving warrant for its flak campaigns, Veritas paper-clips nebulous and incoherent conspiracy hand-waving about deep State machinations to snide assertions about left-liberalism that is imagined as (somehow, monolithically, indivisibly) capturing the resolutely capitalist media industries (O'Keefe, 2018).

Veritas' attacks on "mainstream" news media are made-to-order to be placed side-by-side with self-congratulation over its own performance. On one hand, "The Project Veritas journalist has a profound faith in the power of a free people to make their own decisions regarding what is best for them" (O'Keefe, 2018, para. 46). On the other hand, O'Keefe rants in a register of self-aggrandizement that Veritas contrasts with "mainstream media that detest free people" (2018, para. 47).

O'Keefe asserts that Veritas and like-minded platforms constitute a U.S. version of *samizdat*. Indeed, O'Keefe's premise of equivalence between the contemporary United States and the Soviet system is unmistakable from his tome's title, *American Pravda*. The right-wing "alternative" media that O'Keefe extols does not, however, present the strengths of mainstream news media, such as professional technique that at least prioritizes getting facts mostly straight (Silverman et al., 2016). O'Keefian alternatives also indulge faults that mainstream news media habitually do not; for example, refusal to self-correct, however egregious an inaccuracy.

The lack of baseline professionalism at Veritas led to the collapse of its attempt to plant the specious "Roy Moore-teen abortion" story in the *Washington Post* in 2017. In this episode, Veritas was outclassed by the mainstream media because it assumed that mainstream organizations behave as it does as concerns naked ideological partiality. One upshot of Veritas' failure around the Moore pseudo-story was that it made mainstream media look like champs. Veritas' flak trap implosion puts off the day when mainstream news media will become more independent by displaying the woeful inadequacy of current rightist alternatives to the mainstream. In this media ecosystem, mainstream news has far less need to raise its game.

Real Fakery: Jamie-Gate

On the morning of November 27, 2017, via Twitter, Trump sardonically proposed the creation of a "Fake News Trophy." By the afternoon of the same day, one of Trump's preferred sources had collapsed over the finish line for the fake news gold medal when one of Veritas' stunts had itself become an embarrassing news story (Pilkington, 2017). *The Washington Post*'s Shawn Boburg, Aaron C. Davis, and Alice Crites, open their account of events as follows:

> A woman who falsely claimed to *The Washington Post* that Roy Moore, the Republican U.S. Senate candidate in Alabama, impregnated her as a teenager appears to work with an organization that uses deceptive tactics to secretly record conversations in an effort to embarrass its targets.
>
> In a series of interviews over two weeks, the woman shared a dramatic story about an alleged sexual relationship with Moore in 1992 that led to an abortion when she was 15. During the interviews, she repeatedly pressed *Post* reporters to give their opinions on the effects that her claims could have on Moore's candidacy if she went public. (2017, paras. 1–2)

The backstory of this flak episode concerned Alabama Republican Roy Moore's U.S. Senate special-election candidacy in autumn 2017. While Alabama had not elected a Democrat to the U.S. Senate in a generation, Moore's candidacy was wobbling in the weeks before Election Day. Moore faced accusations from a series of by-then middle-aged women who claimed that he had approached them about dating, decades earlier when they were as young as 14 while Moore was in 30s. The alleged activity was first reported in *The Washington Post*. Alarming in themselves, the credible accusations also did not square with Moore's confrontational brand of public religious piety. Veritas' flak project against the *Post* appears to have been launched to support Moore while his campaign was showing signs of stumbling.

Beth Reinhard's initial story on accusations against Moore was published in the *Post* on November 9, 2017. The following day, Reinhard received a cryptic email from a woman who proffered a shocking scoop. Jamie Phillips claimed to have been impregnated as a 15-year old by a middle-aged Moore in the early 1990s—a situation that, she claimed, led to an abortion. Phillips also pressed *Post* reporters for assurances that her story would guarantee an electoral loss for Moore to Democrat Doug Jones (which is what happened on 12 December). The demand for assurances reads as an attempt to bait a trap to make the *Post* appear eager to intervene in the election rather simply reporting it.

On performing due diligence in parrying Phillips' story, red flags were quickly evident. Phillips' claims to the *Post* about where she had lived and work did not jell. Her social media accounts were observed to have made abrupt pirouettes from "hearting" Trump to honoring John F. Kennedy (Reinhard, Davis, & Ba Tran, 2017). Moreover, a *Post* researcher discovered a crowd funding page in the name of Jamie Phillips from May of 2017 that read:

> I'm moving to New York! […] I've accepted a job to work in the conservative media movement to combat the lies and deceit of the liberal MSM [mainstream media]. I'll be using my skills as a researcher and fact-checker to help our movement. (Boburg, Davis, and Crites, 2017, para. 41)

On a hunch and in the knowledge that Veritas had recently advertised openings, *Post* staff staked out Veritas' offices in uber-wealthy Mamaroneck, New York. Phillips was observed entering the office.

Shortly afterwards, in an arranged meeting in Virginia, Phillips was confronted with the evidence that the *Post* staff had gathered on her apparent flak trap at which time she was also informed that she was being recorded.

The *Post* video was published unedited, *contra* Veritas practice, along with informing the subject of the camera's presence (*The Washington Post*, 2017b). In the resultant video of the encounter, Phillips makes a shambling retreat from the *Post* reporter after she had tried to sucker the newspaper into the flak trap.

The *Post* made further discoveries about Phillips as the staff unwound the caper. Phillips had been attempting to insinuate herself into the lives of the paper's staff since July 2017. She attended at least two gatherings of *Post* staff outside the office in "efforts that went much further than the [later] effort to plant one fabricated article" (Reinhard, Davis, & Ba Tran, 2017, para. 5). Phillips maintained a discourse with one *Post* employee over text message across weeks, seeking dinner appointments. To all appearances, Phillips instrumentally feigned sympathy over a grave family problem in the effort to set a flak trap: "Let me know if I can do anything to help, even if just to talk or something small. We'd like to send flowers or a donation [...] Thoughts and prayers" (*The Washington Post*, 2017a, paras. 7–8).

At a going-away party on September 18, 2017, Phillips covertly recorded *Post* reporter Dan Lamothe while interacting with him under the alias of "Jamie Gibson," a "graduate student" seeking help with her "research." Phillips/"Gibson" followed up with emails and invitations. When the flak trap was exposed, Lamothe commented, "I regret being so open with strangers [...] I'm generally an open, friendly person, but I need to be more cautious" (quoted in Reinhard, Davis, & Ba Tran, 2017, para. 52).

As emphasized throughout this book, flak drains resources (time and effort, funds) from its targets. In considering Lamothe's brief but poignant comment, further social dimensions of flak come into view. In a milieu of pervasive flak, the drawbridge goes up in a moat strategy, suspicion rather than solidarity flows more easily toward the stranger or new acquaintance, toxins circulate since one never knows what another person's project may really be—all redolent of a *Stasi*-esque regime. Moreover, a successful flak trap that, however unfairly, costs someone his or her reputation or employment, leaves the target even more devastated for having in some degree taken the bait and having credulously participated in the stunt.

Flak Falling Action

In the denouement to the dumpster fire stunt with Phillips, O'Keefe posted an article on Veritas' website entitled, "*The Washington Post* Fails to Run Both

Sides of My Story"—and pours gallons more of high-octane discourse into the dumpster. He asserts that, "The premise that Project Veritas was attempting to plant a false story is incorrect [...] We just wanted the meeting and wanted to talk politics" (2017, paras. 3–4). The claim is baldly insulting to the intelligence of any attentive observer as well as contradicted by a decade of Veritas stunt traps. And, to entertain the counterfactual for a moment: If the claim were true, "meeting [...] to talk politics" could have been readily accomplished by picking up the phone or tapping out an email, rather than staging the elaborate bullshit around Phillips's activities. Despite the implosion of this stunt, Veritas published videos on its *Post* covert recordings, cleansed of mention of the Moore flak flop. Osita Nwanevu describes reactions among the flak mill-faithful as they were "coming in on YouTube: '*Fuck* the Washington Post. *Fuck Jeff Bezos. MAGA. Great Job Veritas!*' reads one representative comment" (original emphasis, para. 6).

Simple professionalism and fact-checking foiled the sordid attempt at a flak trap set for Moore's immediate benefit that would have bolstered right-wing meta-ideology around "liberal media" favoring Democrats. As for the *Post*, one can almost forgive the triumphal tone of its coverage of the story, given professional pride and *esprit-de-corps* implicated in repelling a malicious attack. In this vein, the *Post*'s Erik Wemple implores *Post* readers to "Watch as Phillips fumbles and bumbles her way out of her interview, watch as O'Keefe and his wingmen bluster and filibuster" when another *Post* reporter confronts them about Phillips (Wemple, 2017, para. 12). However, Wemple is also cognizant of the opportunity costs around defenestration of Veritas' flak trap: "Yet consider, too, that this whole enterprise required the contributions of McCrummen, Reinhard, Crites, Shawn Boburg, Davis and others working behind the scenes—resources that might otherwise have been deployed investigating other senators, chief executives or potentates" (2017, para. 12).

Flak diverted an organization from its core mission; although, in this case, the *Post* at least seems to have received gratification from dishing out comeuppance. The *Post*'s staff was also garlanded with the Pulitzer Prize for its reporting on the 2017 Alabama campaign in which further dirty tricks had been in play (Lakshmanan, 2018). Nevertheless, the alpha and omega of journalism's mission is to examine a whole range of potentates, beyond flak mills; a broader mission of cross-examining power on behalf of the public for which we need the *Post* and its news media colleagues to double down, without complacency.

Conclusion

Veritas has in recent years been subject to demonstrable pushback against it; for example, the *ProjectVeritas.Exposed* (PVE) web site. PVE is a collaboration between two organizations, the Undercurrent and American Family Voices, that both self-characterize as politically left-of-center. Both share office space with Democracy Partners, hence were in proximity to the 2016 Creamer flak trap, and neither commands Veritas-proportioned resources. PVE characterizes Veritas as engaged in "political espionage" in its infiltration tactics and provides a 13-point rubric for ferreting out flak agents burrowing into an organization (*ProjectVeritas. Exposed*, 2019). The web site also presents original documents from 13 current and previously filed lawsuits against Veritas, as well as two current requests (by former U.S. Senator Claire McCaskill and League of Conservation Voters) to state attorneys general requesting criminal investigations into Veritas.

While heightened scrutiny has been devoted to Veritas' activities without resorting to its cheap-shot methods, there is no room for complacency on the flak front. As noted, news organizations with wide reach have in recent years commented critically on Veritas—even as they have recirculated its product. Moreover, with the advent in 2014 of its political advocacy arm, Project Veritas Action, Veritas is a flak mill that has been expanding as well as training new recruits who could readily improve upon O'Keefe and colleagues' level of competence.

To the extent that other organizations, such as Democracy Partners, have been compelled to combat Veritas in court, they have been blown off-course from their core functions. By contrast, Veritas as a flak mill has no further purpose than disrupting its targets. In the paradoxical world of the flak mill, even a loss in court can be a qualified "win" in interrupting a flak target's main flow of activity—thereby fulfilling the essential purpose for which the flak mill exists, notwithstanding cloying pretexts about rarefied quests for transcendent truth. Moreover, the mere fact that *ProjectVeritas.Exposed* features advice on how to avoid malicious actors demonstrates that the elite "swamp" is not being drained; but, under the flak regime, time, effort and basic trust in each other as political subjects assuredly is.

Notes

1. Further expansion: Veritas was also trained in "intelligence" in 2017 with the assistance of Erik Prince, best known as the founder of the infamously violent "security firm"

Blackwater USA (Scahill, 2013). It is not apparent whether the training yielded any notable result. One trainer whom Prince appointed claimed that Veritas staff "wasn't capable of learning" about intelligence (Cole, 2019, para. 56). The episode nonetheless prompted O'Keefe to tweet photos of himself in a steely pose pointing a gun at a snowy hilly in Wyoming, with a tagline that claimed that Veritas was destined to be the "next great intelligence agency."

2. The UK's Channel Four investigation of Cambridge Analytica (CA) can be taken as a notable and recent exception where deception may pass muster (Channel Four, 2018). In this case, the journalists were, firstly, dealing with a secretive organization operating in the shadows with ties to intelligence agents who assisted CA's work. Secondly, in contrast with Veritas' series of videos shown to be nothing-burgers on further examination, Channel Four's investigation revealed viably actionable legal matters that the United States Department of Justice and the United Kingdom Information Commissioner's Office have pursued. Channel Four's investigation may present an exception to the not-to-be-taken-lightly rule of straightforward reportorial probing over deception that meets the condition of having no other viable method for investigation.

References

Baker, S. (2011). Does raw video of NPR exposé reveal questionable editing and tactics? *The Blaze*, 10 March. Retrieved from www.theblaze.com/news/2011/03/10/does-raw-video-of-npr-expose-reveal-questionable-editing-tactics/

Benen, S. (2014): Congress finally declares victory over ACORN. MSNBC, 8 August. Retrieved from www.msnbc.com/rachel-maddow-show/congress-finally-declares-victory-over-acorn.

Bennet, W.L. (2001). *News: The politics of illusion* (4th ed.). New York: Addison Wesley Longman.

Boburg, S., Davis, A.C., & Crites, A. (2017). A woman approached *The Post* with dramatic—and false—tale about Roy Moore. *Washington Post*, 27 November. Retrieved from www.washingtonpost.com/investigations/a-woman-approached-the-post-with-dramatic--and-false--tale-about-roy-moore-sje-appears-to-be-part-of-undercover-sting-operation/20-17/11/27/0c2e335a-cfb6-11e7-9d3a-bcbe2af58c3a_story.html?utm_term=.dba03ed0e309.

Chafets, Z. (2011). Stinger: James O'Keefe's greatest hits. *The New York Times Magazine*, 27 July. Retrieved from http://www.nytimes.com/2011/07/31/magazine/stinger-james-okeefes-greatest-hits.html.

Channel Four. (2018). Cambridge Analytica uncovered: Secret filming reveals election tricks. *YouTube*, 19 March. Retrieved from www.youtube.com/watch?v=mpbeOCKZFfQ.

Cole, M. (2019). The complete mercenary. *The Intercept*, 3 May. Retrieved from theintercept.com/2019/05/03/erik-prince-trump-uae-project-veritas/.

Del Prado, C., & Economidy, J.M. (2014). *Review of compliant on using voter registration information* (N°.2014-W-0128). Bexar County, TX. Retrieved from www.scribd.com/document/216868925/Special-prosecutors-review-of-complaints-in-Texas-v-Battleground-Texas#fullscreen&from_embed.

Dickson, C. (2014). Inside a Hollywood hit job. *Daily Beast*, 22 June. Retrieved from www.thedailybeast.com/inside-a-hollywood-hit-job-how-sting-artist-james-okeefe-tried-to-set-his-latest-trap-and-got-stung-himself.

Folkenflik, D. (2011). Elements of NPR gotcha video taken out of context. National Public Radio, 14 March. Retrieved from www.npr.org/2011/03/14/134525412/Segments-Of-NPR-Gotcha-Video-Taken-Out-Of-Context.

Gerstein, J. (2018). Court green-lights Democrats' suit against Project Veritas. *Politico*, 4 January. Retrieved from https://www.politico.com/story/2018/01/04/project-veritas-lawsuit-democrats-324976.

Goss, B.M. (2013). *Rebooting the Herman and Chomsky propaganda model in the twenty-first century*. New York: Peter Lang.

Harding, L. (2017). *Collusion*. New York: Vintage Books.

Hasen, R.L. (2012). *The voting wars*. New Haven: Yale University Press.

Kroll, A. (2014). Colorado Dems: We caught James O'Keefe and his friends trying to bait us into approving voter fraud. *Mother Jones*, 20 October. Retrieved from http://www.motherjones.com/politics/2014/10/colorado-dems-james-okeefe.

Lachman, S. (2015). Latest James O'Keefe sting video targeting Clinton campaign flops. *Huffington Post*, 1 September. Retrieved from www.huffingtonpost.com/entry/james-okeefe-video-clinton_us_55e5c0a8e4b0aec9f35481a8.

Lakshmanan, I.A.R. (2018). *The Washington Post* won a Pulitzer Prize for fighting fake news with facts. Poynter Institute, 17 April. Retrieved from https://www.poynter.org/ethics-trust/2018/the-washington-post-won-a-pulitzer-for-fighting-%C2%93fake-news%C2%94-with-facts/.

Marley, P. (2018). Attorney General Brad Schimel concludes for the second time Project Veritas videos show no voter fraud by Dem activist. *Milwaukee Journal Sentinel*, 14 May. Retrieved from eu.jsonline.com/story/news/politics/2018/05/14/attorney-general-brad-schimel-concludes-second-time-controversial-video-shows-no-voter-fraud-dem-act/607073002/.

Mayer, J. (2016). James O'Keefe accidently stings himself. *New Yorker*, 30 May. Retrieved from www.newyorker.com/magazine/2016/05/30/james-okeefe-accidentally-stings-himself.

McCaskill, N.D., Isenstadt, A., & Goldmacher, S. (2016). Paul Manafort resigns from Trump campaign. *Politico*, 19 August. Retrieved from www.politico.com/story/2016/08/paul-manafort-resigns-from-trump-campaign-227197.

Meares, J. (2011). O'Keefe teaches media a lesson (again). *Columbia Journalism Review*, 15 March. Retrieved from archives.cjr.org/campaign_desk/okeefe_teaches_media_a_lesson_again.php.

Media Matters. (2016). James O'Keefe's October surprise shows he's still a hack, not a journalist. 12 October. Retrieved from www.mediamatters.org/research/2016/10/12/james-okeefes-anti-clinton-october-surprise-shows-hes-still-hack-not-journalist/213783.

Millbank, D. (2015). Clinton's accusers are running out of ammunition. *Washington Post*, 1 September. Retrieved from www.washingtonpost.com/opinions/clintons-accusers-are-running-out-of-ammunition/2015/09/01/ea43091e-50e6-11e5-933e-7d06c647a395_story.html?utm_term=.f7dcd426a3f6.

Miller, Z. (2015). Clinton campaign on alert for undercover conservative sting. *Time*, 21 August. Retrieved from time.com/4006454/hillary-clinton-video-project-veritas.

Murphy, B. (2017). The incompetence of Brad Schimel. *Urban Milwaukee*, 2 May. Retrieved from urbanmilwaukee.com/2017/05/02/murphys-law-the-incompetence-of-brad-schimel/.

Nuzzi, O. (2015). James O'Keefe takes aim at Hillary, stings self. *Dailey Beast*, 1 September. Retrieved from https://www.thedailybeast.com/james-okeefe-aims-at-hillary-stings-self.

Nwanevu, O. (2017). James O'Keefe's bungled *Washington Post* sting will not hurt him one bit. *Slate*, 28 November. Retrieved from www.washingtonpost.com/blogs/erik-wemple/wp/2017/11/27/the-washington-post-turns-the-tables-on-project-veritas/?utm_term=.23d3c8f1f8d6.

Office of the Attorney General. (2010). *Report of the Attorney General on the activities of ACORN in California*. Sacramento, CA: California Department of Justice.

O'Keefe, J. (2016). The mainstream media is dead: We won. *FrontPage Mag*, 6 December. Retrieved from www.frontpagemag.com/fpm/265043/james-okeefe-mainstream-media-dead-we-won-frontpagemagcom.

O'Keefe, J. (2017). *The Washington Post* fails to run both sides of my story. *Project Veritas*, 6 December. Retrieved from www.projectveritas.com/2017/12/06/the-washington-post-fails-to-run-both-sides-of-my-story/.

O'Keefe, J. (2018). *American Pravda*. Retrieved from www.amazon.com/American-Pravda-Fight-Truth-Fake-ebook/dp/B071YLKMBD#reader_B071YLKMBD.

Palma, B. (2017). 'Sting' video maker James O'Keefe hit with $1 million federal lawsuit. *Snopes*, 3 June. Retrieved from https://www.snopes.com/news/2017/06/03/james-okeefe-federal-lawsuit/.

Payton, B. (2015). Video shows Clinton taking campaign contribution from Canadian woman. *The Federalist*, 2 September. Retrieved from thefederalist.com/2015/09/02/video-shows-clinton-campaign-taking-contribution-from-canadian-woman/.

Pilkington, E. (2017). Project Veritas: How fake news prize went to rightwing group beloved by Trump. *The Guardian*, 29 November. Retrieved from www.theguardian.com/us-news/2017/nov/29/project-veritas-how-fake-news-prize-went-to-rightwing-group-beloved-by-trump.

Potter, S. (2017). Scott Foval speaks out about Veritas video. *Isthmus*, 18 May. Retrieved from isthmus.com/news/news/democratic-operative-scott-foval-says-sting-that-brought-him-down-was-a-fraud/.

Project Veritas. (2008). Non-gay men with girlfriends get married to each other. *YouTube*, 16 November. Retrieved from www.youtube.com/watch?v=Ruh3TZvdkQ0.

Project Veritas. (2011a). NPR Muslim Brotherhood investigation part I. *YouTube*, 8 March. Retrieved from www.youtube.com/watch?v=xd9OYJMX9t4.

Project Veritas. (2011b). To catch a journalist: *New York Times*, Clay Shirky, Jay Rosen. *YouTube*, 27 October. Retrieved from www.youtube.com/watch?v=qBFOmUXR080.

Project Veritas. (2014a). James O'Keefe as Osama bin Laden crosses border from Mexico to US. *YouTube*, 11 August. Retrieved from www.youtube.com/watch?v=fB37TCDcZBg.

Project Veritas. (2014b). Hollywood celebrities caught on hidden camera accepting money from "Middle Eastern oil interests." *YouTube*, 20 May. Retrieved from www.youtube.com/watch?v=KOX5ehfFF7I.

Project Veritas. (2014c). Battleground Texas illegally copying voter data. *YouTube*, 19 February. Retrieved from www.youtube.com/watch?v=gXKwQI_0kDI.

Project Veritas. (2015a). Hidden camera captures officials shredding Constitution at Vassar College as it 'triggers' students. *YouTube*, 3 November. Retrieved from www.youtube.com/watch?v=3PZAzLTQlX8.

Project Veritas. (2015b). Hidden cam: Hillary's national marketing director illegally accepting foreign contribution. *YouTube*, 1 September. Retrieved from www.youtube.com/watch?v=-qxF7Z2N7Y4.

Project Veritas. (2016). Rigging the election: Video I. *YouTube*, 17 October. Retrieved from https://www.youtube.com/watch?v=5IuJGHuIkzY.

Project Veritas. (2017). New York teacher alleged to have sexually assaulted students with knife—may still be at large. *YouTube*, 14 March. Retrieved from www.youtube.com/watch?v=09-Q1PqRzNI.

Project Veritas Exposed. (2019). Ops & methodology. Retrieved from www.projectveritas.exposed/operations.

Reinhard, B., Davis, A.C., & Tran, A.B. (2017). Woman's effort to infiltrate *The Washington Post* dated back months. *Washington Post*, 29 November. Retrieved from www.washingtonpost.com/investigations/womans-effort-to-infiltrate-the-washington-post-dates-back-months/2017/11/29/ce95e01a-d51e-11e7-b62d-d9345ced896d_story.html?utm_term=.eb91fccccf36.

Scahill, J. (2013). *Dirty wars*. London: Serpent's Tail.

Silverman, C., Strapeigel, L., Shaban, H., Hall, E., & Singer-Vine, J. (2016). Hyperpartisan Facebook pages are publishing false and misleading information at an alarming rate. *Buzzfeed*, 20 October. Retrieved from www.buzzfeednews.com/article/craigsilverman/partisan-fb-pages-analysis#.vi7WmEkMM.

Smith, A. (2016). Experts: Actions of Democratic operatives in latest undercover James O'Keefe video likely not violation of law. *Business Insider*, 25 October. Retrieved from nordic.businessinsider.com/james-okeefe-project-veritas-hillary-clinton-donald-duck-2016-10/.

Society of Professional Journalists. (2014). SPJ code of ethics. Retrieved from www.spj.org/ethicscode.asp.

SourceWatch. (2018). David Horowitz Freedom Center, 14 August. Retrieved from www.sourcewatch.org/index.php/David_Horowitz_Freedom_Center.

State of California Department of Justice. (2010). Brown releases report detailing a litany of problems with ACORN, but no criminality, 1 April. Retrieved from oag.ca.gov/news/press-releases/brown-releases-report-detailing-litany-problems-acorn-no-criminality.

Washington Post, The. (2017a). Text Messages with Project Veritas operative and *Post* employee show sustained effort to befriend newspaper employee. 29 November. Retrieved from https://www.washingtonpost.com/graphics/2017/investigations/project-veritas-text-messages/?utm_term=.607d44e4ec47.

Washington Post, The. (2017b). Listen to full exchange between *Post* reporter and woman who made false accusations. 27 November. Retrieved from www.washingtonpost.com/video/national/listen-to-full-exchange-between-post-reporter-and-woman-who-made-false-accusations/2017/11/27/2aa9cb14-d3c6-11e7-9ad9-ca0619edfa05_video.html?utm_term=.f4a2f80b3d5a.

Weigel, D. (2015). New James O'Keefe video: Clinton campaign allowed a foreigner to acquire official swag. *Washington Post*, 1 September: Retrieved from www.washingtonpost.com/news/post-politics/wp/2015/09/01/new-james-okeefe-video-sting-catches-clinton-campaign-being-kind-to-a-canadian/?utm_campaign=pubexchange_article&utm_medium=referral&utm_source=huffingtonpost.com&utm_term=.f2ace39c16f5.

Weigel, D. (2016). Two Democratic operatives lose jobs after James O'Keefe sting. *Washington Post*, 19 October. Retrieved from www.washingtonpost.com/news/post-politics/wp/2016/10/19/two-democratic-operatives-lose-jobs-after-james-okeefe-sting/?utm_term=.c951aa369192.

Wemple, E. (2017). *The Washington Post* turns the tables on Project Veritas. *Washington Post*, 27 November. Retrieved from www.washingtonpost.com/blogs/erik-wemple/wp/2017/11/27/the-washington-post-turns-the-tables-on-project-veritas/?utm_term=.23d3c8f1f8d6.

Part III
FLAK ISSUES AND CONCLUSIONS

· 5 ·

VOTERS AS "THIEVES AND FRAUDSTERS": FLAK AGAINST ELECTIONS

> In politics as in everything else it makes a great difference whose game we play. The rules of the game determine the requirements for success […] and go to the heart of political strategy.
>
> E.E. Schattschneider (quoted in Minnite, n.d., p. 16)

Introduction: Three Million Imposters

In the queasy, immediate aftermath of November 8, 2016, it was largely overlooked that Trump claimed the prize through the eighteenth-century technicalities of the Electoral College that negated a three million vote deficit in the popular vote. While four other presidential elections in the previous 200 years produced a similar Electoral College/popular vote split, most recently in 2000, the magnitude of the difference in 2016 was galling to those who noticed. A handful of counties in Michigan, Wisconsin and Pennsylvania delivered the White House to Trump as he tallied the right number votes in the right places for Electoral College sums.

Three days later, an obscure former state government official and right-wing activist assayed to "explain" the slippage between the Electoral College and the popular vote as the efflux of criminality. Via Twitter, Gregg Phillips laconically lobbed this claim: "Completed analysis of database of 180 million voter registrations. Number of non-citizen votes exceeds 3 million. Consulting legal team" (quoted in Lusenhop, 2017, para. 11). The number of ineligible voters that Phillips cites approaches two-percent of the electorate and aligns—closely, magically—with Trump's deficit in popular votes in the election days earlier. The totemic three million number was also invested with the implicit message that *all* of the allegedly illicit votes tilted against Trump. According to one election specialist exercising common-sense, Phillip's lightning collation of voter records could not plausibly have been conducted so rapidly, since records of this sort are not immediately available (Lusenhop, 2017). Undeterred, in his first week in office in January, Trump recirculated Phillips' arithmetic blitz in his own tweet: "Gregg Phillips and crew say at least 3,000,000 votes were illegal" (quoted in Chan, 2017, para. 2). In short order, Trump announced plans for a (later aborted) commission to investigate election integrity in the United States, with seats at the table for some of the most aggressive pushers of electoral fraud memes.

Despite a shady résumé that includes investigations into his own integrity (Woodward, 2017), Phillips was judged to merit television interviews on CNN and ABC in January 2017. Notwithstanding White House support, integrity commissions proposed partly on the basis of his claims, as well as attention from mainstream news, could it be that Phillips' startling claims were constituted by baseless flak-in-discourse? Could it be that the claims served no purpose beyond shoring up the optics around Trump's popular vote total? And could it also be that the "three-million non-citizens" meme stood taller on the shoulders of an ongoing, multi-faceted flak campaign to problematize or harass selected voter demographics?

During the CNN interview, a defensive Phillips seemed to confuse even himself. He not only furnished no evidence or methodology to ground his "three million non-citizen voters" assertion, despite repeated prompts to do so—but seemed gobsmacked that anyone would even ask for evidence (Cable News Network, 2017). Phillips has also been surprised to learn that he is registered to vote in three states: "Why would I know or care?," he protested (quoted in Walker, 2017, para. 4). While it is legal to have multiple registrations, it presents the kind of electoral sloth that right-wing flaksters have regularly pegged as a fount of electoral corruption (Fund, 2008). Vann Woodward concludes his portrait of Phillips by observing that his "claims are unverified," to say nothing of baldly implausible. Nonetheless, through phantom flak, "perhaps the damage has already been done" to confidence in election results (2017, para. 31). Indeed, damage done, regardless of whether there is any evidence behind it, is a core objective of flak.

In this chapter, I will consider flak around elections that has engendered contradictory elements. On one hand, Republican Party flak discourse has usually refrained from impugning the whole system since the party regularly wins elections. On the other hand, the political right has pushed the narrative of significant voter fraud—all of it coded as "liberal"—for the flak-in-action objective of ever-tightening ballot regimes that effectively downsize the franchise. In the first half of the chapter, I present evidence that the alleged wave of voter fraud has, on rigorous examination, been found to be as microscopic as 1 in 33 million voters (Levitt, 2014). Flak narratives gain traction by dwelling on anecdotes, exceptional cases, exaggerations, suspicions, and later retracted stories to contrive a ballot-box crime wave. For purposes of illustration, I cross-examine the Heritage Foundation booklet *Does your vote count* as a brief case study of standard flak in-discourse-talking points. While these contrived talking points circulate, real weaknesses in the United States' haphazard election system remain unaddressed.

The second half of the chapter takes up a more extended flak case study of John Fund, a leading election flak merchant. Fund's brand of flak postures as affable and avuncular—even as his discourses are factually challenged and resolutely partisan. I conclude by briefly considering ways in which elections may be more directly gamed, beyond the flak regime.

Beyond the Carnival Barkers: Another Look at "Election Fraud"

Surveying the evidence, Rutgers University political scientist Lorraine C. Minnite bluntly characterizes the electoral fraud landscape: "The claim that voter fraud threatens the integrity of American elections is itself a fraud" (n.d., p. 5). Minnite's appraisal of the likelihood of election fraud has been corroborated by a battery of empirically-oriented, large-scale investigations (Brennen Center for Justice, 2017; Hasen, 2012; Khan & Corbin, 2012; Levitt, 2007, 2014). In the light of evidence, the fraud banner is waved as part of a flak-in-discourse strategy toward shaping impressions and mobilizing flak-in-action against ready access to the franchise.

But, what specifically constitutes voter fraud? Following U.S. Department of Justice's guidelines, Minnite characterizes election fraud as corruption in any moment of the electoral process that implicates registering voters, marking ballots, counting votes, or certifying results. Voter fraud is, in turn, a sub-category of election fraud in which a person who is not a qualified voter knowingly corrupts the process by casting a ballot. As for voters who are eligible, they may commit fraud by accepting payment for voting or by participating in a conspiracy to orchestrate voter fraud (n.d., p. 6). Minnite posits that most of what is flagged as fraud is subsequently found to reduce to sour grapes from losing candidates or to unwitting errors by election administrators or voters. Moreover, where legally-recognized fraud is concerned, motive matters. Inadvertent errors (stray marks on ballots, not knowing the minutia of complicated voting laws) do not constitute fraud (Minnite, n.d., p. 6).

While inadvertent errors by officials or by voters during elections are by definition random, to repeatedly assert the existence of pervasive fraud is not at all capricious. Minnite explains that, "There is a long history in America of elites using voter fraud allegations to restrict and shape the electorate" (n.d., p. 3). In the nineteenth century, when Republicans were the party of Lincoln, "it was the Democratic Party that erected new rules said to be necessary to respond to alleged fraud by black voters" (n.d., p. 3). In the twenty-first century, in a distinctly different environment, "the use of baseless voter fraud allegations for partisan advantage has become the exclusive domain of Republican Party activists" (n.d., p. 3).

The Republican Party's current wager on voter fraud flak may be driven by losing the popular vote six times in the past seven presidential elections, while facing increasingly unfavorable voter profiles (notably, from young people and Latinos and Latinas entering the voter pool). The response on the right has been to rewire the rules of the game with strategically selective, restrictive voter laws. In a hair-on-fire statement that defies the evidence on individual voter fraud, Republican National Committee chair Reince Priebus (2011–2017) channeled right-wing flak memes about the franchise. He charged that Democrats opposed "standing up for potential [vote] fraud—presumably because ending it would disenfranchise at least two of its core constituencies: the deceased and double-voters" (quoted in Mayer, 2012, para. 9).

Priebus' tough talk notwithstanding, "The intent of the exaggeration" of election fraud "is to intimidate the general public and even law makers into believing that American elections face a security threat from a rising tide of deceitful and criminal voters" (Minnite, n.d., p. 22). There is a hefty prize for flak-in-discourse that simulates flak-in-action against easy access to the ballot for eligible voters. Strategically-tailored laws may decisively shape the contours of the electorate by placing obstacles between, for example, low-income populations or students and the ballot box. Flak toward these ends is baldly undemocratic while it aligns with Schattschneider's epigram as concerns tailoring the rules of the game in order to structure its outcome.

As in other instances of flak-in-discourse, claims need not cohere, but can appreciate in perceived truth-value through sheer repetition. Flak-in-discourse against the franchise also gains traction as "common sense" by overlooking even obvious considerations. To wit, while an individual's impersonation voter fraud can engender considerable penalties if caught, it is vanishingly unlikely to change the course of an election. Impersonation fraud is, in this view, a textbook instance of an unappealing low-reward/high-risk endeavor. By contrast with individual voter fraud such as impersonating an eligible voter, manipulating election procedures at the "back end" *can* make a difference; for example, misconduct in counting ballots by election officials is far more likely to produce nefarious outcomes.

Consider that, in 2018 in North Carolina, "consultant" Leslie McCrae Dowless was hired by congressional candidate Mark Harris—party: Republican—to coordinate absentee ballot matters in an election. Dowless was a curious choice for a sensitive campaign position for having a criminal record that included felony fraud. In turn, Dowless and others whom he directed collected almost 1,000 absentee ballots in Democrat-leaning precincts with the promise of delivering them to the election office. Instead, Dowless' operation altered or disposed of the ballots, to his client Harris' advantage. These actions went far beyond individual fraud and were meant to disenfranchise swaths of trusting voters to swing a tight election. The caper unraveled Harris was compelled to recant the election result from the witness stand in the subsequent legal process or face the distinct possibility of perjury under oath (Clark, 2019). Notice that calling this seedy episode voter fraud is also a misnomer insofar as the disenfranchised voters were victims. This form of fraud at the back end of the election that impacts the vote count is the kind of scam that *can* make a difference in an election outcome, in contrast with the dedicated right-wing emphasis on individual voter impersonation. Such wider mischief also proves difficult to conceal, as evidenced by the annulment of the tainted electoral result in North Carolina.

Flak around voter impersonation has additional appeal for flak-mongers since it does not leave fingerprints as Dowless' caper did. Loudly raising the false flag of fraud can in itself chill segments of the electorate from electoral participation through the prospect of hassles from authority around voting; a flak-driven chill that leaves even fewer fingerprints. Moreover, one of the US' most populated states, Florida, enacted registration laws that are sufficiently tight, with fines and criminalization for even minor bureaucratic slips that the widely respected League of Woman Voters has withdrawn from voter registration (Berman, 2011). The bureaucratic clampdown straightforwardly disables wider voter registration and loads the deck for fewer votes—with already marginalized populations who are less likely to be registered the first to be left behind.

The public may readily be confused about electoral fraud, given the anecdotes and conflicting claims that have circulated. To begin unpacking the issue in empirical terms, I will analyze a flak-driven discourse that assertively pushes fraud memes. To wit, the Heritage Foundation's *Does your vote count?* booklet presents one-stop shopping for contemporary flak-in-discourse tropology that is designed to prompt flak-in-action measures around the ballot box.

Zombie Apocalypse

Heritage's 21-page *Does your vote count?* booklet is relatively light on written text. Substantial space is devoted to close-up images of serious-looking types staring soulfully toward the camera, presumably contemplating cascades of voter fraud. In turn, claims about voter fraud are conveyed with gut-punch concision. Despite its ominous state-by-state catalogue of fraud cases going back decades, the booklet's references cite a paltry nine sources to back its assertions, one of which was composed by Heritage staff (John Fund and Hans von Spakovsky).

In *Does your vote count?*, Heritage intones, "As an eligible citizen, you must be guaranteed the right to vote"—verily—"and it must be guaranteed that your vote is not stolen or diluted by thieves and fraudsters" (Heritage Foundation, n.d., p. 2). Heritage's central premise is that electoral thievery and fraud is commonplace. Furthermore, the pamphlet's readers are furnished with a victimization frame as concerns the alleged theft of their rights by shady others lurking by the electoral urn.

In conjuring a crime wave, Heritage's booklet follows the standard flak technique of the bullet-pointed list, designed to flood the zone and suggest that outrageous happenings are ubiquitous (n.d., pp. 8–15). The reader may be startled by datum such as, "1.8 million voters are dead" (n.d., p. 5). The phrasing ambiguates whether Heritage is observing that there are dead people inertly included on voter rolls—or (the more ominous and literal reading) that this many dead people have been "voting" posthumously, in line with a long-cultivated right-wing trope. Fraud *is* happening, Heritage avers. In this view, procedures must be tightened to repel vote moochers from the ballot box.

The booklet's final flak-in-discourse appeal is action-oriented, as it assays to steer discourse toward flak-in-action. In doing so, the booklet conjugates verbs in the imperative: "Talk to your family and friends […] about the danger of voter fraud," "Distribute copies of this booklet" along with writing letters to the editor, calling talk radio, and pressing the panic button over vote fraud in public meetings. Heritage recruits readers to deputize themselves as polling place volunteer watchers to arrest the crime wave that it insists to be in motion (n.d., p. 19).

What Is Wrong with This Picture?

Notwithstanding the booklet's George A. Romero-style scenario of (un)dead voters lumbering across the electoral landscape with armloads of completed ballots in hand, the evidence is scant. For example, when asked to furnish particulars about votes from the dead, election flak merchant—and Heritage Foundation "Senior Legal Fellow"—Hans von Spakovsky pointed to a study by the *Atlanta Journal-Constitution* in 2000 that claimed 5,400 such instances. The situation sounds grim; but, following further examination, the *Journal-Constitution* concluded that all the presumed-as-dead voters were accounted for by clerical and other errors (Mayer, 2012).

South Carolina in 2012 provides another instance in which an investigation of assertions of massive improprieties negated the zombie voter tropology. Following instruction to investigate from the state's attorney general, the South Carolina State Election Commission (SEC) examined 207 alleged cases of dead voters. In reporting the findings, SEC Executive Director Marci Andino notes the drain on resources the investigation generated: "Nearly half of the SEC staff has spent more than 200 hours working over the past four weeks to gather the necessary information and examine each record to make determinations, if possible" (2012, p. 1); an effort that clearly interfered with the office's normal functioning. The SEC's investigation could not locate the zombie voters clotting polling sites across South Carolina: "The investigation found that 197 of these instances are not cases of votes being cast fraudulently in the name of deceased voters" (Andino, 2012, p. 1). Instead, the SEC discovered clerical errors, confused data matching (around, e.g., "Junior" and "Senior"), participation errors (such as stray marks on voter roll sheets)—and three cases of voters who died after (*not before*) having mailed an absentee ballot. That left ten cases of "insufficient information in the record to make a determination," mainly surrounding voters' signatures that appear to speak more to what could not be known with certainty than a crime wave (Andino, 2012, p. 2).

When Heritage's booklet turns to "Types of Voter Fraud" on page 6, "Impersonation Fraud at the Polls" tops the list. While absentee ballot fraud is more common, if still rare, evocations of impersonation are made-to-order to agitate for voter identification at the polls. Ergo, Heritage presses for "Photographic government-issued identification to vote" (n.d., p. 17). While voter ID laws are a "solution" to an empirically non-existent problem, Jane Mayer reports that 11-percent of the U.S. population—one person in nine—does not have the type of ID that meets muster under the strictest state voting regimes. Moreover, these figures are more than 50- and 100-percent higher among elderly and African-American citizens (2012, para. 23). With respect to this "solution" to a non-existent problem that generates significant election participation problems in its own right, one can connect the dots.

Felons also make Heritage's electoral threat list, as the booklet claims "convicted felons [...] are not eligible to vote" (n.d., p. 7). The claim is inaccurate, since each state can codify its own procedures with respect to felons who have served their time. Maine, for example, restores felons' voting eligibility following their sentences (Minnite, n.d., p. 39). However, according to *Business Insider*, "Nearly every state restricts the rights of people with felony convictions to vote in some way" that has led to six million Americans left on the electoral sidelines, in many instances for non-violent drug offenses (Panetta and Gal, 2018, para. 10). Inaccuracy aside, Heritage situates hardened criminality in close proximity to voting behavior, drenching the polling site with seething *film-noirish* connotations.

Continuing in a register of fanciful claims, Heritage's *Does your vote count?* asserts that vote fraud prosecution has been "low priority" for law enforcement (n.d., 16). Recent history says otherwise: "According to the attorney general [John Ashcroft], since the inception of the [Ballot Access and Voting Integrity Initiative] program in 2002, 'we've made enforcement of election fraud and corruption offenses a *top priority*'" (emphasis added, quoted in Minnite, n.d.,

p. 8). Law professor and elections specialist Richard Hasen characterizes the Bush administration's mobilization toward finding and prosecuting election fraud as "unprecedented" (2012, p. 52). From the inside, U.S. Attorney for New Mexico (2001–2007) David Iglesias observes in an interview that, in summer 2002, he and all 92 of his peer U.S. Attorneys received messages "asking us to work with state and local officials to prevent election fraud" (Horton, 2008a, para. 4). Despite the priority placed on election integrity, and the fact that election offenses are rigorously codified in law, scant convictions followed from the Bush-era campaign. As Mayer observes, "In 2005, for example, the federal government charged many more Americans with violating migratory-bird statues than with election fraud" (2012, para. 32).

Rules of the Game

While ostensibly discussing the same topic as Heritage, News21's Natasha Khan and Corbin Carson are 180-degrees removed from the crime-wave atmospherics of *Does your vote count?* In particular, "A News21 analysis of 2,068 alleged election-fraud cases after 2000 shows that while fraud has occurred, the rate is infinitesimal and in-person voter impersonation on Election Day, which prompted 37 state legislatures to enact or consider tough voter ID laws, is *virtually non-existent*" (emphasis added, 2012, para. 1). The investigation was conducted over seven months and implicated 2,000 records requests and a team that reviewed nearly 5,000 court documents. Khan and Carson also appealed for more information from the public, in the spirit of summoning the wisdom of crowds. In contrast with Heritage's litany of largely unsourced examples, News21 performed systematic, original research.

Following extensive contacts with local authorities, Khan and Carson found ten cases of voter impersonation among the country's roster of 146 million voters—or, about *one impersonation fraud for every fifteen million voters*. In other words, it is simply not possible for voter impersonation fraud to have turned an election result in the period under examination. However, Kahn and Carson's investigation finds 207 cases of other forms of fraud for each voter impersonation, even as Heritage and the wider fraud discourse prioritize voter impersonation. Absentee ballot (491 cases) and registration fraud (400 cases) were the leading forms of misconduct that Khan and Carson discovered. In any event, by Khan and Carson's numbers, *all* forms of fraud in aggregate impact about 0.00001-percent of votes, notwithstanding its central place in the right-wing universe of election discourse.

As for tighter ID laws, Khan and Carson suggest a reason why Republicans have insisted on them, despite the vanishingly slight occurrence of voter impersonation: "In a video that went viral in June [2012], Republican Mike Turzai, Pennsylvania's House majority leader, spoke approvingly at a Republican State Committee meeting of the state's new voter ID law 'which is going to allow Governor Romney to win the state of Pennsylvania—done'" (2012, para. 21). While Turzai's prediction about the 2012 election turned out wrong, the seemingly reasonable-on-their-face ID laws present a subtle procedural means by which to sculpt—and thus better predict and control—the pool of eligible voters on election day.

The case of Pennsylvania, an electorally competitive swing-state begs more scrutiny in the framework of flak against the vote. According to Pennsylvania's Departments of State and of Transportation, nine-percent of the state's eligible voters did not possess acceptable ID at the time the law that Turzai referenced was passed. Translated from percentages to raw numbers, an estimated 758,000 citizens did not have qualifying ID in Pennsylvania; a sum well within the margin of even a moderately competitive election. Moreover, people less likely to have IDs tend to be from marginalized groups and less likely to vote Republican in general. Beyond Republican electoral interests, the law answered to no demonstrated need as Pennsylvania's Attorney General could name no cases of impersonation fraud to justify it (Khan and Carson, 2012).

According to the American Civil Liberties Union, the Pennsylvania law was, "one of the most restrictive in the nation and did not allow many commonly used identification cards for voting" (2014, para. 4). It was, in turn, answered with three trials and a preliminary injunction, before Commonwealth Court Judge Bernard L. McGinley dismissed the law in strong language. He wrote that it "does not pass constitutional muster because there is no legal, non-burdensome provision of a compliant photo ID to all qualified electors"; the judge calls the law that was passed by the legislature "fraught with illegalities" (quoted in American Civil Liberties Union, 2014, para. 3). McGinley adds, "Inescapably, the Voter ID Law infringes upon qualified electors' right to vote" (quoted in American Civil Liberties Union, 2014, para. 3).

While ensconced in high-minded catchphrases about the sanctity of the vote, ID laws are effective for the purpose of subtly shaping the electorate for partisan advantage—particularly when there is no concomitant stipulation to make the qualifying voter ID easy to obtain for all. In turn, the partisan quality of "ballot security" initiatives are evident in the distribution of voter ID bills at the state level. From 2010 to 2012, Khan and Carson report, 62 ID bills were introduced in state legislatures with Republican majorities—and only in Rhode Island did a Democratic majority take up the cause. Moreover, ID laws have been crafted to empower some selected voter blocs over other blocs through the mechanism of ID regulation; thus, in Texas, a concealed handgun license is a qualifying ID, but a student ID is not (Leber, 2014).

Despite the notably weak empirical basis for ID laws, they have gained traction as flak-in-action. Significant investment of time and effort, plus costly legal action, is necessary to confront restrictive laws once passed by legislatures. As always, the expenditure of time, effort and cash is a core flak objective to drain flak targets of all three.

Real Problems

Khan and Carson report some dire circumstances around U.S. elections, even if individual voter fraud is not one of them. The system that they find in their investigation is chaotic due to the crazy-quilt of local laws and voting apparatuses that characterize the country's 3,145 counties. For this reason, Khan and Carson perceive considerable honest confusion among U.S. voters. Ballots can indeed be given in error to ineligible voters who may not know they are ineligible, as elections administered by non-professional and/or cursorily trained local personnel generate unwitting mistakes. Khan and Carson also flag problems with voter registration groups that are prevalent in the United States and that pay employees for reaching targeted numbers of registrations. The current system, with numerous privatized registration drives, perversely incentivizes fake registrations. Even if "Riggan Thomson" or "Amy Winehouse" are very unlikely to actually show up at the polls, the fake registrations are a further drag on an already poorly designed U.S. electoral system that lacks centralized coordination and apolitical professionalism.

When one construes all forms of election process failure as troubling, it focuses attention on systemic solutions to really-existing problems in U.S. elections—and not the phantom problems that flaksters contrive. In this vein, Hasen posits that, "partisan discretion, lack of uniformity, and inadequate training on the local level are this country's most serious problems with running elections" (2012, p. 197). Effective election administration implicates professional and technical competence in a wide array of domains; to wit, understanding the hardware and software of voting machines, training workers, tabulating results, conducting recounts if needed, all the while communicating with the public. However, elections are typically administered by figures who are not hired for their competencies, but are themselves elected officials, with a partisan and personal interest in the processes they oversee.

There are, in other words, significant problems with U.S. elections. The problems simply do not correspond with what right-wing flak discourses assert them to be. In drilling down further into the particulars of flak around elections, I will examine leading flak merchant John Fund who has long agitated about the recondite criminal tendencies he perceives around the voting booth.

Fraud *Fund*amentalism

John Fund (born 1957, Arizona) may be characterized as the doyen of right-wing election fraud pundits—an ensemble that Hasen dubs the "fraudulent fraud squad," devoted to manufacturing flak around elections (2012, pp. 41–73). Fund spreads flak memes through mass media appearances, social media, books, and regular platforms at *National Review* and *American Spectator*. He formerly worked for *The Wall Street Journal* for two decades. Fund's book collaborators have included Rush Limbaugh and, more recently, Hans von Spakovsky who oscillates between acting as a state bureaucrat and a think tanker.

Georgia congressman and 1960s civil rights warrior John Lewis regards von Spakovsky as "the moving force behind photo I.D." laws. In Lewis' appraisal, von Spakovsky has "been hell-bent to make it more difficult—always, always—for people to vote," with the justification of rampant voter impersonation (quoted in Mayer, 2012, para. 26). However, I have elected to emphasize Fund's flak-in-discourse as a case study as he has been a more flamboyantly public exponent of election fraud flak tropes. While mindful of his institutional affiliations, I interpret Fund as a flak merchant. That is, he has been an entrepreneurial figure in spreading flak while roving across several platforms. Fund's flak-in-discourse auteur signature presents as far more emollient, faux-cheery and avuncular than the often angry products of flak mills like Heartland and Veritas. Fund's seemingly palatable flak is, nonetheless, flak—and it pivots on wildly contentious interpretations and inaccuracies, while resolutely pursuing divisive partisanship.

Below, I telescope in on the second edition of Fund's book, *Stealing Elections* that was published in 2008. The book appears to have been timed to (unsuccessfully) rally Republicans and demoralize Democrats with doses of flak tropes prior to the 2008 election. Fund's contradictory project in *Stealing*

Elections reverberates with that of other electoral flaksters on the right. On one hand, Fund in effect defends the status quo of low voter participation and shabby electoral infrastructure, as if U.S. culture and laws prescribe such. On the other hand, Fund sounds alarms around U.S. elections in partisan terms. He visions the voting booth as having regularly been breached by imposter voters—a situation that demands an ever-narrower path to the voting booth. *Stealing Elections'* title and cover image also scream recognizably partisan flak tropology. The cover depicts a felon passing a ballot between prison bars while another vote is handed out of a coffin. These are the same tropes that Priebus and countless other rightists have channeled around voter fraud—coded as the dedicated work of Democrats, despite the striking paucity of factual backing that I have already considered.

Overview of Stealing Elections

Like the Heritage booklet discussed earlier, Fund generally avoids systematic "big picture" investigation of fraud and gravitates toward assuming its existence, *writ large*—and then enters examples and anecdotes into the record, one after another, an apparent daisy-chain of fraud. In Fund's narration, all forms of election mishaps, from actual mischief to ineptitude and accidents, to uncorroborated stories, are shepherded toward the flak-driven premise that fraud is everywhere, always already happening.

Fund asserts that, particularly since 1993's National Voter Registration Act ("Motor Voter Act") assayed to ramp up voter registration, the United States has witnessed "an explosion of phantom voters" (2008, p. 28). Fund nonetheless makes sideways admission of the weakness of the evidence around voter impersonation. While he celebrates the 2008 *Crawford v. Marion County Election Board* Supreme Court case that affirmed voter ID laws in Indiana, Fund acknowledges that "the record showed no evidence of impersonation fraud in Indiana" (2008, p. 90). He further observes, "My research found that the number of people who have actually spent time in jail as a result of a conviction for vote fraud is shockingly low" (2008, p. 11)—although, not quite for the reasons that Fund implies. As noted, a lack of criminal convictions has not been for lack of effort in ferreting out crimes, but for a paucity of crimes in the first instance.

Notwithstanding unconvincing rhetorical efforts to inoculate himself from appearing partisan (2008, pp. 15–22), Fund strongly articulates Republicans to lawful rigor as concerns elections. He maintains that, "Republicans tend to pay more attention to the rule of law and the standards and procedures that govern elections" (2008, p. 15)—although the "rule of law" deficit was what, for example, Judge McGinley, slapped down vis-à-vis Republican-driven ID laws in Pennsylvania. Filling in the other side of the dichotomy that he constructs, Fund assails Democrats for alleged electoral sloth, self-interest, and willingness to stoop to fraud—a tropology that, as noted, saturates the book starting with its cover. Democrats are mainly driven by grubby self-interest, as Fund "helpfully" explains: "Democrats might do better than to look for ways to reform the voting system that would actually improve elections, instead of just making sure the laws do not benefit Republicans" (2008, p. 46). In this view, measures such as the Motor Voter Act, designed to enable participation in elections, are a self-evident detriment to the electoral process; a bizarre position to assume in a country that defines itself as apotheosizing electoral democracy.

Fund acknowledges Republican efforts to short-circuit voter participation—provided that incidents can be framed as having occurred in the mists of centuries past, for example, in 1986 (2008, pp. 24–25). "Since then," he asserts, "the national GOP has been terminally gun-shy of launching any programs that could be characterized as trying to prevent minorities from voting, but the perception that they are doing so lingers" (2008, p. 25). In Fund's narration, the problem is one of perception while the Republican Party is too debilitated with self-defeating politically correct fevers for its own good.

On this score, Fund's message was not convincing in 2008—or in the time period since then. Consider a TV ad message delivered in Spanish to voters in 2010's tight election climate in Nevada. The message intones, "This November, we need to send a message to all politicians. If they didn't keep their promise on immigration reform, then they can't count on our vote. Democratic leaders must pay for their broken promises and betrayals." Following this tee-up, the ad concludes, "Don't vote this November. This is the only way to send them a message" (translated by and quoted in Hasen, 2012, pp. 75–76). "Paid for by Latinos for Reform" was the attribution for a message that presents as tough-talk that jabs at Democrats from a staunchly politically-left posture. However, Latinos for Reform was headed by Robert de Posada, an operator "with deep Republican ties," via service for the Bush administration as well as for Republican congresspeople—and the ostensible "group" Latinos for Reform shared a post-office box address with the producers of the pro-Bush/anti-Kerry "swift boat" flak ads of 2004 (Hasen, 2012, p. 76). Rather than trying to win Latin votes that may be largely beyond reach for the Republicans for undisguised hostility toward Latinos and Latinas, the next best approach is to demobilize those same voters from casting ballots. While a potential vote that is *not* cast against you is effectively the same in the electoral sums as one more vote in your favor, the Latinos for Reform ad is driven by cynical flak logic that hijacks the spirit of electoral democracy.

More recently, in 2018, Georgia Secretary of State Brian Kemp, Republican and self-proclaimed Trumpian, endeavored to make the underhanded Latinos for Reform flak ploy look like an advanced civics lesson. While radiating standard issue vote fraud flak memes in public, as Georgia's Secretary, Kemp implemented an exact match policy on voter registrations. The policy signified that hyphens, accents, and even typographical errors (!) had to present identical match to state records—a policy that previously had been declared illegal in the state. As a result, Emory University professor Carol Anderson (2018) writes that, from 2016 to 2018, almost 11-percent of names were culled from Georgia's voter rolls. Immediately prior to the 2018 election another 53,000 new registrations were held-up by exact match concerns—and 70-percent of the holds were African-Americans.

The punchline? Kemp was not only managing the election as Georgia Secretary of State, he was simultaneously the Republican candidate for the state's highest office of governor—and was facing off against an African-American woman, Democrat Stacey Abrams, to boot. He also refused to step down from one position to run for the other. Journalist and former Republican operative Elise Jordan observes election conditions in Georgia that, in *some* districts, included "broken voting machines, or functional machines with missing power cords, or too few machines." If the same selective obstacles to voting had arisen in Afghanistan or Zimbabwe as in Kempian Georgia, Jordan avers that, "American election monitors would protest the result" (2018, para. 4).

Fund's narrative about Republicans having masochistically sacrificed themselves for electoral political correctness assays to deflect attention from right-wing flak around voting. The narrative also defies facts on the ground—both before and after *Stealing Elections*. Moreover, the evidence against Fund's claims are not a loose examples or anecdotes but go systematically toward how elections have been administered.

What Is to Be Done? Or, a Passion for Purges

Fund alludes to many legitimate problems with U.S. elections, such as the haphazard patchwork of local voter rolls. However, he consistently denies the most straightforward solution—federal standardization—as unconstitutional intrusion into localities. Fund's animus even extends to declaring Election Day a federal holiday since, one assumes, any reform that makes voting more likely is understood to contradict current Republican Party interests. It bears mention that Fund does praise a modernized, professionally-administered election system that strives for ballot security and high participation via easy access to registration—when that system is located in Mexico (2008, pp. 6–7).

By contrast with Fund, Hasen envisions U.S. elections in which "a voter should be able to walk into any polling place, anywhere in the country, and see the same voting equipment and same ballot format" (2012, p. 198), as in other former British colonies and mature democracies Canada and Australia. "Registration should be uniform as well," Hasen argues. In a modernized system, registration would be triggered when someone finishes high school, with a centralized national voter identification number, portable regardless of where one moves in the US.

Fund insists that improvements in the US' current creaking system as largely off-limits, under a tendentious reading of the law. *Stealing Elections* finally endorses a seemingly modest platform of "simple procedural changes" that collapse into familiar Republican talking points (2008, p. 12). To wit, Fund proposes the remedies of "purging voter rolls or requiring a photo ID at the polls, combined with secure technology and more vigorous prosecution of fraud" (2008, p. 12). Interestingly, purging and punishment are prominent pillars of Fund's reverie of electoral order.

More recently, Fund repeats these talking points, darkly intoning that "voter rolls are breeding grounds for potential fraud"—rather than a fount of democracy (2017b, para. 1). In Fund's vision of purging, voters who have moved out of the district would be removed from the rolls. The purging solution seems benign and commonsensical on its face. In practice, false positives that surround people with common or semi-common names—say, Michael Dawson, Alicia Palmer, Ana García—readily disenfranchise eligible registered voters once purging commences. In Florida at the turn of the millennium, voter roll purges of felons were performed to scandalously loose standards (first four letters of the first name, 90-percent of last name and approximate match on date of birth). The algorithm facilitated scatter-shot false positive purging of qualified voters (Minnite, n.d., p. 25). As a result, "at least two thousand eligible voters were removed from the rolls" in a state that determined the outcome of the 2000 federal election by an official 537-vote margin (Hasen,

2012, p. 28). The recklessness of the purging procedures belies right-wing narratives about protecting the sanctity of the vote.

Along with giving exalting ID laws and extolling voting roll purges, Fund pivots to attack measures that are likely to *increase* the prevalence of legitimate voting such as easier registration and an election day holiday (2008, pp. 27–30). Nevertheless, in displaying a chimerical posture toward elections, Fund unleashes a hymn to "the communal aspect of citizens voting together"—provided, one must assume, citizens are on lunch break, not on a shared election day holiday (2008, p. 41). For sentimentalized inspiration, Fund rallies to a Norman Rockwell painting "showing people lining up outside churches and schools to vote" (2008, p. 37). Interestingly, Rockwell's painting—"America at the Polls" from November 4, 1944's *Saturday Evening Post*—also features an all-white electorate. And no voter IDs in sight.

Politicizing the Politicization

In discussing elections, Fund (2008) circles several times around the U.S. Attorneys scandal in the George W. Bush era—and each time delivers a notably nebulous account of its troubling politicization of parts of the justice system. Prominent human rights lawyer Scott Horton noted in 2008 that, "Perhaps the hallmark of the administration of justice in the Bush era is its complete politicization." As Bush-era Senate hearings revealed, "virtually every political staffer in the White House had been authorized to meddle with criminal investigations and prosecutions"—including cases around elections (Horton 2008b, para. 7).

In Fund's account, the sacking of U.S. Attorneys David Iglesias (New Mexico) and John McKay (Washington), along with seven others, was "ham-handed." Fund simultaneously contends that the sackings were for "failing to prosecute vote fraud cases" (2008, p. 16). He thereby assigns blame on the U.S. Attorneys for their ostensible lack of vigor as prosecutors, rather than on a lack of legitimate voter fraud cases to pursue.

Let us consider the case of Iglesias, a highly regarded conservative lawyer. As a United States attorney, Iglesias followed up on instruction from the Department of Justice in Washington to prioritize election fraud by establishing a task force, convening regular meetings, and setting up a tip hotline. Moreover, according to the Department of Justice's investigation of Iglesias' sacking by the White House, "The chief of the Public Integrity Section's Election Crimes Branch, Craig Donsanto, told us that he thought Iglesias pursued voter fraud cases vigorously and fairly" (Office of the Inspector General/Office of Professional Responsibility, 2008, p. 190). Indeed, the Department of Justice's investigation into the firings maintains that the White House's stated rationales for firing Iglesias—poor management of the office—were contradicted by all evidence that instead indicated high regard for Iglesias' conduct (2008, pp. 187–197). After two years of attention to electoral fraud in New Mexico (following leads from the public, consulting with the FBI), Iglesias' office had not found a single case of vote fraud that merited prosecution. It is impossible to imagine the same being said of any other category of crime if that category had been prioritized for scrutiny (e.g., labor law violations). In other words, the lack of prosecutions from Iglesias' office was not for lack of vigor on election fraud, *contra* Fund's glib contentions and vagueness on the topic. Rather, the putative voter fraud crime wave conjured by flak mills and flak merchants is not what they assert it to be.

Fund's narrative also effaces the story of U.S. attorneys who *did* bulldoze into the electoral processes through aggressive, if specious and tangential fraud charges. In Wisconsin, US Attorney Steven Biskupic's fraud case against a state employee was, to all appearances, a means of indirectly tarnishing incumbent Democrat governor James Doyle's reelection bid. The alleged corruption was around a state-tendered travel contract (Cohen, 2007). Flaws in the prosecution were legion. There was nothing unusual about the bidding on state travel contracts and the alleged offenses had not even occurred in Biskupic's district. Moreover, details about the case were not only leaked to the press by prosecutors against proper Justice Department practice, but were leaked in alignment with the electoral calendar. Iglesias similarly claimed in congressional testimony that he faced pressure to make prosecutions align with election season to benefit Republicans (Horton, 2008b). In the Wisconsin case, the timing appears to have been an effort to contrive linkages between the suspect and Governor Doyle who, in any event, did not appoint the supposedly corrupt employee.

The suspect spent four months in jail prior to a hearing before the United States Court of Appeals for the Seventh Circuit. The case was, in turn, dismissed by the judges in an extraordinary 20 minutes for which a written opinion was deemed unnecessary. Judge Diane Wood chastised the zealous prosecutor, positing "Your evidence is beyond thin" (Cohen, 2007, para. 3). Nonetheless, the process soiled an innocent person's reputation and deprived her of liberty in jail while flaking Doyle's campaign by extension on absurd grounds. In constructing the flak narrative about voter fraud, Fund is not only resolutely selective; he is also silent on this troubling case of prosecutorial overreach that was implicated in an election campaign, while asserting a lack of vim and vigor on the part the U.S. attorneys.

Flak Finesse for Florida

Alongside his penchant for uncannily selective accounts of events, Fund (2008, pp.95–110) makes a seemingly curious move to re-litigate the narrative around Florida in the 2000 presidential election. Flak-in-discourse can, however, be utilized to bend narrative recollections of the past into alignment with meta-ideological positions (right vs. left), with an eye toward impacting the present and future. Recall that Fund's book is called *Stealing Elections*. However, rather than positing an election as "stolen" in this chapter, Fund insists that the system works (i.e., when Republicans prevail). Fund rallies to the "official story" around Florida 2000 while stripping out or delegitimizing the many peculiarities of this electoral episode (discussed in Goss, 2003).

In dismissing doubts around Bush's election in 2000, Fund cuts and pastes his sources as needed. Fund writes, "in fact, every single recount of the votes in Florida determined that George W. Bush had won the state's twenty-five electoral votes and therefore the presidency" (2008, p. 96). It is the bluntest of several repetitions of this misleading claim (2008, p. 44, p. 98). The recounts that Fund references were carried out in 2001 by a consortium staffed by eight media outlets (including *The New York Times*) and University of Chicago academics. The *Times*' Ford Fessenden and John R. Broder's report on the consortium's 10-month, one million dollar investigation indeed opens as follows:

> A comprehensive review of the uncounted Florida ballots from last year's presidential election reveals that George W. Bush would have won even if the United States Supreme Court had allowed the statewide manual recount of the votes that the Florida Supreme Court had ordered to go forward. (2001, para. 1)

Although the United States was at the start of active military conflict in Afghanistan at the time of the report in November 2001, Fessenden and Broder quickly introduce important qualifications. Specifically, in "looking at a broader group of rejected ballots than those covered in the court decisions, 175,010 in all," the consortium "found that Mr. Gore might have won if the courts had ordered a full statewide recount of all the rejected [machine-unread] ballots" (2001, para. 4). While Fund bluntly dismisses any doubts around the outcome from the after-the-fact recount, the findings of the source he cites "indicate that Mr. Gore might have eked out a victory if he had pursued in court a course like the one he publicly advocated when he called on the state to 'count all the votes'" (2001, para. 4). The consortium identified "any of seven single standards [...] combined with the results of examination of overvotes" in which Gore would have carried Florida (2012, para. 27). Despite the white-knuckle demands of propping up Bush's legitimacy immediately after September 11, 2001, the *Times*' strongly implies that Al Gore may also have lost due to the inclusion of late absentee ballots (i.e., baldly illegal votes), in addition to surreal snafus around ballot design—factors that have been corroborated by other investigators (Hasen, 2012; Tapper, 2001).

With further flak fervor in support of the election's official outcome, Fund dismisses the post-Florida discourse over the intersection of race demographics and voting booth technology. It is an attempt to write race out of the administration of U.S. elections that continues into Fund's more recent writing (2017b). As concerns race in Florida 2000, Fund belittles the very idea that there is anything at issue: "Machine errors cannot be a cause of discrimination since the machines do not know the race of the voter." Next, Fund hunkers down as gallant defender of minority voters: "Is it not bordering on racism in the first place to assume that those who spoil ballots are necessarily minority voters?" (2008, p. 98). Fund clinches the passage off by referencing the United States Commission on Civil Rights' report (2001). He claims the report found that machine error "accounts for about one error in 250,000 votes cast" (2008, p. 98).

Once again going to the source, what does the report that Fund cites actually say? The Commission notes that in Florida 2000, five types of voting systems were employed. In turn, the different systems had vastly different rates of failing to read ballots. In particular, optical scan with precinct tabulation presented very low spoilage rates, as the counting system "kicked out" ballots that were not filled in correctly or were unreadable. This mechanism enabled another attempt to fill out a readable ballot, as the law permits, before the voter left the premises.

"Machines do not know the race of the voter," Fund thunders. However, we know that precincts are demographically distinct from each other—and that they do not vote on remotely comparable machines. In this vein, the Commission reports that, "The Governor's Select Task Force on Election Procedures, Standards and Technology stated in its March 2001 report that error—or 'spoilage'—rates in Florida's November 2000 election varied widely by type of voting system." For this reason, "every voter does *not* have the same chance to have his or her vote counted accurately"; a situation that, in turn, "creates substantial questions about equal protection" (Governor's Select Task Force, quoted in United States Commission on Civil Rights, 2001, ch. 8, para. 7). In other words, equal protection of the ballot across the state's precincts and populations is what is at stake—and some voters had far more reliable devices at their fingertips.

How much more reliable? Moving to the data in the report that Fund pegs as his source, one finds that Gadsden County used an optical scan with central (not *local*) tabulation system. The county's spoilage rate of 12.4 percent meant that *one vote in every eight* in the county was uncounted—a surreal contrast with Fund's hand-waving figure of one in "250,000 votes cast." By contrast, "on the other side of the Ochlockonee River" from Gadsden (2001, para. 8), Leon County's optical scan, precinct-level (local) tabulation system recorded the lowest spoilage rate among Florida's counties at 0.18 percent (or, one in 550 ballots); an almost 70-fold (7,000 percent) difference from Gadsden. It bears mention that Gadsden is also Florida's only African-American majority county.

The Commission cites a *New York Times* estimate that African-American precincts across Florida were two-to-four times more likely to have votes not counted due to substandard voting apparatuses as compared with Latino and Euro-American population centers—implicating a sum of voters effectively disenfranchised that dwarfed the final margin of 537 votes by which Bush officially prevailed. Nevertheless, Fund huffily talks over the facts of the US' race- and class-division that extends down to electoral infrastructure that effectively intervened in the 2000 election by silently blotting out votes. The systemic problems with voting infrastructure were sufficiently egregious for passage of the Help America Vote Act in 2002 to address some of the problems, notwithstanding flak campaigns that bang on endlessly about individual voter fraud.

Plus ça change: The Continuing Career of a Flak Merchant

In recent years, Fund has continued to put out his stall as a merchant of partisan flak-in-discourse to set up flak-in-action (such as laws and commissions). During the 2016 U.S. presidential campaign, from his regular column in *National Review*, Fund found no basis for criticism of Trump's candidacy. It would not have been difficult to find matters for concern. For example, Paul Manafort was forced to resign as campaign manager in August 2016 for implication in the shady world of Russo-Ukrainian politics that later became a cascade of felony convictions (as noted in Chapter 1). Unmoved by this story among others, Fund problematizes Hillary Clinton's campaign and its allegedly depthless corruption. The resultant faux flak memes have become more uproariously ironic from the vantage point of even modest hindsight.

Fund recirculates flak articulations already forged in the broader right-wing discourse concerning alleged machinations around the Clinton Foundation (Fund, 2016d) and "sleazy Clinton emails" (2016c, para. 1). These phantom flak-*cum*-"scandals" propel Fund toward conjuring a Watergate-proportioned, Clintonian "cover-up"—of *something bad*, but as yet unknown (2016b, para. 1). Fund channels Nostradamus as he assays mightily to make his assertion into a criminal conviction: "Once the details of the [Clinton] Foundation's activities come to light, there will likely be evidence of it engaging in massive solicitation and operating frauds" (2016c, para. 11). While his discourse is destitute of established facts, despite 25 years of hostile scrutiny of the Clintons' public and private life (cf., Brock, 2002), Fund concludes with the spine-tingling prospect of phantom flak: "Who knows what else will be belatedly revealed should she win the White House?" (2016c, para. 16).

This faux flak trope bids to preemptively render hollow a Clinton electoral victory and to demobilize and demoralize Democratic voters—as well as to symmetrically excite *National Review* readers with flak memes. The Democratic Party is also honey-combed with intractable division, in Fund's narration. He falsely pins the "birther" flak sham against Barack Obama on Clinton's 2008 campaign (2016a). By 2016, *PolitiFact* seems almost fatigued with addressing this partisan porkie: "*PolitiFact* and our friends at *FactCheck. org* and the *Washington Post* Fact-Checker have debunked this zombie claim multiple times. There is no evidence that Clinton or her 2008 campaign ever floated the theory" (Greenberg and Qiu, 2016, paras. 9–10).

During autumn 2016, Fund also fretted in a flak register that the prospect of a Clinton presidency would weaken the United States at home and abroad via scandals and blackmail opportunities (Fund 2016b); a grimly hilarious prognostication given prevailing conditions in the Trump era, abetted by the administration's widely reported secrecy and defiance around security vetting of officials. In this vein, Sabrina Siddiqui and Adam Gabbatt report on presidential son-in-law Jared Kushner's high-level security clearance: "Intelligence officials had further warned that Kushner might be a target for manipulation by at least four foreign governments based on his business dealings, lack of foreign policy experience and financial debt" (2019, para. 19). Fund cannot, of course, be faulted for not seeing the future with 20/20 acuity. However, Fund missed no chances to flak at Clinton with wild flak merchant hyperbole and invention—even as Trump's campaign rehearsed its later scandals and presented a wide-open target for criticism that Fund never ventured.

Integrity Warriors

Following the 2016 election, Fund participated in the discourse on the (in the end, aborted) electoral integrity commission that was referenced at the start of this chapter. Under the title "Why are Democrats afraid of the Election Integrity Commission?" Fund primes *National Review*'s readership with memes of how vexed and confused, thus illegitimate, the "left" is. Fund grabs at the gaslight with both hands by asserting that (unnamed) "smart liberals" are already aligned with him in supporting the commission (2017a, para. 5), evidently beholden to the belief that people will agree with his avuncular guidance in order to appear "smart." Fund ventures further pacifying "assurances" in noting that Democratic Secretaries of State Bill Gardner (New Hampshire) and Matthew Dunlap (Maine) were appointed to the panel; more on how that worked out in a moment.

In an effort to seal the deal at his flak stall, Fund insists, "If liberal critics are right that voter fraud doesn't exist save for trace elements, then the commission will come up empty-handed" (2017a, para. 3)—ignoring the series of careful investigations that have *already* made this determination and largely mooted the need for more (Brennen Center for Justice, 2017). Moreover, figures whose resumes have amply demonstrated themselves to be ideologically-driven do not readily come up "empty-handed" when there are flak points to be scored. Given enough trash barrels to sift through, the flak merchant will metaphorically find the "smoking gun" in the form of, let us say, burnt toast.

Who, in particular, could already have demonstrated himself to be ideologically-driven over election integrity and its flak opportunities? Fund enthused in 2017 that Kansas Secretary of State Kris Kobach was one stalwart member of the commission. In turn, Kobach "already pursued nine cases" of fraud in Kansas, a number even less impressive than it seems on further examination (Fund, 2017a, para. 4). Kobach is in the vanguard of vote fraud flak hysteria, while his record of prosecution in Kansas has been more suspect than stellar. Despite extravagant claims about tidal waves of fraud in Kansas, Kobach's nine convictions in the state for vote irregularities have mainly been against older people with more than one residence who were confused about in what jurisdiction they can vote; trivial, sadistic and tendentious cases that included uncounted provisional ballots, such that local Kansas authorities did not see the need for prosecution before Kobach bulldozed in with a flak hardhat (Strauss, 2017).

Fund's collaborator von Spakovsky, discussed earlier, was also appointed to the commission. In addendum to his long record of election fraud flak (Mayer, 2012), von Spakovsky summed up the partisan spirits that he insisted should drive the Commission in a leaked email: "There isn't a single Democratic official that will do anything other than obstruct any investigation of voter fraud." In von Spakovsky's appraisal even "mainstream Republicans" would doom the commission to "abject failure" vis-à-vis the militancy in assuming vote fraud (quoted in Huseman, 2017, para. 13). By their prior words and deeds in government, Kobach and von Spakovsky brought the electoral fraud flak hardline to the commission, for flak-in-action purposes, rather than the betterment of elections.

By the end of 2017, the integrity commission collapsed in shambolic fashion over doubts around its own integrity. In particular, the commission faced a barrage of eight lawsuits, accusations of violations around statutes on bipartisan advisory commissions, as well as the disgrace of a commission staff member's arrest on child pornography charges. The aforementioned Democrat commissioner Matthew Dunlap sued the commission *of which he was a commissioner* for withholding documents and pertinent communications from him. Trump administration lawyers, in turn, argued that the commission member had no reason to expect to see that same commission's paperwork or to know about its activities (Huseman, 2017); a very strange concept indeed of a "bipartisan" commission. Notwithstanding Fund's pieties on the matter, Democrat participation was instrumentalized as partisan window-dressing for photo-op purposes. Even as U.S. elections are clearly in need of modernizing reform, flak designs were sufficiently telegraphed by the right's long record of partisan discourse and action vis-à-vis voting to make the Election Integrity Commission untenable.

Conclusion: Beyond Flak

Right-wing flak hystericizes over the spectral figure of the ineligible voter charging at the electoral urn with a clutch of ballots, as democracy herself cowers undefended in the corner. Nevertheless, politically-driven, structural injustice is being embedded in the U.S. electoral system by gaming the system, beyond the archaic electoral college that guarantees that each person's vote does not have equal weight; injustice that extends beyond the perimeter of flak.

At book-length, David Daley (2017) examines the impact that gerrymandering of districts has had on the United States' representative bodies. Daley observes that Obama achieved reelection with a majority of 3.5 million votes in 2012, while the Democratic Party prevailed in three-quarters of U.S. Senate races that are statewide and thus undistricted. In the same election cycle, Democrats also claimed 1.4 million more votes for the House of Representatives—but came away with a steep 33-seat deficit in the congressional body in which districts can be drawn to political specifications. Notice that this slippage (more votes nationally, fewer seats in the House) is aberrational and not occurred in more than a generation (since 1972).

The central factor that transformed more votes into fewer seats was that some Republican state legislatures utilized spread-sheet engineering of congressional districts. The technique of "packing" and "cracking" districts can artificially maximize one party's representation. Table 5.1 presents a simple illustration of how packing and cracking works, using an example of nine voters (56-percent of whom vote X, while 44-percent vote Y) sorted into three districts. In this example, two districts have been designed to be Y majority for a commanding two-to-one majority of elected seats—even as Y is the minority of 44-percent across the whole electorate. With hundreds of thousands of voters in play, there are many more creative techniques to pack and crack districts to, for example, dilute X and empower Y. Congressional districts can be tailored down to the neighborhood and street level, in defiance of fair, equitable representation of communities of shared interest.

As noted earlier, Heritage angers over having one's vote cancelled out by a fraudulent vote—and suppresses the evidence that individual fraud is a "man-bites-dog-while-both-are-humming-'Ice-Ice-Baby'" happenstance, as well as the degree to which gerrymander can effectively cancel the electoral

Table 5.1: Less is more—or packing and cracking to transform a minority of voters into a majority of seats

District 1: X X X (packed district): X wins the seat
District 2: X Y Y (cracked district): Y wins the seat
District 3: X Y Y (cracked district): Y wins the seat

voice of millions. In gerrymandered Pennsylvania, voters delivered a majority of votes for the House to Democrats in 2012—and claimed *five out of 18 House seats* due to pack-and-crack microsurgery on the state's mapping of congressional districts (Daley, 2017, pp. xxi–xxiii). Arizona, Michigan, North Carolina and Wisconsin also exhibited strong skews between popular vote and the state's delegation (pp. 182–184). On the Democratic side, Illinois and Maryland have enacted Democrat-favorable gerrymanders, in an undesirable "arms race" situation.

Finally, the electoral vehicle of the U.S. right, the Republican Party, has in some notable cases brazenly blown far beyond flak and gerrymander. In recent years, Republicans have legislated to at least partly negate elections in the immediate aftermath of electoral defeats. In 2016, upon losing the governor's race in North Carolina, spurned incumbent Republican governor Pat McCrory refused to acknowledge defeat for an extended period. Next, the Republican majority in the North Carolina legislature passed a series of bills before the new, Democratic Party governor took office in January 2017 in order to downsize the authority of the office. For example, Republicans reduced incoming Democrat Roy Cooper's number of appointees to several consequential panels (State Board of Elections, appellate court) and radically reduced the governor's roster of appointed positions from 1,500 to 425. Siphoning the office's authority after the "wrong" party won the gubernatorial election was enacted with precision. Republicans in the legislature shifted control of North Carolina's Industrial Commission, with its wide-ranging portfolio, from Democrat Cooper's cabinet to the state's insurance commissioner—who was a Republican (*Ballotpedia*, n.d.). What was shocking aberration may now be called a pattern: the same script played out in Wisconsin after Republican Governor Scott Walker was sent packing from the governor's office by the electorate in 2018 in favor of Democrat Tony Evers (Davis, 2018).

These actions extend beyond flak as they attempt to rewire the rules of governance on the fly to crude partisan specifications. Doing so is grotesquely undemocratic as the public does not get what it had voted for just weeks earlier—for example, a fully-empowered Democratic governor—by redefining the office according to partisan calculus. These are not the actions of a normal political party, governing for all the people; an argument that has already been made by former Republican Congressional aid, analyst, and apostate Mike Lofgren (2011) following his twenty-eight-year career in Washington. In this view, ugly flak tactics and strategies around voting and elections by no means represents the full dimensions of right-wing hostility to the will of voters and to the nation's norms and mores.

References

American Civil Liberties Union. (2014). Pennsylvania's voter ID law found unconstitutional. 17 January. Retrieved from www.aclu.org/news/pennsylvanias-voter-id-law-found-unconstitutional.

Anderson, C. (2018). Brian Kemp's lead in Georgia needs an asterisk. *The Atlantic*, 7 November. Retrieved from www.theatlantic.com/ideas/archive/2018/11/georgia-governor-kemp-abrams/575095/.

Andino, M. (2012). Dear Mr. Attorney General […]. 22 February. Retrieved from images2.americanprogress.org/campus/web/South%20Carolina%20Election%20Fraud%20Report.pdf.

Ballotpedia. (n.d.). Conflicts between Gov. Roy Cooper and the North Carolina General Assembly. Retrieved from ballotpedia.org/Conflicts_between_Gov._Roy_Cooper_and_the_North_Carolina_General_Assembly.

Berman, A. (2011). The GOP's war on voting. *Rolling Stone*, 30 August. Retrieved from www.rollingstone.com/politics/politics-news/the-gop-war-on-voting-242182/.

Brennen Center for Justice. (2017). Debunking the voter fraud Myth. 31 January. Retrieved from www.brennancenter.org/analysis/debunking-voter-fraud-myth.

Brock, D. (2002). *Blinded by the right*. New York: Three Rivers Press.

Cable News Network. (2017). Man behind debunked voter fraud claim: Proof is coming. 27 January. Retrieved from www.youtube.com/watch?v=LIYHIycbWb8.

Chan, M. (2017). Meet the man who may have convinced president Trump voter fraud exists. *Time*, 27 January. Retrieved from time.com/4651634/gregg-phillips-voter-fraud-donald-trump/.

Clark, D.B. (2019). The tearful drama of North Carolina's election-fraud hearing. *New Yorker*, 24 February. Retrieved from www.newyorker.com/news/dispatch/the-tearful-drama-of-north-carolinas-election-fraud-hearings.

Cohen, A. (2007). A woman wrongly convicted and a United States Attorney who kept his job. *New York Times*, 16 April. Retrieved from www.nytimes.com/2007/04/16/opinion/16mon4.html.

Daley, D. (2017). *Ratf**cked*. New York: W. W. Norton.

Davis, D.L. (2018). Wisconsin Republicans gave GOP governor more power, but that's changing with new Dem governor. *PolitiFact Wisconsin*, 3 December. Retrieved from www.politifact.com/wisconsin/statements/2018/dec/03/wisconsin-republican-legislative-leaders/wisconsin-republicans-gave-gop-governor-more-power/.

Fessenden, F., & Broder, J.M. (2001). Examining the vote. *New York Times*, 12 November. Retrieved from www.nytimes.com/2001/11/12/us/examining-vote-overview-study-disputed-florida-ballots-finds-justices-did-not.html.

Fund, J. (2008). *Stealing elections*. San Francisco: Encounter Books.

Fund, J. (2016a). Sidney Blumenthal, birtherism, and the law of unintended consequences. *National Review*, 14 November. Retrieved from www.nationalreview.com/2016/11/birtherism-sidney-blumenthal-white-house-correspondents-dinner-trump-victory/.

Fund, J. (2016b). History repeats: A Nixonian cover-up in the home stretch of the campaign. *National Review*, 30 October. Retrieved from www.nationalreview.com/2016/10/hillary-clinton-richard-nixon-cover-ups-lying-enemies-list/.

Fund, J. (2016c). WikiLeaks dumps will mean Hillary's presidency would be tainted from day one. *National Review*, 27 October. Retrieved from www.nationalreview.com/2016/10/clinton-foundation-scandal-wikileaks-discredit-hillary-presidency/.

Fund, J. (2016d). Déjà vu: Time for the GOP to stop a "blank check" for a Clinton. *National Review*, 20 October. Retrieved from www.nationalreview.com/2016/10/republicans-hillary-clinton-congress-2016-donald-trump-bob-dole-1996/.

Fund, J. (2017a). Why are Democrats afraid of the Election Integrity Commission? *National Review*, 15 May. Retrieved from www.nationalreview.com/2017/05/election-integrity-commission-trump-democrats-attack-ignore-fraud-evidence/.

Fund, J. (2017b). Obama's final whopper as president. *National Review*, 22 January. Retrieved from www.nationalreview.com/2017/01/obama-lies-voter-id-many-countries-require-it/.

Goss, B.M. (2003). The 2000 US Presidential Election in Salon.com and *The Washington Post*. *Journalism Studies*, 4(2), 163–182.

Greenberg, J., & Qiu, L. (2016). Fact-checking Donald Trump's claim Hillary Clinton started Obama birther movement. *PolitiFact*, 16 September. Retrieved from www.politifact.com/truth-o-meter/statements/2016/sep/16/donald-trump/fact-checking-donald-trumps-claim-hillary-clinton-/.

Hasen, R.L. (2012). *The voting wars*. New Haven, CT: Yale University Press.

Heritage Foundation. (n.d.). *Does your vote count?* Washington, DC: Author.

Horton, S. (2008a). "Six Questions for Former U.S. Attorney David Iglesias, Author of *In Justice*". *Harper's Magazine*, 23 July. Retrieved from harpers.org/blog/2008/07/six-questions-for-former-us-attorney-david-iglesias-author-of-_in-justice_/.

Horton, S. (2008b). The gathering storm at Justice. *Harper's Magazine*, 15 March. Retrieved from harpers.org/blog/2008/03/the-gathering-storm-at-justice/.

Huseman, J. (2017). Trump voter fraud commission is sued—by one of its own commissioners. *ProPublica*, 9 November. Retrieved from www.propublica.org/article/trump-voter-fraud-commission-dunlap-lawsuit.

Jordan, E. (2018). I've worked in Republican politics. The party's voter suppression in the midterms has been a disgrace. *Time*, 15 November. Retrieved from news.yahoo.com/ve-worked-republican-politics-party-142624012.html.

Khan, N., & Carson, C. (2012). Comprehensive database of U.S. voter fraud uncovers no evidence that photo ID is needed. *News21*, 12 August. Retrieved from /votingrights.news21.com/article/election-fraud/.

Leber, R. (2014). In Texas, you can vote with a concealed handgun license—but not a student ID. *The New Republic*, 20 October. Retrieved from newrepublic.com/article/119900/texas-voter-id-allows-handgun-licenses-not-student-ids.

Levitt, J. (2007). *The truth about voter fraud*. Brennen Center for Justice: New York.

Levitt, J. (2014). A comprehensive investigation of voter impersonation finds 31 credible incidents out of one billion ballots cast. *Washington Post*, 6 August. Retrieved from www.washingtonpost.com/news/wonk/wp/2014/08/06/a-comprehensive-investigation-of-voter-impersonation-finds-31-credible-incidents-out-of-one-billion-ballots-cast/?utm_term=.5c5969ee3629.

Lofgren, M. (2011). Goodbye to all that. *Truthout*, 3 September. Retrieved from truthout.org/articles/goodbye-to-all-that-reflections-of-a-gop-operative-who-left-the-cult/.

Lusenhop, J. (2017). Gregg Phillips: The man claiming 3M illegal votes. *BBC News*, 31 January. Retrieved from www.bbc.com/news/world-us-canada-38774428.

Mayer, J. (2012). The voter fraud myth. *New Yorker*, 29 October/5 November. Retrieved from www.newyorker.com/magazine/2012/10/29/the-voter-fraud-myth.

Minnite, L.C. (n.d.). *The politics of voter fraud*. Project Vote: Washington, DC.

Office of the Inspector General/Office of Professional Responsibility. (2008). *An investigation into the removal of nine U.S. Attorneys in 2006*. Washington, DC: Department of Justice.

Panetta, G., & Gal, S. (2018). Floridians with felony convictions are now beginning to register to vote after the state restored voting rights to 1.5 million felons. *Business Insider*, 7 November. Retrieved from www.businessinsider.es/felony-disenfranchisement-states-florida-amendment-4-voting-rights-2018-11?r=US&IR=T.

Siddiqui, S., & Gabbatt, A. (2019). Trump ordered officials to give Kushner top-secret security clearance—report. *The Guardian*, 1 March. Retrieved from www.theguardian.com/us-news/2019/feb/28/jared-kushner-donald-trump-security-clearance-report.

Strauss, B. (2017). Kris Kobach came after me for an honest mistake. *Politico*, 21 May. Retrieved from www.politico.com/magazine/story/2017/05/21/kris-kobach-voter-fraud-investigation-prosecution-215164.

Tapper, J. (2001). *Down and dirty*. Boston: Little, Brown and Company.

United States Commission on Civil Rights. (2001). *Voting irregularities in Florida during the 2000 presidential election*. Retrieved from www.usccr.gov/pubs/vote2000/report/main.htm.

Walker, P. (2017). Donald Trump's electoral fraud expert Gregg Phillips was "registered to vote in three states". *The Independent*, 31 January. Retrieved from https://www.independent.co.uk/news/world/americas/donald-trump-electoral-fraud-expert-gregg-phillips-registered-to-vote-three-states-alabama-texas-a7554551.html.

Woodward, V. (2017). Trump's favorite voter fraud activist hedges his claims. *The Atlantic*, 31 January. Retrieved from www.theatlantic.com/politics/archive/2017/01/gregg-phillips-trump-voter-fraud/515046/.

· 6 ·

"INDOCTRINATION," "PERSECUTION," "CONTROL": FLAK GOES TO COLLEGE

> Central European University "has been forced out [of Hungary]. This is unprecedented. A U.S. institution has been driven out of a country that is a NATO ally. A European institution has been ousted from a member state of the EU.
> —Central European University President and Rector Michael Ignatieff (quoted in Central European University Newsroom, 2018, para. 3)

Introduction: School's Out

Central European University (CEU) was founded in 1991 in the aftermath of the revolts against command socialism and the Soviet Union. Originating with funds from Hungarian-born George Soros, a longtime magnet of furious right-wing flak, (cf., Emery, 2018; Goss, 2013, pp. 159–164), the avowed mission of the campus has been to advance classical liberalism and democracy in the post-Soviet epoch. As professor and public intellectual Cas Mudde observes of his time at CEU earlier in his career, the campus is a "uniquely international, world-class university which [has] attracted talented faculty and graduate students from across Europe and the world" (2018, para. 2). According to CEU's web page, the campus can boast three programs rated in the top 50 globally (Central European University, 2019) and is also the region's most successful applicant for European Union research grant funds (Central European University, 2018, para. 3).

The shuttering of the highly regarded campus in Budapest can be called flak against an organization. Fidesz, the hard-right party of Hungarian President Viktor Orbán, has been bold in capturing key institutions during the 2010s by, for example, changing the country's constitution after only months in power and taking command of ninety-percent of Hungarian media via direct State ownership or through close allies (Beauchamp, 2018). As CEU's degrees are U.S.-accredited, Orbán's government introduced a law demanding that CEU have a campus in the United States as well as in Hungary, a law contrived to apply to CEU and only to CEU. In journalist Zack Beauchamp's appraisal, these were "sneaky regulations aimed at forcing out CEU without needing to formally ban them"; in other words, flak at an organization through made-to-order, legalistic red tape (2018, para. 6). After making an arrangement with Bard College to deliver courses with approval from New York state educational authorities, Orbán's government still refused approval for CEU to continue to admit students.

CEU will not perish but assume a new form as operations are scheduled to move to Vienna, Austria in September 2019; a transnational relocation under duress that exacts enormous strain on CEU's staff and students. EU-member Hungary joins explicitly authoritarian states—Belarus, Russia, Turkey—in harassing and shuttering universities on ideological grounds. Moreover, as Mudde observes, "Two years ago"—during the Obama administration—"it would have been completely unthinkable that the United States would accept the closure of a U.S. institution by another government" (2018, para. 7). Flak against higher education presents as an authoritarian motif.

In considering higher education, it is empirically true that left-of-center views hold more sway with faculty on the United States' campuses. In a 2007 study of 1,417 full-time professors from two- and four-year campuses, college faculty identified as 46-percent moderate, 44-percent liberal, and nine-percent conservative (Jaschik, 2017b, para. 6); a five-to-one liberal-to-conservative ratio, although the plurality of academicians self-characterize as moderates. Despite being demonstrably out-numbered and the occasional anecdote to the contrary, Scott Jaschik reviews evidence that "faculty members who are Republicans are succeeding and finding happiness in academic careers"—and are indeed more likely to answer affirmatively as to whether they would be a college professor if they could take the decision over again (2017b, paras. 39, 43–44)!

While it is correct to claim that there are more center-left voices in the faculty, the implications of that fact are not obvious. In this view, the ratio of liberal and conservative faculty is by no means trivial, but it is not game-over for robust discussion on campus. While professors are often memorable figures for students and pillars of the campus, students' encounters with each other during immersion in the college milieu are surely more influential than what the most eloquent man or woman at the podium avers during class. Moreover, faculty members who present themselves as driven by ideology regularly encounter eye-rolling and pushback—even from students who may be inclined to agree with much of what they are saying. Debt heaps with which students graduate are far more likely to impact (and constrain) their choices about their futures than professorial posturing in the seminar room. Moreover, as concerns the composition of the faculty, there is evidence of self-selection in entering academics. Left-leaning students are more likely to opt for (low wage, high precarity) graduate school, whereas conservatives are more attracted to finance and other professional degrees (Jaschik, 2017b).

Despite these considerations, in many right-wing narratives on the university, it as an article of faith that the campus is a hostile territory of relentless ideological pogroms against the right. The resultant flak against the university system assumes more overt shadings of victimization than other variants of flak—even as it "goes on offense" against higher education, rather than "playing defense," as we will see in the case study to come.

In addressing flak against the university, this chapter begins by considering the current conditions of higher education. The impact of neoliberalism on the university occupies a prominent place in the analysis. After a brief survey of earlier flak campaigns directed at higher education, I take up the chapter's case study, the *Campus Reform* web site. In drilling down into a specific case, I seek to avoid hand-waving generalities and identify the characteristics of a significant flak mill's discourse in detail. Whatever the faults of universities in the present, the daily reportage from *Campus Reform* goes much further in pursuing its flak project. *Campus Reform*'s discourse presents as an effort to, day-by-day, delegitimize higher education as a macabre left-wing circus *cum* ideological boot-camp. Following backstory on the *Campus Reform* website, I examine its flak-in-discourse with emphasis on the double standards by which the university is problematized and flaked in its coverage—most notably, around speech issues.

A Brief Survey of Contemporary Higher Education

Champions of the university rally to its enrichment of both individual lives and society. Benjamin Ginsberg maintains that, "The university can be a subversive institution in the best sense of that word, showing by its teaching and scholarship that new ways of thinking and acting are possible" (2011, p. 3). Nick Couldry similarly celebrates the social mission of higher education. He writes, "The idea of the university represents the shared commitment" to "practical access to the widest range of human knowledge and creativity [that] should not be restricted by social class or family wealth" (2011, p. 37). Affirmations such as these are driven by educators' direct encounters with the transformative experience of education, first as students in their younger days and later as instructors.

Alongside the attachment to and high hopes for the university's pro-social impacts, it is also apparent that the campus is deeply embedded within its time and place. While universities channel some of the best features of the societies that summon them into being, they inevitably become implicated in their parent society's problematic realities by reproducing deeply inscribed inequalities and conflicts—or by assaying to (even partly) ameliorate them. Depending on where and when one looks on campus, both reproduction of the status quo and (subtle or unsubtle) subversion of it may be playing out. During the Cold War, for example, some academics enlisted in the battle by making their scholarship and investigation serviceable to the State (Simpson, 1994) while students in many instances resisted Cold War logics.

From a European perspective, Joan Pedro-Carañana (2016) argues that university curricula are designed to mobilize the kind of student/subject that societies value at a given time. In his analysis, current European priorities have pivoted away from a humanist emphasis and toward producing flexible workers for a fluid, neoliberal milieu. Noting that the campus on which he labors evokes a steel and concrete bank aesthetic, Neil Faulkner (2011) similarly argues that, within-living-memory, the university has become more business-like and buttoned-up "serious" than in the 1960s and 1970s—but not necessarily better. He posits the curriculum as in retreat from the liberal arts, with deep context and consideration of radical perspectives as casualties. At present, market-induced pressures have shifted the university toward a tamer (if, at times, still unruly) version of itself, one that more readily reproduces the prevailing social order of markets *über alles*.

Antecedents to Contemporary Flak

Flak against universities and their professors is not a recent invention, even as it arises from new platforms on new issues. Prior to the tenure system in the early twentieth century, it was easier to cleanse the campus of ideologically unpalatable faculty. In the late nineteenth century, for example, teaching evolution could get a professor bounced from campus (Ginsberg, 2011, pp. 137–141). Following the rise of the tenure system and its attendant professionalization in the mid-twentieth century, Ginsberg observes that faculty were substantially insulated from undue ideological pressure.

However, new flak fronts arrayed against the university were becoming visible. William F. Buckley's *God and Man at Yale* (1951) excoriated the secularism and (for Buckley, effectively Marxist) Keynesian economics that prevailed at his *alma mater*. The notoriety of Buckley's book, in turn, furnished a platform for founding the still extent *National Review*. Buckley's regular column for that journal, "The Ivory Tower," continued *God and Man*'s project of scrutinizing and surveilling the academy for deviationism from market economics, within a McCarthyist milieu (Goss, 1996). From the vantage point of the present, Buckley's jaded discourse toward the university presents a prototype for platforms that could deliver what we now call flak.

Fast-forward to the late 1980s and early 1990s when hyperkinetic arm-waving about political correctness came into vogue, and the bookshelf heaves under the weight of polemical tomes on the university (e.g., Bloom, 1987; D'Souza, 1991). Within this genre, Charles Sykes' *ProfScam* (1988) made notable contributions to surveilling, problematizing and flaking the university. Like *God and Man* almost 40 years earlier, *ProfScam* was published by right-wing publishing house Regnery. Sykes' volume is not a work of subtlety nor is it crafted from infinitely weighed judgements as its sets out to delegitimize the contemporaneous university. By page 4, following a bullet-pointed account of dystopia on campus, Sykes is quaking with derisive energies:

> In the midst of this wasteland stands the professor. Almost single-handedly, the professors [...] have destroyed the university as a center of learning and have desolated higher education [...] No understanding of the academic disease is possible without an understanding of the Academic Man [sic], this strange mutation of twentieth-century academia who has the pretensions of an ecclesiastic, the artfulness of a witch doctor, and the soul of a bureaucrat. His [sic] greatest accomplishment has been the creation of an academic culture that is one of society's most outrageous and elaborate frauds. (1988, p. 4)

And so Sykes continues in a register of miserablism for another 300 pages. His central criticism of the academy concerns his perception of its retreat from the classroom. However, Sykes' polemical concatenation of anecdotes seldom ventures beyond "Research I" campuses (mainly, Ivy League and Big Ten) in which research is indeed the center of gravity for tenured and tenure-track faculty. Sykes writes as if agnostic to the extent to Research I campuses are high profile, but the exception—*not* the rule—for their research intensity within the variegated world of U.S. academe. Sykes' analysis also indulges the slothful practice of judging research by the titles of research reports, pre-emptively appraised as trivial. In line with the 1980s–1990s genre of which *ProfScam* is a part, the thrust of the book's flak assessment is toward root-and-branch reformation of the illegitimate university.

The New Structure of the Ivory Tower Workplace

Among earlier waves of flak against universities, Sykes is at least attentive to status distinctions within the academic profession—although he effectively yells over his own potentially interesting observations by eschewing structural analysis in favor of polemic. At the same time that Sykes railed against a cardboard-cutout *homo academicus*, David Harvey (1990) analyzed neoliberal ("free market") dynamics of workforce composition in western capitalist economies. During the 1980s, neoliberal reorganization of the structure of work was superseding the previous Keynesian model that featured greater attention to labor rights and a degree of wealth redistribution.

Harvey argues that, as neoliberalism gained momentum, the structure of the workforce was increasingly defined by "just-in-time" logics of production. The remodeled workplace featured a smaller core group of employees, with more temporary, sub-contracted, and contingent employment—more precarious work, in other words—to fill in around core workers as needed. The result has been enhanced flexibility for the employer to absorb and discard workers as needed in the "just-in-time" milieu that is posited as ever-alert to oracular market signals. After decades of empowerment of these logics, they extend to the precarities of, for example, delivery service (Deliveroo), with "no fuss" disposable, non-unionized, devoid-of-benefit workers subject to high levels of performance surveillance.

The composition of university employment has been notably re-ordered in alignment with the neoliberal model. Whereas part-time faculty composed 31-percent of the roster in 1976, the figure spiked to 48-percent less than thirty years later. In other words, the faculty shifted from predominantly full-timers by a two-to-one ratio, to a situation in which the full-time to part-time ratio is one-to-one (Ginsberg, 2011, p. 19). The new composition of the faculty leaves many doctorates who studied their discipline into their thirties under-employed and compensated to precarious specifications.

Another important feature of work under neoliberalism implicates middle management. In Gérard Duménil's and Dominque Levy's account (2011), during the Keynesian period after World War II, middle management oriented more to workers and their concerns than to the upper reaches of management. However, in the neoliberal era, middle-managers have pivoted toward shared interest with higher management and identify less with workers.

The university has similarly succumbed to managerialism. Ginsberg posits that, "As recently as the 1960s and 1970s, American universities were heavily influenced, if not completely driven, by faculty ideas and concerns." By contrast, today's "institutions of higher education are mainly controlled by administrators and staffers who make the rules and set more and more of the priorities of academic life" (2011, p. 1). In turn, administrative priorities are not as likely to embed teaching and research at the heart of the institutional mission. Ginsberg notes that faculty at University of Texas at Austin were gobsmacked to discover that their administration apportioned $200 million to improving the campus' athletic facilities. When administrators are less likely to be accomplished academics and more likely to be corporate-style paper-pushers, the busy-work, ballyhooed but banal reports, and managerial mishaps pile up. Since 1975, growth in administration and tertiary staff has far outdistanced growth in professorial appointments that have remained closely yoked to student enrollment numbers (Ginsberg, 2011, p. 25).

Even as the professorate's role in steering the university has diminished, flak against the professorial profession and its individual members has surged. Polemics that place the professor at the center of the university's universe present an over-simplification—but it is an over-simplification with a purpose as it conjures an easier target in the figure at the podium. Flak accusations are thusly endowed with a face, with a name. Emphasis on the professor produces personalized flak that can, in turn, be read back to the putative defects of the profession and higher education writ large. As flak narratives pile up in the compilations curated by flak factories dedicated to the cause, they come to signify a seemingly amok profession and dysfunctional higher education system. At the same time, professor-centric flak brackets out structural considerations that shape the university from inside and outside the campus; to wit, the broad impact of neoliberal economics and the attendant craze for hypertrophic management.

Looking Away from Pay-to-Play

The explosion of the U.S. admissions scandal in spring 2019 underscores these observations. The admissions scandal begins with parents within a deeply class-divided society who went far beyond pushy to advance their offspring's interests over everyone else's children. Thereafter, the scandal did not implicate the professorate, but revolved around athletics coaches and directors as well as some administrators willing to participate in the pay-to-play (or pay-to-be-admitted) hustle. The admissions scandal encompassed faked standardized test scores and fabricated athletic prowess (with the assistance of bribed coaches) to facilitate students' admission.

However, beyond baldly illegal activity, the everyday legal ways in which universities can reproduce society's flaws also surfaced in some accounts of the admissions scandal. In particular, parents bent on getting their children into a prestigious (or quasi-prestigious) university can pay up to US$1.5 million for an above-board five-year college admission consultancy—or make "donations" denominated in the millions to the college of choice for Junior (Hoffower, 2019). Daniel Golden first broke the story of Jared Kushner's admission to Harvard University that shocked his high-school counselors. Kushner's admission was greased by his (super-rich and later incarcerated) father's meetings with the university president—alongside a donation of US$2.5 million. On the topic of affirmative action for the wealthy, Golden writes, "decades of investigating college admissions have led me to conclude that, for rich and famous families" college admission is "more like a television game show, 'Who Wants to Be an Ivy Leaguer?'" The privileged contestant is endowed "with lifelines for those who might otherwise be rejected. Instead of phoning a friend or asking the audience, the wealthy benefit from advantages largely unavailable to middle-class and poor Americans" (2019, para. 12). Golden posits that, "The best-known and most widespread of those preferences is conferred on alumni children, known as 'legacies'" who follow in parents' footsteps to campus and "who tend as a group to be disproportionately white and well-off" (2019, para. 12). Right-wing flak directed at the university elides this version of "affirmative action" (e.g., D'Souza, 1991) as well as favoring tropes of "radical" academicians "hijacking" campus discourse toward convening a "people's republic" from inside the US.

The college admission scandal does not readily align with right-wing storylines about what is wrong with higher education; and so *Campus Reform*, considered in detail later in this chapter, ignored the story of 46 indictments around college admissions that begins with pushy, ultra-rich parents. Instead, *Campus Reform* maintained dedicated focus on right-wingers ostensibly hounded on college campus in the week after the admissions scandal story broke on March 12, 2019. For example, *Campus Reform* covered the story of a student "who took aim"—thankfully only with words—"at Clemson's administration for failing to provide any defense for conservative ideas on campus" (Washington, 2019, para. 16). The admission scandal's dramatizations of classism that reaches criminal proportions simply does not affirm prevailing, right-wing flak talking points.

Flak Moves Online

Flak directed at the university and its professors is a growth industry. For instance, in late 2016, Turning Point USA (TPUSA) launched a webpage with the at once over-the-top and ominous title, *Professor watchlist*. The web site describes its remit in April 2019 in the following, notably confused terms:

> TPUSA will continue to fight for free speech and the right for professors to say whatever they wish; however students, parents, and alumni deserve to know the specific incidents and names of professors that advance a radical agenda in lecture halls. (*Professor watchlist*, 2018, para. 3)

TPUSA founder Charlie Kirk describes the organization as itself radical in promoting "true free market values" and describes himself as a rad-man willing to "fight to the death" for unfettered expression (Schuman, 2016, para. 5). In other words, TPUSA claims the chimerical mission to champion free speech even as it is devoted to making free expression problematic. If it was a free speech champion, like the American Civil Liberties Union, TPUSA and its *Professor watchlist* platform would actively take up and support the difficult cases, such as defending professors who harbor iconoclastic ideas that may need to be heard and/or have been harassed and harangued for it. Instead, *Professor watchlist* draws from ideologically-aligned flak mills such as *Campus Reform* and recirculates exaggeration, misinterpretation, and context-indifferent assertion.

One example will suffice: A University of Texas professor is on the watchlist for stating, "I don't believe there will be any serious progress toward eliminating men's violence against women if we do not address the toxic notions about masculinity in patriarchy—masculinity understood as rooted in control, conquest, aggression" (*Professor watchlist*, 2016, para. 1). The 35-word statement is left to speak for itself, without grounding in evidence, argument, and context. Moreover, the professor's comments have no obvious bearing TPUSA's self-proclaimed "free market" mission. As for whether the statement is "radical," *Professor watchlist* does not even venture an argument. The quote is marshaled, and the reader is cued to assume it is manifestly, glowingly radical—if not, why would it be included on a serious web page? Some putatively beyond-the-pale radicals are even more worrisome. Ergo, as of April 2019, the *Professor watchlist* landing page continues to present a gallery of "featured" professors that adopts the semiotics of mug-shots and the substance of personalized flak.

While online flak mills such as *Professor watchlist* deride the university, their resolutely one-sided, ideologically-driven performances suppress any sign that higher education has often been judged as being equal to its difficult mission. Ginsberg (2011, p. 55) observes that a scant nine-percent of Americans who were surveyed report a "great deal" of confidence in large corporations, despite the private sector's constant promotional campaigns for its wares and for the profit motive in general. By contrast, 48-percent of respondents reported a great deal of confidence in higher education—confidence that exceeded churches (44-percent) and far outdistanced confidence in health care professions (26-percent). Students in the United States claim, by a wide margin, that the monetary debt that higher education generates is their central concern about university study. By contrast, ostensible bias from instructors is rated as less of a student concern than drinking on campus (Nelson, n.d.)! Nevertheless, right-wing flak campaigns fixate on ostensible bias and the term "indoctrination" flows very freely.

The divergence between the concerns of most students and the concerns of flak mills leads straightforwardly to this chapter's flak case study: *Campus Reform*.

Confronting "The Evil Empire": Introducing *Campus Reform*

Campus Reform (CR) debuted in 2009 as a spin-off from Leadership Institute. In turn, Leadership Institute was established in 1979 to groom young right-wingers for government and media positions. The founder of both Leadership Institute and CR, Morton C. Blackwell, is a former staff member in the Ronald Reagan White House (Leadership Institute, 2017a). Blackwell has long assayed to recruit youth to the right as he was formerly the executive director of College Republicans. Notice that Blackwell's interest in higher education is, however, that of an avowed enemy of the university as currently constituted; he denounces higher education as "a left-wing indoctrination center" (quoted in Schmidt, 2015, para. 10).

CR is tight enough with the Leadership Institute that it shares office space in Arlington, Virginia. The Leadership Institute draws annual revenue of $15 million and claims a network of 1,600 right-leaning organizations on campuses across the United States (Schmidt, 2015). As for CR, it is staffed by an editor-in-chief, three full-time staff, and five interns, in addition to about 50 correspondents prowling campuses and paid $50 an article to report on what they perceive as higher education's leftist rampage. In 2014, the site received 9.3 million page views (about 25,000 per day), demonstrating the reach that a small group can have when its flak is backed by stable institutions and carefully packaged.

As the CR site generates no advertising revenue, its funding stream arrives via the Donors Capital Fund, Donors Trust and the Charles Koch Foundation. Donors Capital Fund and Donors Trust share the same address in Alexandria, Virginia (*DeSmogBlog*, n.d.) and have been characterized as the "dark money ATM for the conservative movement" (Vogel, 2017, para. 9) while also furnishing secrecy about who in particular is writing the checks. Despite its proximity to elite funders—the Koches are likely the wealthiest family in the world—CR's editor-in-chief Sterling Beard insists that, "Campus leftists cast themselves as plucky, victimized underdogs" (2017b, para. 7). Although it claims the underdog status for itself, with just two few clicks from the CR landing page, one arrives at the Leadership Institute's "Balance in the Media Funding Form" (Leadership Institute, 2017b). It is that easy to apply for largesse from right-wing interests to spread the gospel, in handsomely-subsidized vox pop flak fashion.

CR's content may be characterized, in Angela Nagle's terms (Nagle and Wilson, 2017) as "alt-light" since it skirts away from the more incendiary "alt-right." In this vein, CR's Beard denounces notorious race-hustler Richard Spencer as "repulsive" (2017a, para. 9). Nonetheless, the substance of CR's discourses present strains of alt-right DNA for their constant attention to identity that implicates bodily-marked as well as ideologically-defined identities. In its discourse, CR is not centered on understanding the complex world of the campus. Rather, CR constructs a delegitimizing caricature of higher education, flak-in-discourse that may prepare flak-in-action.

In this vein, an unsubtle flak agenda bleeds from a manifesto, "The evil empire: Leftist abuses and bias," posted on CR's web site. Blackwell is the signed author and, as founder of CR's parent Leadership Institute as well as CR, the text has the look and feel of a mission statement. The document is also striking for its Manichean flak-in-discourse vision that closes with a flak-in-action appeal: "If you experience any kind of leftist abuse or bias on campus [,] contact Campus Reform at www.CampusReform.org or contact@campusreform.org" (n.d., p. 4).

In the course of 780 words, "The evil empire" uses the term "leftist" 25 times, starting with the document's title (Blackwell, n.d.). No effort is made to even provisionally define who or what is "leftist"—as if the term is self-evident, even as the left-of-center tradition extends from John Stuart Mill to Karl Marx, from Amnesty International to the Castro regime in Cuba. Nonetheless, Blackwell's assertion that "large numbers of student organizations [are] supported by major, national leftist organizations" is innocent of evidence or specifics (n.d., p. 1). In describing "leftists"—whomever and whatever they may be—Blackwell describes their program on campus as "indoctrination" (n.d., p. 1), "persecution" (n.d., p. 1), "control" (n.d., p. 1) and "domination" (n.d., p. 1). A colorful litany of verbs and verb phrases animates Blackwell's characterizations of the political left: they "denigrate" (n.d., p. 1), "suppress" (n.d., p. 1), "penalize" (n.d., p. 3), "clamp down" (n.d., p. 3), "shout down" (n.d., p. 3), and "ridicule" (n.d., p. 4). In what specific areas of campus life are these leftist campaigns acted out? Blackwell marshals a list that is as long as it is untroubled by conditions and qualifications: campus leftists mobilize oppression through "compulsory student fees" (n.d., p. 1), the composition of journalism faculties, guest and graduation speakers, library collections, orientation programs, student judicial processes, graduate and undergraduate admissions, resident assistant programs, faculty hiring, tenure decisions, faculty salaries, examinations, and "special bathrooms." In Blackwell's flak memes, campus leftism has constructed an almost seamless matrix of tyranny. The university is relentless in its harassment of conservative sensibilities, even when the lights are off. Blackwell intones that the right is further hounded by a peepshow ambiance of "College rules which authorize overnight guests in dorm rooms with people of *either* sex—rules which force offended roommates either to witness these sexual couplings or to find somewhere else to spend the night" (emphasis added; n.d., p. 4). That conservatives may be the ones (sometimes? predominantly?) getting laid escapes Blackwell.

Beyond its founder, CR more generally conjures a flak-memed cartoon world in which the left is always an aggressor, while the right struggles to defend itself and keep order. The Manichean narration leads to strikingly selective coverage in CR and notable blind spots in its discourse. For example, an alarming wave of sexual assault accusations at a conservative-branded campus—Baylor University in Waco, Texas—merits no mention in CR. As professor of sports law Michael McCann observes, the situation is more disturbing in the light of the Baylor administration's apparent effort to suppress accusations about suspected crimes, in defense of the university's (mediocre) football team (McCann, 2017). The accusations were credible enough for Baylor to fire head football coach Art Briles and for a juridical process to go forward. However, the Baylor story does not fit the right-wing flak narrative of what is wrong with higher education—ergo, it literally does not exist in CR's universe, as revealed by use of the site's search function. At the same time, CR indulges all manners of triviality and contrivance in filling its daily news hole. Baylor's football apparatus is not news in CR's judgement, but a poster by a campus bathroom merits rhetorical gasps of indignation (Gockowski, 2017c).

CR also maintained complete silence over the weekend of August 11–12, 2017 (and immediately after) when a crowd of more than 500 right-wing activists attending "Unite the Right" marched on the grounds of the University of Virginia. While the rightists were ostensibly in Charlottesville to rally for an off-campus Confederate statue, University of Virginia was also implicated; campuses have indeed become irresistible targets for rightists, as noted by the Southern Poverty Law Center (2017). While chanting slogans that included the Nazi standard "blood and soil," the Unite the Right mob menaced students on the campus around a statue of Thomas Jefferson, according to eye-witness accounts (Stripling, 2017). The following day in downtown Charlottesville, one counter-protester to Unite the Right was killed and 19 more injured by a 20-year old, avowed neo-Nazi who weaponized a car against a crowd. James Alex Fields, Junior was subsequently convicted of murder (Durkin, 2018). Despite its ostensible focus on campus intimidation, CR did not address the mayhem on and around the Virginia campus—even as the story and its tense aftermath saturated U.S. news discourse for several days. Instead, on 14 August for example, CR snidely denounced a Portland State University professor's writings on obesity (Airaksinen, 2017a); timely, hard-hitting stuff.

Along with regularly trawling for triviality, CR has realized at least a measure of success in its flak project. *Chronicle of Higher Education*'s Peter Schmidt reports on the whiteboard in CR's office that tallies its metrics of success in 2015. To wit, 70 interviews on television to spread the word (27 of them on Fox News) and 15 "victories"—a term CR applies to any situation in which a college "changes a policy, fires someone, or otherwise responds to concerns raised by the reporting on its site" (2015, para. 4). The organization's center of gravity can thusly be described as flak-in-discourse that aims to stimulate flak-in-action.

CR's formula depends on stories that move into circulation and achieve repetition across media platforms. As Chris Quintana and Brock Read report, "Review enough such cases of faculty polemic gone viral, and an archetype starts to emerge—an assembly line of outrage that collects professors' Facebook posts, opinion essays, and classroom comments and amplifies them until they have become national news. Often, at the start of that line, you'll find *Campus Reform*" (2017, para. 3). In other words, after CR's product ricochets around larger right-wing niche sites (*National Review*, *Daily Caller*), it may be picked up by still larger and more prominent mainstream entities—and, in this way, flak memes enter society's discursive bloodstream. While specific careers may be blown off-course or policies changed as a result of CR's flak, the bigger and longer-term prize is to place higher education *writ large* on the defensive.

General Tendencies of *CR*'s Discourse

Having considered the organization, I will now pivot to particulars of CR's flak discourses. The central purpose of the CR webpage is to furnish a steady drumbeat of flak, with daily doses posted on the web site. The faithful reader is recruited to an unswervingly consistent vision: Class session by class session, from one semester to the next, indoctrination is downloaded into the student brain and intimidation by militant faculty and "regime thug" students is the rule. Hence, CR's bio-sketch tagline for each of its "student correspondents" employs identical phrasing, positing that he or she "reports liberal bias and abuse on college campuses for *Campus Reform*"—"abuses" understood to constitute the sum total of what occurs on campus, and to be at once clownish *and* menacing. Curiously, the campus correspondents often report from campuses other than their own, unwittingly interrupting the notion that the correspondents are filing eyewitness dispatches from the frontlines.

As discussed earlier, U.S. universities face serious challenges; and, through it all, U.S. universities continue to be a global attractant for students and faculty members. To read CR is, however, to gaze through a kaleidoscope of dystopia. In CR's narration, there are no discoveries in the domain of new knowledge, no skills learned, no minds expanded in contact with other minds, no lives endowed with enhanced purpose and opportunity, no high fives and smiles, among other quotidian happenings within the Ivory Tower. In contrast with CR, publications such as *Inside Higher Ed* and *Chronicle of Higher Education* report on and interpret academia across a panoramic view of its activities, rather than grinding an axe in most every story.

Content Analysis of CR's product

After reading a corpus of 124 articles published on CR's web site between 15 April and May 15, 2017, I reviewed the material and developed six categories into which to sort the stories: "Left-Wing Speech" (including speaking badly or too much, in CR's view); "Left-Wing Activism" (including resolutions from student governments): "Left-Wing Suppression of Speech"; "Right-Wing Victimization"; "Right-Wing Heroes and Triumphs"; and "Miscellaneous." These are "rough-and-ready" categories and not as irreducibly distinct as biological differences between vertebrates and invertebrates. In this vein, the difference between "Right-Wing Victimization" and "Right-Wing Heroes" can be a matter of perceived emphasis in the article and its headline (since, for instance, a martyr can be construed as at once a victim and a hero).

In Table 6.1's data, one finds that 69-percent of the articles (a shade more than two-thirds) focused on what CR judges to be left-wing activity.

Table 6.1: Content analysis of CR (15 April–May 15, 2017)

Category	Raw Total of Articles	Percentage
Left Activism	42	34
Left Suppression	23	19
Left Speech	20	16
Right Victimization	17	14
Right Heroes	16	13
Miscellaneous	6	5
Total	124	101 (due to rounding)

By contrast, 27-percent of stories employed right-wing figures as protagonists, while five-percent of stories were judged "Miscellaneous." However, if the thrust behind flak is to surveil and problematize *them*, it follows that most of the discourse is, indeed, about the liberal-leftist Other—and their faults, their excesses, their aggressions and their misdeeds. Moreover, the stories with a center of gravity in alleged right-wing victimization (14-percent) compliment CR's vision of liberal reign of (t)error on campus. The resolute emphasis on "feel-bad news" is also striking as right-wing heroes constitute a scant 13-percent of the discourse.

The content analysis also demonstrates that, although ostensibly focused on academic institutions, CR almost never engages with the published content of academic endeavor—notably, scholarly books and articles—hence there was no need to include a salient category in this content analysis. Instead, CR orients to supposedly dodgy course titles, notices posted on campus message boards, professors' hand-written comments on student papers (and so on). One exception that proves the rule of avoiding academic scholarship is a book review (Airaksinen, 2017c) that quotes Camille Paglia at length (categorized as an instance of a "Right-Wing Hero"). Thus, in the corpus of 124 articles supposedly about the university, decoding academic literature is a vanishingly faint presence.

The results of the content analysis suggest that, in CR's construction of the campus, the left is convening a monologue—speech that is not only menacing for CR, but whiny. In this vein, a student "campus correspondent" denounces a group that he construes as left-leaning (Clemson University's Sexuality and Gender Alliance) for "demanding," "complaining"—and, through these whiny performances, leaving others "intimidated" (Gunter, 2017a, paras. 7–8). Students indulge in "protests and cry-ins" when they are constructed as having been seized by leftism (Sharpstene, 2017, para. 1). By contrast, right-leaning students cited by CR come off as young Abraham Lincolns reincarnated, with exquisitely measured expression as they sagely survey the wreckage wrought by the left on campus.

At noted earlier, the CR web site features Blackwell's four-page itemization of "Leftist Abuse and Bias on Campus" that flags 16 bullet-pointed signs of "Persecution of Conservative Students and Organizations." In taking up the assumption of persecution, small-bore events often suffice to fill CR's news hole. Ergo, two CR's student correspondents flag a case of alleged right-wing victimization that would read as *The Onion*-style satire if not for CR's white-knuckle insistence on academic dystopia: "A student at the University of Florida became a victim of collegiate political correctness when his *History of Water* professor [...] deducted points from his essay for use of the word 'man' [...] as opposed to its gender neutral alternative 'humanity'" (Long & Wilfong, 2017, para. 1). The professor added the following note to the bottom of the student's paper: "Thoughtful paper, although the writing mechanics are killing you" (2017, para. 3)—ominous "liberal-fascist" code words, the reader is to infer. CR furnishes a scan of the paper as a show of evidence for this putatively explosive episode. A victimization frame is reprised for a similar case at Northern Arizona University (Gottry, 2017), as lexical persecution is deemed a viral contagion.

Is there a more straightforward interpretation of events, besides a victimization frame? Try this: One may posit the instructor's comments as aligned with formal English that has, since at least the 1980s, eschewed gendered language where possible. Indeed, a professor who is inattentive to gratuitous use of ungrammatical forms (e.g., "ain't"), or non-standard subcultural lexicon ("illin' and chillin'"), or obscenity, would be negligent toward—wait for it—*his or her* students. As a matter of enlightened self-interest, the student should be cued to internalize correct formal conventions of the language; a point often made with considerable piety to speakers of non-standard English and/or immigrants. To state the obvious, in these instances, free speech "martyrdom" is not in play; but attempting to coach students to express themselves as educated and not bores is at stake.

As concerns particular right-wing personages as victim, CR rallies in 2017 to the defense of Trump. One article rails against "a highly paid, far-left professor at Cornell," of whom the university should be "ashamed," over what is asserted to be a professorial "tendency" to bring "political opinions in where they don't belong" (Sharpstene, 2017, paras. 2 and 5). In this case, what are flagged as "opinions" are asserted to not belong in a course on government (!) that had yet to be delivered (!!); but, from the course description, was set to evaluate the erstwhile "reality" TV performer's vision with regard to, for example, the exercise of soft power.

Ideological Cross-Dressing

Despite the generalized right-wing orthodoxy of CR's discourse, the effort to summon dreary visions of the university prompts CR to deviate from some bedrock positions; valorizing wealth and opposing redistribution of it, for example. Cabot Phillips explains with evidence-free assertion: "As *Campus*

Reform has reported extensively, professors at these eight [Ivy League] schools have a special propensity for using their power to indoctrinate students in leftist ideology" (2017, paras. 1–2). In looking at facts on the ground, however, Ivy League professors' "power to indoctrinate students" appears to be sufficiently unsuccessful as to place its existence in considerable doubt. Graduates of note from Ivy League schools include standard bearers of "leftist ideology" such as the aforementioned Trump (University of Pennsylvania, 1968), George H.W. and George W. Bush (Yale, 1948 and 1968), William F. Buckley (Yale, 1950), George F. Will (Princeton, 1968), Steven Mnuchin (Yale, 1985), Anne Coulter (Cornell, 1984), *ad infinitum*. Moving from particular names to broad tendencies across Ivy League graduates, the mid-career annual income averaged across the eight universities is estimated at almost $117,000 (PayScale, n.d.)—a sum that can subsidize closets full of stylish Che Guevara berets for these successful players in the capitalist system. Although an ordinary Ivy League graduate can reasonably expect to become a millionaire, leftist indoctrination *must be happening*, as demanded by conveniently summoned populist flak memes, in defiance of facts and common sense.

The Ivy League pedigree generates symbolic and economic wealth for its graduates—and, through the affirmative action of "legacy admission," maintains that wealth from one generation to the next. Nonetheless, CR's Anthony Gockowski is willing to combat Ivy hegemony with hard-core socialist levelling. Gockowski approvingly discusses legislation that would mandate Ivies to devote "investment earnings to financial aid or share the proceeds with other universities" (2017e, para. 4). Gockowski concludes by endorsing free-ride scholarships to all Ivy League students for the next 51 years that he insists is feasible in the light of the universities' endowments. I, for one support that concept—then again, I posit all education should be free or at nominal cost, as a matter of long-standing commitment toward egalitarianism. In CR's case, however, these passages illustrate the extent to which even sacrosanct capitalist principles are sacrificed in the effort to problematize any part of the university system.

CR's zeal in its flak mission leads to further deviation from commitment to the capitalist market. In particular, CR is outraged when university administrators engage in what it calls "capitulation to [student] demands" rather than taking the unswerving hard line against uppity undergraduates (Zupkus, 2017a). While attentiveness to student demands may follow from multiple reasons, administrators' core priorities include maintaining enrollment and keeping fee-paying students more satisfied than not; obvious considerations in any service-based industry.

In a similar vein, students and prospective students are often attracted by the aura of diversity and inclusiveness on a campus as a positive value in itself, in contrast with atavistic retreats into tribalism. Visions of the world convened in one place drive many campus' appeals to students. Diversity as an attractant may also (in less lofty terms) be read back to multiculturalism in commodified forms in the neoliberal era, given the compatibility of multiculturalism and marketing products with distinction. Furthermore, for U.S. university administrations, attracting students from abroad can constitute vital revenue enhancement within a highly competitive industry.

In the light of these straightforward, even obvious considerations, it is strange to read CR's fury at Furman University for initiating faculty awards to recognize, "Furman's value of diversity and inclusion, and multiculturalism on campus" (Cooley, 2017, para. 2). CR rallies to one student's semi-coherent-if-wholly-sour assertion that, "Furman should be about equal opportunity rather than singling out diverse groups" (quoted in Cooley, 2017, para. 7). CR's discourse is once again animated by the desire to flak the university and pathologize its practices—including those that enact the enlightened self-interest of inclusiveness, in what can also be (at least partly) read back to marketing and customer service terms.

Flak Versus Journalism Ethics and Accuracy

CR presents itself as an exemplar of journalism, beginning with the titles it bequeaths to its staff. The college students who constitute the majority of CR contributors use the byline of "campus correspondent." Staff member Anthony Gockowski sports the vainglorious title of "investigative reporter," although the content of his stories evoke a cubicle-bound scribe. Nevertheless, in the sample of 124 articles, CR exhibits only a handful of moments in which the organization does what it purports to do: to wit, report on and examine the higher education system with a measure of dispassion. In one moment of straightforward reportage, Jackson Richman (2017) eschews flak impulses in an account of a George Washington University student government vote on divestment from firms doing business with Israel. The article presents the student government as animated by the rigors of self-governance on a significant issue.

Like Project Veritas, CR regularly flaunts the Society of Professional Journalists' "SPJ Code of Ethics." The code charges members of the profession to, "Provide context. Take special care not to misrepresent or oversimplify in promoting, previewing or summarizing a story." Moreover, in pursuit of fairness and accuracy, journalists are enjoined to, "Avoid stereotyping. Journalists should examine the ways their values and experiences may shape their reporting" (Society for Professional Journalists, 2014, p. 1). Part of the ethical code also addresses minimizing harm and considering whether the news may harshly impact the subjects of its stories. In particular, journalists are charged to, "Consider the long-term implications of the extended reach and permanence of publication. Provide updated and more complete information as appropriate" (Society for Professional Journalists, 2014, p.1). CR contradicts, at the very least, the spirit of these ethical charges. The organization mobilizes pre-judged, contentious discourse with the objective of achieving the CR whiteboard "victories" that, in turn and by evident design, harm careers cultivated across their targets' adult lives.

CR's deficits as a journalistic enterprise are at times channeled through headlines that read as inaccurate and right-wing sensationalist with respect to the content of the article. In this vein, an article presents the blaring headline, "Students demand Pomona rescind offer to prof because she is white." Notwithstanding the clickbait title, the article mainly concerns student unease with the visiting professor hire over "methods that have endangered her research participants, [and] encouraged the hyper-policing of Black communities" (Airaksinen, 2017e, para. 13). For support, the students in the article cite other academics' criticisms of the hire's research.

Exaggeration for impact also drives CR's discourse, as is evident when one compares student newspaper texts available online with CR's caricatures of them. A Wesleyan University student's 2017 editorial is characterized in CR's headline and introductory bullet point as making "demands" that "men 'step back' in class discussions" as they are "oppressing their female peers" (Airaksinen 2017d). Far from the castrating caricature conjured in CR, *The Wesleyan Argus* op-ed treads carefully and at no point frames its arguments in terms of "oppression." The editorialist posits gender disparity during in-class discussion as "complicated," "rarely intentional," "not entirely the students' fault"; many students are even "blissfully unaware" about patterns of classroom discourse, the editorialist suggests in a series of carefully calibrated claims supported via citation of academic studies (Joy, 2017, paras. 4–6). The editorial by the college student is thoughtfully measured while CR's supposedly professionalized account of it depends on asserting flak tropes of man-hating campaigns.

College newspaper editorials may seem like very small potatoes, an intramural matter. However, in contrast with the 1980s when I covered basketball and soccer for the same campus newspaper, a *Wesleyan Argus* editorial in the internet era can become a world-wide story, far beyond the Middletown, Connecticut campus. Events and opinions that formerly played out locally can rally flak-mongers from all corners. *Breitbart*, *Turning Point USA*, and Milo Yiannopolous subsequently rushed to the scene of the 2017 *Wesleyan Argus* editorial on gender in the classroom; indeed, their flak-imbued accounts of it furnish some of the first results when the student's name and school are entered into Google as of July 3, 2017. In any event, the teenage college student exhibits far more intelligence and sophistication than the parties flaking her (see, e.g., Allen, 2017)—and the behavior of CR, in particular, strains stated ethical standards around fairness and minimizing harm. Moreover, it requires no imagination to see the traumatizing chill on speech when a flak echo chamber is convened against a young person's thoughtful expression.

In several cases on which CR has published, a platoon of right-wing web sites have further fanned the flames of flak that have led to abuse, up to death threats; and credible death threats are, of course, not protected speech but criminal in themselves. As Quintana and Read observe, "about those threats: They've become increasingly common. The assembly line of outrage doesn't just expose faculty statements to a national audience; it also calls forth an id" (2017, para. 8). Beyond CR, the platoon of websites that regularly traffic in alleged horror stories from campus include *The blaze*, *The daily caller*, *Accuracy in academics*, and the aforementioned *Professor watchlist*. Echo-chamber-style convergence on tendentiously narrated stories have generated harm by summoning mobs speaking malice; behavior that defies the caution advised by the SPJ code, as well as against common-sense concepts of proportionality and decency.

Doubling Down on Double Standards

Double standards are perhaps the lynchpin CR's discourse and illustrate the extent to which its scrutiny of academia presents not the quest for "reform," but a one-sided flak project. Under the regime of double standard, what is supposed to be a wrong regardless of who commits an act is instead construed as wrong *conditioned* on whether it implicates members of an unfavored group—while other, similar instances are exonerated, even celebrated when enacted by members of a favored group. For example, CR announces its disapproval toward African-American and Latino graduation ceremonies at Harvard as "self-segregation," even as it is noted that the same students will participate in the general university graduation (Hall, 2017). At the same time, CR betrays anxiety about University of Rochester's efforts to ameliorate self-segregation that would implicate fraternities and sororities far more extensive practices on this score (Gockowski, 2017b). Fraternities and sororities are, indeed, the lone beacon of light that CR founder Blackwell (n.d.) can locate on the campus in his manifesto, discussed earlier. CR addresses cases that present as self-segregation through the shape-shifting optics of double standard, and not principled consistency.

In this vein, Gockowski rails against "Social Justice Advocates" among students that University of Arizona plans to appoint. Gockowski asserts, accurately or otherwise, "that the school was effectively paying its students to 'tattle on others'" (2017a, para. 3). While Gockowski's use of the past tense is strange as the plan had yet to be implemented, something else is striking from the double-standard perspective. To wit, CR openly recruits students to "tattle" on their universities for a global audience as an integral part of its business model; student correspondents furnish a large share of the site's content. "Tips" is also one of six tabs on CR's landing page menu as of July 2017, which makes it easy to file bulletins (tattle) from the campus front lines with the flak command center at CR.

Where Are the Opiates of the Masses When You Need Them?

As noted in the introductory chapters, activism can be distinguished from flak. At the same time, when flak-driven, ideologically-grounded double standard enters the discussion, activity may be celebrated as brave activism—or flaked as beyond-the-pale.

In this vein, CR turns a generally jaundiced eye toward campus activism and social justice when they enter the flak gaze. CR snidely derides a Student Government Association in South Carolina as "stooping to" advocacy for "unwanted social justice activism" (Gunter, 2017b, para. 12). In another article, Senator Kamala Harris' graduation speech at Howard University urges graduates to "speak truth and serve": "We need you. Our country needs you. And the world needs you. Get out there and do your thing" (Airaksinen,

2017b, para. 16). It reads as an inspiring message for new graduates in tumultuous times—but the activist call to serve receives a bitter response from *CR* as a demand for students to be "just like her" (2017b, para. 12). The article's headline also denudes the speech of inspiration in favor of a miserabalist vibe: "Senator Harris paints dystopian picture in commencement address." Scanning the U.S. landmass, *CR* also finds that Oberlin College undergraduates who take activist interest in work conditions in the dining hall rise to the level of red menace. *CR*'s alarmism begins with the headline, "Oberlin students seek to socialize dining halls" (Zehnder, 2017)—within the (unmentioned, unmentionable) context of the $70,000 per year (tuition and fees) campus steadfastly reproducing market relations, albeit to a degree that evidently does not satisfy *CR*'s demands (*College simply*, 2019).

Through double-standard, right-wing activism is, however, spared similar dismissive treatment. A chapter of Young Americans for Freedom, for example, put on a pointless and dumb stunt near University of Texas that it called an "affirmative action bake sale." The "activists" set prices based on bodily-marked identities—and are lauded by *CR* as free speech titans (Sabes, 2017a). Another article returns to the victimization frame to complain that a "Students for Life chapter was assigned a table directly behind its pro-choice counterpart in what members call an 'intentional way' to silence pro-life voices" (Gockowski, 2017f). The "silencing" of *CR*'s preferred activists at California State University at Dominquez Hills is, in turn, "exposed" via three ostensibly hard-hitting photos from the scene. Unfortunately for this flak gambit, the photos make it apparent that no one would have trouble strolling up the pro-life table's aisle unless one actively avoided doing so. To follow *CR*'s flak meme in this case requires that one annul the evidence of one's own senses, within a broader devotion to double-standards around activism.

First Amendment Fudges

As for the First Amendment, it can readily be called one of the United States' best known and most highly regarded inventions. The vaunted amendment leads off the Bill of Rights and has been characterized as the fount of all the nation's liberal, Enlightenment freedoms. The amendment's 45-word text has also enduringly provoked contention in the United States, accompanied by a stream of court cases to sort out what it means in practice. Refinements that have evolved through judicial processes across centuries have established an array of carefully calibrated qualifications around speech. These restrictions surround, for example, intellectual property such as copyright, as well as restrictions that concern obscenity and libel or slander (Campbell, 2003). Moreover, speech can also be judged as incompatible with security (personal or collective), as credible death threats are not protected speech for the injuries they inflict on a person in having been uttered. Given rising tides of diversity alongside a rising taste for confrontation in many parts of the world, the interest in a wise calibration of free expression has become an international issue of compelling interest (see, e.g., Todorov, 2010). At present, expression on campus is a hot button issue for the complications around enabling speech while cultivating an ambiance of dignity and respect.

CR regularly covers speech issues—and, in doing so, manufactures microwave-ready right-wing flak, rather than thoughtfully addressing the topic. In this vein, CR's editor-in-chief fumes that on today's campus, "Dildo juggling *is a valid form of protest*"—however, "hosting a panel of non-leftists *will bring the shrieking ninnies out*" (original emphasis; Beard, 2017a, para.). In line with Beard's stern rebuke to the dildo jugglers and the ninnies, CR assays to transmit the impression that it is a militant free speech champion, driven to bravely stare uncomfortable truths in the face. However, in a low voice and without flagging these moments as such, CR cancels its speech absolutism whenever right-wing flak imperatives demand it.

Double standard and blind spots abound. In order for its flak narratives to hang together, CR is silent on evangelical colleges that lean conservative—and often expressly demand adherence to very particular codes of belief, behavior and expression by faculty and students. An evangelical job notice that fits the pattern reads, "Genuine affirmation" of the campus' "Life Together Covenant' is required" as a condition of being on faculty (Taylor University, 2017, para. 2). In turn, along with laudable passages on community, the Covenant exceeds the "totalitarian" campus codes about which right-wing flak-mongers solemnly warn. The Covenant codifies proscriptions around gayness, pre-marital sex, most forms of dancing, what the campus construes as immodest dress, profanity, and use of alcohol. The code further regulates what one should do and not do on Sunday.

Of course, no one has to submit to a code such as this unless he or she elects to enroll or toil in an institution that regulates itself thusly. However, the same may be said of the immeasurably looser mores to which students and faculty at non-evangelical campuses are subject—and that CR relentlessly problematizes. Moreover, while ethical language is commonly employed by other religiously-oriented campuses (including the Jesuit-order Catholic one at which I work), the same kind of totalizing prescriptions around expression are not made on students and faculty. CR is silent on what would be flaked as the evangelical "politically correct militancy" if remotely similar practices prevailed at an Ivy League or Big Ten campus—elision that disrupts CR's ostensible free speech absolutism.

Pantomiming Censorship

As the content analysis discussed earlier shows, CR engages regularly with what it construes as the university's stifling of speech. However, there is reason to believe that right-wing activists actively bait many of these speech conflagrations. For example, at Saint Louis University (SLU) in Missouri, College Republicans and Young America's Foundation invited Fox News performer Allen B. West to speak on the campus. In a "bait-and-switch" move shortly before the address, the sponsors changed the previously declared title of the talk from a general interest politics topic to a more provocative title on "radical Islam" (Mary Rachel Gould, personal communication, October 9, 2017; Sultan, 2016); a topic that would not only slight Muslim students enrolled on the Jesuit campus, but everyone affronted by what (given West's record) augured as a chauvinistic screed from the speaker.

On his blog, West's rails against "the little cupcakes" (students) at SLU who "ask for a 'safe space'" (2016, para. 1). West calls the administrator who flagged the newly minted title of the talk as a concern "the most deplorable embodiment of fascism" (2016, para. 9). West's continues with a string of assertions untroubled by a scintilla of evidence: "if this is a case of the influence of stealth radical Islamic campus organizations such as the Muslim Student Association, an affiliate of the Muslim Brotherhood, then you will be exposed" (2016, para. 14). He adds further vaguely threatening demands that a SLU administrator contact him "unless you're truly the coward I sense that you are!" (2016, para. 16).

Although he speciously claimed to have been censured, West gave his talk at SLU as scheduled. In the event, SLU students filled the auditorium in its entirety—until West took the stage to speak. The "little cupcakes"/students then filed out, one by one, until the audience in the amply-sized auditorium melted away to about two dozen die-hards on a campus of 10,000. It was an elegant rebuke to the speaker who preemptively slurred his audience, but seemed to expect awed deference. The episode also demonstrates that free speech may grant a person the soapbox—but the same classically liberal conventions mandate that absolutely no one is obligated to listen. It is of further note that West's SLU meltdown generates no mention in CR. The fiasco does not fit the script that CR demands for outrage at "'left-wing' abuses."

As for what CR does cover, patently ugly expression mobilizes defense from CR when it emanates from the right. College Republicans at Hood College in Maryland fit the bill when given a turn at filling a student activity display case. Rather than exalting supply-side economics or "thousand points of light" volunteerism, the College Republican display featured alt-right bile and thinly disguised digs at Black Lives Matter. For example, "Let's talk about race": "'Abortion is the number one killer of black lives in the United States' [...] 'The most dangerous place for an African-American is in the womb.'" CR pointedly places characterization of the Hood Republicans' messages as hateful in "scare quotes" (Price, 2017a). The web site also credulously quotes the College Republicans president on the campus as insisting that the "displays were not intended to offend anyone" (2017a, para. 17). CR's headline supports that disingenuous assertion and frames that matter as, "Students say they feel 'threatened' by conservative views." Although the Hood College administration allowed the display to stay up for its full scheduled duration, the College Republicans insist that *they* had been victimized and audaciously assay a guilt trip: "The handling of the situation by the school administration"—a situation transparently planned and contrived to manufacture a flak storm—"has demonstrated the extreme bias against free speech and diversity of thought for conservative views on campus" (2017a, para. 20).

The purpose of a manipulative stunt such as this is to demean others *and* to feign persecution—regardless of whether or not one's exhibit was finally taken down for being a weeping sore of an embarrassment to the campus. With CR's assistance, the Hood College Republicans do what fanatics yearn to do. To wit, fanatics force choices between one's principles (in this case between free expression and blunting empty, undignified speech) in the knowledge that fanaticism will either enable a cheap claim to martyrdom—or enable rubbish to circulate. *Heads I win and tails you lose* enables the flak to flow, with CR ready as a channel in which to disseminate the resultant memes against Hood in particular, higher education in general.

When Speech Codes Go Good

If one assumes that CR always rallies to the principal of free expression as a categorical imperative, one will be disappointed. CR's support of free expression depends not on principle, but on the identity of the parties involved. In order to advance flak purposes against unfavored groups, affirmations of free expression can be turned on and off like a light switch as circumstances demand. Even as it rallies to defend bile from behind the free expression shield (e.g., toward African-Americans), CR supports a speech code resolution around anti-Semitism at Chapman University.

Chapman's statement is substantially the same as other codes that have assayed to thread the needle between open expression and regulating hate speech that takes shelter within liberal speech rights. After listing some of the disgusting tropes that have long been directed at Jewish people, CR's account of the resolution reads, "Chapman University Student Government Association unequivocally condemns all forms of anti-Semitism, and rejects attempts to justify anti-Jewish hatred or violent attacks as an acceptable expression of disapproval or frustration." The student government avers that it "will not facilitate, promote, fund, or participate in any activities that directly or indirectly promote anti-Semitism or undermine the rights of the Jewish people to self-determination" (Sabes, 2017b, paras. 3–4). The report presents a rare case of "good news" in CR's reportage, as its headline declares, "A university resolves to take stand against anti-Semitism"; an affirmation of speech policing that would otherwise be a cue for indignation over political correctness.

Posturing aside, CR's support of free expression reduces to who is implicated and what flak objective may be at stake. Embracing double-standard with gusto, CR disparages an editorial from Wellesley College's student newspaper. The editorial is, in turn, far less stringent about hate speech than the Chapman resolution—that is, when one actually reads the Wellesley editorial that stresses education, and not speech restrictions around identity issues (*The Wellesley News* Staff Editorial, 2017), rather than reading CR's hysterical account of the same editorial (Price 2017b).

In a similar vein of evaluating speech standards based on who is harmed, a campus correspondent reports on an incident at American University (AU). Nooses with bananas bearing the message "AKA free" were hung around campus; obvious references to lynching, sickening racial tropes, as well as to AU's new student government president, an African-American member of Alpha Kappa Alpha (AKA) sorority. While letting the hideousness of the incident speak for itself, CR nevertheless trains its headline fire on "AU students [who] *exploit* racist incident for progressive causes" (emphasis added; Zupkus, 2017b). CR delegitimizes subsequent student demands as "ostentatious" as the reaction—and not the cowardly, abusive messages—are discovered to be problematic (2017b, para. 5).

Big "Buts" on Free Expression

CR's resolute commitment to double-standards on speech—and not to classically liberal free expression—can be illustrated via a paired example of professors using new media badly. One of the professors was an avowed man of the left and the other of the right. It is a difference that determines the contours of CR's subsequent discourse as concerns, on one hand, denunciation of intemperate expression—and, on the other, equally indignant pantomimes of speech absolutism.

In late 2016, Drexel University's George Ciccariello-Maher startled holiday revelers by tweeting, "All I want for Christmas is white genocide." He followed in short order with apparent celebration of whites killed during Haiti's eighteenth-century slave rebellion. CR's reaction was predictably horrified—as well as gleeful to report administration and alumni displeasure with the tweeting professor. CR's discourse is suddenly seized by concerns around standards of decency as well as fretting over the university's corporate "brand" considerations sullied by Ciccariello-Maher's outbursts (Airaksinen, 2017f).

Slate's Matthew Dessem comments that the Ciccariello-Maher "story quickly went as viral as dysentery," as other right-wing sites joined the frenzy and "death threats crashed into Drexel" (2016, para. 2). In defense, Ciccariello-Maher observed that "white genocide" is a white supremacist term for activity such as miscegenation. Ciccariello-Maher is adamant that Twitter readers need do further research on the term. The professor displays dubious judgement in assuming that the concision and non-seminar room atmospherics of Twitter square with "further research"—or that his gesture at provocation would not excite what Dessem sardonically terms "the internet's winged monkeys" (2016, para. 8). Moreover, even if common sense was not a brake on Ciccariello-Maher's rush to the keyboard, Drexel's administration had cautioned him previously on his social media use (Flaherty, 2017). In any event, Ciccariello-Maher presents a convenient flak villain from central casting for CR. Following the abuse directed at him, Ciccariello-Maher resigned from Drexel's faculty.

The contrasting case concerns Marquette University's John McAdam. In this instance, CR pirouettes one-hundred eighty degrees to free speech absolutism in defense of an avowed man of the right, in unmissable contrast with Ciccariello-Maher. On his blog, McAdam slammed a Marquette graduate teaching assistant who was said to have glossed over a question about gay marriage from an undergraduate during class. Although the right in general, and *CR* in particular, relentlessly accuse universities of indoctrination as part of its delegitimation tactics, the teaching assistant eschewed the opportunity to install a party line. Instead, she redirected the class to the day's topic of John Rawls' philosophy (Jaschik, 2015, 2017a). Anyone who has actually delivered university classes further cognizes that redirecting discussion away from digression or attempted discursive hijacking by a prolix student is a basic classroom skill.

McAdams' blog attacks on the graduate student metastasized over the internet into a wider campaign of abuse against her. Threats reached sufficient intensity that a campus security agent was assigned to stand by the door of her class. Not surprisingly, she eventually left the university (Jaschik, 2015). The ugly chain of events began with glossing over a comment in class that was followed by McAdams' online paroxysms. McAdams charged that the graduate teaching assistant with "using a tactic typical among liberals" to allegedly suffocate discussion (quoted in Jaschik, 2017a, para. 12). In turn, McAdams' standard issue, flak rant could be accessed by anyone in the world with an internet connection.

McAdams publicly and by name attacked a colleague on the campus—a clear redline in an academic community. After Marquette tried to suspend him, McAdams' sued his employer—and lost. *CR* rallied to McAdams' with an article accompanied by a banner illustration that depicts a kangaroo court judge childishly banging a gavel while asserting injustice against McAdams and his rights to free expression. With unswerving one-sidedness, *CR*'s account of events leaves out the grievous impact on the graduate student in order to insist on McAdams as victim—even as McAdams put the ugly situation into motion with his decision to publicize the mundane incident and to harshly attack a colleague by name on a globally available platform. No matter: McAdams is given the final word in *CR*'s account, as he laments the "increasing unwillingness of colleges to stand up for free speech" (Gockowski, 2017d, para. 10). The right to speech is air-brushed out of *CR*'s Ciccariello-Maher discourse—a right that also includes the right to *not* speak and gloss over a question as the graduate student did, a possibility that *CR* never entertains, thus never addresses.

Whereas the American Association of University Professors consistently defends academic freedom, and the American Civil Liberties Union is steadfast on even the tough cases around free expression, *CR*'s position is demonstrably contingent. Notwithstanding its First Amendment bromides, for *CR*, free expression is wholly contingent on the question of *whose* rights need to be defended. From the logics of double standard, free speech absolutism flows for us (McAdams, Hood College Republicans, American University race hustlers, and so on)—but not for those with whom we disagree, who are not us, who must be flaked. It is a tendency apotheosized by CR's "maximum leader," Trump, who has *both* publicly angered for more punitive libel laws (obviously meant to criminalize critics) alongside free speech absolutism on college campuses to empower alt-right monologues; although free speech on campus *about* Trump is outside the perimeter of free expression, in CR's considered view.

Heads Up. Two articles published on the same day (April 19, 2017) speak once again to CR's unprincipled and unacknowledged double-standard on free expression. In the first article, under the headline "College: A 'Safe Space' for Censorship," Beard delivers standard flak talking points: "Even mere affirmations of commitment to free speech [on campus] get shot down on the grounds that they could create '*an unsafe space*'" (original emphasis, 2017b, para. 2). The same day's flow of CR campus dystopia includes a story about a faculty art exhibit that takes readers all the way to University of Alaska at Anchorage. In this case, the narrative arc careens from "free speech *now!*" to "free speech *but.*"

In particular, a painting at the Alaska exhibit depicted Captain America brandishing Trump's disembodied head. The presence of Captain America flags that this is work in the genre of a cartoon, albeit an obviously political one. CR responds by quoting, at length, from a Facebook post by a former University of Alaska professor, moved to stare solemnly into an abyss of Shakespearian complexities around free expression: "As a free speech advocate, everyone has a right to express their opinion the way the way you [sic] want to express them [sic]" (quoted in Athey, 2017, para. 9). Can you feel the *"but"* coming from CR, channeled through the Facebook post? Here it is, right on cue: "But as a parent and a citizen, there's a discussion. In a university setting, what's appropriate?"

Common-sense decency and standards of "what's appropriate" are expressed to the point of exhaustion toward speech that pejoratively judges entire groups of people. In the case of Captain America versus Trump, however, CR suddenly conjures mitigating circumstances—whether the art was state-funded suddenly becomes a matter about which to wring one's hands in anguish—and daisy chains of "buts" abruptly cloud the vision of free expression absolutism. Either way, universities are targets of flak opportunity in CR's consistently inconsistent scrutiny—damned if you do *or* do not permit controversial expression, depending on *who* said it about *who*—that is part-and-parcel to problematizing of the campus.

Conclusion: The Right-Wing Sublime

If CR's project was to be a news source with a mission of informing and educating the public, its discourse simply would not assume the specifications that it does. To wit, CR's resolute dedication to specifically right-wing flak is not an occasional, added-on detail of its discourse—it is central feature, enacted day-by-day, in article after article.

As noted, flak is often directed at individual faculty as it is likely to register palpable impact such as internal investigation, leave of absence, or termination. However, the flak target may be interpreted to be far bigger. In flak discourses against higher education, in CR and beyond, the professorial monad can be readily recast as the synecdoche of a rotten system. Given the extent of the dystopia on campus that CR posits, the implicit message is that the university needs to be re-engineered from the ground up and replaced with some (unspecified) form of right-wing regime.

As discussed earlier, neoliberalism has weakened higher education in demonstrable respects, through heightened commodification that impacts students alongside heightened managerialism and precarity for many faculty. However, an even more right-wing project presents as driven by antipathy toward the *very idea* of higher education. This project seeks to plunge the university into demoralized chaos, annul its campaigns for intellectualism over gut instinct and raw coercion, and disable universities as a ladder to advancement and class mobility; a ladder that can, albeit with difficulty, scale over fixed hierarchies. Higher education may further valorize traditional concepts of beauty, accomplishment and decorum. In doing so, it conflicts with what Corey Robin (2011) describes as the right-wing sublime that is viscerally drawn to the ugly, brutish expression of pyramidal pre-Enlightenment hierarchy. Universities may only partly achieve their mission in the best of conditions. However, livid flak campaigns against higher education channel the desire to gut the university's enablement of (often slow-moving, under the radar) subversions of traditional authority's writ through the counter-power of education.

To return to the opening example of Central European University, this U.S.-accredited campus was welcomed by Vienna in continuance of its high-quality educational mission after being banished from Hungary by Fidesz rightists. CEU nonetheless presents a bracing warning about complacency about how far flak against education may extend.

References

Airaksinen, T. (2017a). High white obesity rates jeopardize whiteness, Prof Claims. *Campus Reform*, 14 August. Retrieved from www.campusreform.org/?ID=9581.
Airaksinen, T. (2017b). Sen. Harris paints dystopian picture in commencement Address. *Campus Reform*, 14 May. Retrieved from www.campusreform.org/?ID=9179.
Airaksinen, T. (2017c). Camille Paglia tackles the "tyranny" of "tolerance." *Campus Reform*, 3 May. Retrieved from www.campusreform.org/?ID=9136.
Airaksinen, T. (2017d). Female student demands men "step back" in class discussions. *Campus Reform*, 1 May. Retrieved from www.campusreform.org/?ID=9125.
Airaksinen, T. (2017e). Students demand Pomona rescind offer to prof because she's white. *Campus Reform*, 24 April. Retrieved from www.campusreform.org/?ID=9097.
Airaksinen, T. (2017f). Students, donors fleeing Drexel over prof's inflammatory tweets. *Campus Reform*, 21 April. Retrieved from www.campusreform.org/?ID=9088.
Allen, C. (2017). Wesleyan feminist demands that male students shut up during classroom discussions. *Independent woman's forum*, 2 May. Accessed July 19, 2017, from http://iwf.org/blog/2803553/Wesleyan-Feminist-Demands-That-Male-Students-Shut-Up-During-Classroom-Discussions.
Athey, A. (2017). U Alaska art exhibition displays Trump's severed head. *Campus Reform*, 19 April. Retrieved from www.campusreform.org/?ID=9072.
Beard, S. (2017a). A requiem for free speech. *Campus Reform*, 27 April. Retrieved from www.campusreform.org/?ID=9111.
Beard, S. (2017b). College: A safe place for censorship. *Campus Reform*, 19 April. Retrieved from www.campusreform.org/?ID=9070.
Beauchamp, Z. (2018). An assault on a Hungarian university shows authoritarianism in action. *Vox*, 4 December. Retrieved from www.vox.com/world/2018/12/4/18123754/hungary-ceu-orban-soros-authoritarianism.
Blackwell, M.C. (n.d.). The evil empire: Leftist abuses and bias. *Campus Reform*. Retrieved from www.campusreform.org/img/writings/Left_Bias_and_Abuse.pdf.
Bloom, A. (1987). *The closing of the American mind*. New York: Simon & Schuster, Inc.
Buckley, W.F. (1951). *God and man at Yale*. Chicago: Henry Regnery.
Campbell, R. (2003). *Media and culture*. Boston: Bedford/St. Martin's.
Central European University Newsroom. (2019). CEU Ranks 41st in politics and international studies, among the top 100 in four subjects, 26 February. Retrieved from www.ceu.edu/article/2019-02-26/ceu-ranks-41st-politics-and-international-studies-among-top-100-four-subjects.

Central European University Newsroom. (2018). CEU forced out of Budapest. 3 December. Retrieved from www.ceu.edu/article/2018-12-03/ceu-forced-out-budapest-launch-us-degree-programs-vienna-september-2019.

College simply. (2019). Oberlin College tuition and cost. Retrieved from www.collegesimply.com/colleges/ohio/oberlin-college/price/.

Cooley, L. (2017). Profs get cash prizes for promoting "Multiculturalism" on campus. *Campus Reform*, 26 April. Retrieved from www.campusreform.org/?ID=9106.

Couldry, N. (2011). Fighting for the university's life. In M. Bailey & D. Freedman (Eds.), *The assault on universities* (pp. 37–46). London: Pluto Press.

DeSmogBlog. (n.d.). Donors Trust. Retrieved from www.desmogblog.com/who-donors-trust.

D'Souza, D. (1991). *Illiberal education.* New York: Free Press.

Dessem, M. (2016). Drexel University, apparently unfamiliar with white supremacist lingo, censures prof for "white genocide" tweet. *Slate*, 26 December. Retrieved from slate.com/culture/2016/12/drexel-censures-professor-for-white-genocide-tweet.html.

Duménil, G., & Levy, D. (2011). *The crisis of neoliberalism.* Cambridge, MA: Harvard University Press.

Durkin, E. (2018). James Fields guilty of murder for driving car into crowd. *The Guardian*, 7 December. Retrieved from www.theguardian.com/us-news/2018/dec/07/charlottesville-james-fields-guilty-murder-heather-heyer.

Emery, D. (2018). Was George Soros an SS officer or Nazi collaborator during World War II? *Snopes*, 4 February (updated). Retrieved from www.snopes.com/fact-check/george-soros-ss-nazi-germany/.

Faulkner, N. (2011). What is a university education for? In M. Bailey & D. Freedman (Eds.), *The assault on universities* (pp. 27–36). London: Pluto Press.

Flaherty, C. (2017). Looking into tweets. *Inside Higher Ed*, 18 April. Retrieved from www.insidehighered.com/news/2017/04/18/documents-show-drexel-investigating-professors-tweets-its-unclear-whether-faculty.

Ginsberg, B. (2011). *The fall of the faculty and the rise of the all-administrative university and why it matters.* New York: Oxford University Press.

Gockowski, A. (2017a). U of Arizona to revise "social justice advocates" position. *Campus Reform*, 15 May. Retrieved from www.campusreform.org/?ID=9181.

Gockowski, A. (2017b). Single-gender clubs labeled "discrimination" at Rochester. *Campus Reform*, 9 May. Retrieved from www.campusreform.org/?ID=9160.

Gockowski, A. (2017c). College asks students to contemplate "pee privilege." *Campus Reform*, 8 May. Accessed July 19, 2017, from https://www.campusreform.org/?ID=9156.

Gockowski, A. (2017d). Judge upholds Marquette's suspension of conservative prof. *Campus Reform*, 5 May. Accessed July 18, 2017, from: https://www.campusreform.org/?ID=9149.

Gockowski, A. (2017e). Wealthy universities fear GOP will end their tax breaks. *Campus Reform*, 4 May. Retrieved from www.campusreform.org/?ID=9141.

Gockowski, A. (2017f). Pro-life group hidden by abortion advocates at Social Justice Fair. *Campus Reform*, 1 May. Retrieved from www.campusreform.org/?ID=9124.

Golden, D. (2019). How the rich really play "who wants to be an Ivy Leaguer?" *ProPublica*, 12 March. Retrieved from www.propublica.org/article/college-admission-bribe-rich-parents-ivy-league-how-to.

Goss, B.M. (2013). *Rebooting the Herman and Chomsky propaganda model in the twenty-first century*. New York: Peter Lang.

Goss, B.M. (1996). Right-wing surveillance of the academy: William F. Buckley, Jr.'s *God and man at Yale* (1951) and *National Review* (1955–56). Paper and Address. Midwest Journalism History Conference. Urbana, IL. April 1996.

Gottry, J. (2017). Lumberjacks in northern Arizona sure are touchy these days. *Campus Reform*, 8 May. Retrieved from www.campusreform.org/?ID=9152.

Gunter, M. (2017a). Resolution Demands "Permanent Space" for LGBTQ Students. *Campus Reform*, 10 May. Retrieved from www.campusreform.org/?ID=9161.

Gunter, M. (2017b). Students demand cash-strapped college spend more on diversity. *Campus Reform*, 17 April. Accessed July 18, 2017, from www.campusreform.org/?ID=9065.

Hall, E. (2017). Black Harvard grads to hold separate commencement ceremony. *Campus Reform*, 11 May. Retrieved from www.campusreform.org/?ID=9167.

Harvey, D. (1990). *The condition of postmodernity*. Malden, MA: Blackwell Publishers.

Hoffower, H. (2019). Wealthy parents are paying up to $1.5 million for consultants to help get their kids into college. *Business Insider Deutschland*, 13 March. Retrieved from www.businessinsider.sg/college-admissions-scandal-legal-alternatives-wealthy-parents-paying-consultants-donations-2019-3/.

Jaschik, S. (2017a). Setting a limit on academic freedom. *Inside Higher Ed*, 5 May. Retrieved from www.insidehighered.com/news/2017/05/05/wisconsin-judge-says-marquette-was-justified-punishing-professor-publicly.

Jaschik, S. (2017b). Professors and politics. *Inside Higher Ed*, 27 February. Retrieved from www.insidehighered.com/news/2017/02/27/research-confirms-professors-lean-left-questions-assumptions-about-what-means.

Jaschik, S. (2015). Firing a faculty blogger. *Inside Higher Ed*, 5 February. Retrieved from www.insidehighered.com/news/2015/02/05/marquette-moves-fire-controversial-faculty-blogger.

Joy, T. (2017). Male privilege in the classroom, from an all-girls grad. *Wesleyan Argus*, 20 April. Retrieved from wesleyanargus.com/2017/04/20/male-privilege-in-the-classroom-from-an-all-girls-grad/.

Leadership Institute. (2017a). About Morton Blackwell. May 30. Retrieved from www.leadershipinstitute.org/aboutus/Morton.cfm.

Leadership Institute. (2017b). Balance in the media funding form. Retrieved from www.leadershipinstitute.org/campus/?Resources=4.

Long, S., & Wilfong, A. (2017). UF prof lowers student's grade for using the word "man." *Campus Reform*, 25 April. Retrieved from www.campusreform.org/?ID=9099.

McCann, M. (2017). Breaking down Friday's new Baylor sexual assault lawsuit. *Sports Illustrated*, 28 January. Retrieved from www.si.com/college-football/2017/01/28/baylor-football-sexual-assault-lawsuit-art-briles.

Mudde, C. (2018). The Central European University is the latest victim of the Trump era. *The Guardian*, 4 December. Retrieved from www.theguardian.com/commentisfree/2018/dec/04/central-european-university-latest-victim-trump-era.

Nagle, A., & Wilson, C. (2017). The anthropologist of the alt-right: An interview with Angela Nagle. *Yahoo News*, 21 June. Retrieved from www.yahoo.com/news/anthropologist-alt-right-interview-angela-nagle-155357529.html.

Nelson, C. (n.d.). AAUP president Cary Nelson debates David Horwitz (March 2007). *Cary Nelson*. Retrieved from www.cary-nelson.org/nelson/horowitz-nelson-debate.html.

PayScale. (n.d.). Best Ivy League schools by salary potential. Retrieved from www.payscale.com/college-salary-report/best-schools-by-type/bachelors/ivy-league-schools.

Pedro-Carañana, J. (2017). The menace of Trump and the new authoritarianism: An interview with Henry Giroux. *OpenDemocracy*, 11 April. Retrieved from www.truth-out.org/opinion/item/40188-the-menace-of-trump-and-the-new-authoritarianism-an-interview-with-henry-giroux.

Phillips, C. (2017). Taxpayers shocked by cost of Ivy League handouts. *Campus Reform*, 11 May. Retrieved from https://www.campusreform.org/?ID=9165.

Price, A. (2017a). Students say they feel "threatened" by conservative views. *Campus Reform*, 24 April. Retrieved from www.campusreform.org/?ID=9095.

Price, A. (2017b). Hostility may be warranted to fight "hate speech", students say. *Campus Reform*, 17 April. Retrieved from www.campusreform.org/?ID=9057.

Professor watchlist. (2016). Robert Jensen. 8 November. Retrieved from https://www.professorwatchlist.org/2016/11/08/robert-jensen/.

Professor watchlist. (2018). About us. Retrieved from www.professorwatchlist.org.

Quintana, C., & Read, B. (2017). Signal boost. *Chronicle of Higher Education*, 22 June. Retrieved from www.chronicle.com/article/Signal-Boost-How-Conservative/240423.

Richman, J. (2017). BDS resolution narrowly rejected at George Washington U. *Campus Reform*, 2 May. Retrieved from www.campusreform.org/?ID=9135.

Robin, C. (2011). *The reactionary mind*. Oxford, UK: Oxford University Press.

Sabes, A. (2017a). High school YAF chapter subjected to verbal abuse at UT-Austin. *Campus Reform*, 15 May. Accessed July 18, 2017, from www.campusreform.org/?ID=9180.

Sabes, A. (2017b). CA university resolves to take stand against anti-Semitism. *Campus Reform*, 3 May. Retrieved from www.campusreform.org/?ID=9137.

Schmidt, P. (2015). Higher education's internet outrage machine. *Chronicle of Higher Education*, 8 September. Retrieved from www.chronicle.com/article/Higher-Educations-Internet/232879.

Schuman, R. (2016). Oh good, a "professor watch list." *Slate*, 23 November. Retrieved from www.slate.com/articles/news_and_politics/education/2016/11/professor_watchlist_is_a_grotesque_catalog_of_left_leaning_academics.html.

Sharpstene, L.M. (2017). Cornell to offer course on Trump's "xenophobic nationalism." *Campus Reform*, 3 May. Retrieved from www.campusreform.org/?ID=9139.

Simpson, C. (1994). *Science of coercion*. New York: Oxford University Press.

Society of Professional Journalists. (2014). SPJ code of ethics. Accessed May 27, 2017, from www.spj.org/ethicscode.pdf.

Southern Poverty Law Center. (2017). *The alt-right on campus*. 10 August. Retrieved from https://www.splcenter.org/20170810/alt-right-campus-what-students-need-know.

Stripling, J. (2017). Did UVa miss signs of looming violence? *Chronicle of Higher Education*, 14 August. Retrieved from www.chronicle.com/article/Did-UVa-Miss-Signs-of-Looming/240928?cid=at&utm_source=at&utm_medium=en&elqTrackId=8b482d8c2a4c4d2ebb12457ad34762c4&elq=7051dbd774f049089e2656c8b8e97d58&elqaid=15149&elqat=1&elqCampaignId=6455.

Sultan, A. (2016). SLU students walk out of speech, stand for university ideals. *Saint Louis Post-Dispatch*, 9 October. Retrieved from www.stltoday.com/news/lifestyle/aisha-sultan-slu-students-walk-out-of-speech-stand-for/article_d9d573b1-c180-5d51-80c9-465f436d0ffc.html.

Sykes, C. (1988). *ProfScam*. Washington, DC: Regnery Gateway.

Taylor University. (2014). Life together covenant. Retrieved from www.taylor.edu/about/mission/life-together-covenant.shtml.

Taylor University. (2017). Tenure track in communication. *Chronicle of Higher Education*, 27 June. Retrieved from chroniclevitae.com/jobs/0000374272-01.

Todorov, T. (2010). *The fear of barbarians*. Chicago: University of Chicago Press.

Vogel, P. (2017). The conservative dark-money groups infiltrating campus politics. *Media Matters for America*, 29 March. Retrieved from www.mediamatters.org/research/2017/03/29/conservative-dark-money-groups-infiltrating-campus-politics/215822#dt.

Washington, S. (2019). Clemson student government passes anti-bias resolution. *Campus Reform*, 13 March. Retrieved from www.campusreform.org/?ID=11974.

Wellesley News staff editorial, The. (2017). Free speech is not violated at Wellesley. *The Wellesley News*, 12 April. Retrieved from thewellesleynews.com/2017/04/12/free-speech-is-not-violated-at-wellesley/.

West, A.B. (2016). Folks, I've just been *censored*. *Allen B. West*, 22 September. Retrieved from www.allenbwest.com/allen/folks-ive-just-censored.

Zehnder, K. (2017). Oberlin students seek to socialize dining halls'. *Campus Reform*, 15 May. Retrieved from www.campusreform.org/?ID=9182.

Zupkus, K. (2017a). UC Santa Cruz caves to admin building occupiers' demands. *Campus Reform*, 7 May. Retrieved from www.campusreform.org/?ID=9151.

Zupkus, K. (2017b). AU students exploit racist incident for progressive causes. *Campus Reform*, 3 May. Retrieved from www.campusreform.org/?ID=9140.

· 7 ·

CONCLUSION: PLAY TO WIN

Introduction: Psychotic State

In a recent news item in spring 2019, Alex Jones is being sued for defamation for claims he made on his program *InfoWars* (Sakuma 2019). Along with hawking dubious commodities, Jones can also be called a flak merchant with a particular accent on tendentious conspiracy theories. Across years, Jones has asserted shooting massacres to be staged events featuring "crisis actors," most notably the 2012 Newtown, Connecticut mass murder at an elementary school. Jones' narratives channel unfathomable cruelty after the fact of the massacre toward the extended circle of victims, including bereaved parents who lost children. For Jones, the massacres have been faked to roll-back gun rights in the United States—even as the cascade of massacres have not much moved the needle on legislation and regulation.

When confronted with some of his claims in the high stakes setting of a legal deposition in 2019, Jones was denuded of his *InfoWars* studio props and helpers. Along with some shows of defiance, Jones pirouetted away from significant parts of his own body of work. Most notably, he claimed to have been seized by psychosis when he ranted about massacre hoaxes and crisis actors to his audience. He also claimed to have been seized by a now-disavowed conviction that most everything is staged—a condition that may have been intensified by a feedback loop opened by viewing his own program.

The sequence of events may tell us something about flak as a defective form of discourse. To wit, when truth is slammed in their faces, flak merchants may go rapidly into retreat. Indeed, if the stakes are high enough, even ardent flaksters may disavow their own performances. In Jones's case, he seems gobsmacked during the deposition when presented with videotape of his own previous statements; as if watching someone else who looks like him and answers to his name but is, somehow, a flak-spewing imposter, an efflux of an alien state of mind (i.e., psychosis).

Nevertheless, old flak habits (and profitable shtick) do not easily loosen their grip. During the same time period when Jones disavowed his own mind, he also greeted the news of a bereaved Newtown, Connecticut parent's suicide as yet another hoax (Sakuma, 2019). My point is not to ascertain Jones' state of mind—sorting out what he may think he thinks when presumably thinking un-psychotically presents no intrinsic interest—but to allude to the weakness of the flak endeavor when it is challenged.

When push comes to shove, good faith, rigorous efforts to account for reality can stand on their own degree of merit in terms of evidence embedded within argumentation; flak, as a matter of definition, cannot so readily and must avoid a reckoning. It is also important to reiterate that flak is not merely inadvertent exaggeration or misinformation. As I have conceptualized it, flak is a deliberate—indeed, tactical and strategic—attempt to degrade, delegitimize or disable targets by whatever available means. Moreover, flak is an efflux of power. Whatever its weaknesses in substance, flak arises from a place that has the resources to assert itself in the sociopolitical field.

Don't Believe the "We Believe in Nothing, Lebowski" Hype

This volume has assayed to make a case that a phenomenon called flak, discussed decades ago by Herman and Chomsky (1988), has metastasized into a prominent feature of the current sociopolitical sphere—even as the term flak is rarely used and not understood systematically when it is. As I have characterized it, the project of flak as a form of political harassment is to problematize, demean, undermine or halt the activities of its targets, through belittling discourses and punitive actions. The "communications revolution" that heavily implicates new media has—whatever its other still unfolding impacts—proven to be a potent machine for the incubation and amplification of flak.

The intensification of flak is evident in its boutique form, from putatively well-briefed, expert sources. The spike in flak has been perhaps more evident as vox pop flak that is readily summoned over new media platforms. Having made these claims at length, I acknowledge that this volume is far more centered on characterization and diagnosis than on prescription. I will nonetheless venture a few straightforward points about how people who worship at the altar of truth and human betterment could or should—as well as should not—proceed.

First, it is very seductive to assume that technology and techno-fixes can (somehow) patch over and remedy the dysfunctions of flak and the pre-standing sociopolitical problems that it aggravates. I do not dismiss the help that technology-grounded solutions can furnish toward pro-social ends of neutering flak, such as algorithms designed to downgrade suspect stories on given platforms. Benjamin T. Decker (2019) of Harvard University makes a game attempt to propose an architecture of techno-monitoring, human hands, and information sharing to curb flatly false stories that are often spiked with flak memes. As necessary as new and sophisticated approaches are, every such move to thwart bad informational actors also provokes a variety of countermoves on the same technical terrain. Marc Goodman (2015), a seasoned national and international law enforcement figure with expertise in new communication technology, has made this case at book length.

I am partial toward Sarah Jeong's suggestion that better site moderation or techno-bandages are, in the bigger picture, small-bore answers to deeply seated sociopolitical problems (Jeong, 2018). Arresting flak from spreading in a sphere as vast as the internet is, in this view, like stopping human foibles such as using drugs excessively, gossiping, eating junk food, or falling "in love" with the wrong person, among other common faults that may be blunted but not eradicated. We may dream of techno-silver bullets and magic pills, but they are not readily, if ever, at hand; and the space of the internet is too vast to be patrolled by "white hat" moderators. Rather than deferring to technology with a wave of the hand as if it possesses its own motive force (a techno-determinist idea critically discussed by Winston, 1995), we need to do this ourselves. Doing so may further implicate seemingly "retro," hands-on methods in the sociopolitical sphere to put flak campaigns decisively on the defensive.

In that vein, my second point: If the practices of flak are to be placed on the back foot, it will be because people who care for cultivating the truth and continued betterment in the arc of human endeavors push back against flak mills and their sponsors with a vim and vigor that makes flak not worth the candle. Longer-term, big-picture solutions to the proliferation of flak are not primarily technical and they are not necessarily media- and rhetoric-centered either; mind-blowing erudition and arguments may be necessary but are surely not sufficient to the battles ahead. As I have suggested in this volume, flaksters do not necessarily believe much of what they say, hence, their thundering double standards. In this view, arguing against shape-shifting flak claims can surely be over-emphasized. From a time and place near at hand to the right-wing convulsions of the 1930s' regimes, Hannah Arendt has famously minted wise observations about cynical people who do not believe their own political pantomimes beyond their serviceability to power (2004, pp. 593–615).

To draw on a more recent reference point, flakster charlatans are akin to the anarchists in *The Big Lebowski* (director: Joel Coen, 1997), albeit far less amusing. To wit, the anarchists repeat their refrain of "we believe in nothing" throughout the film—and back that conviction with, for example, crude if painful attempts to pretend that a kidnapping has occurred while exhibiting notable cowardice and ineptitude in the final parking lot confrontation with The Dude's posse. The point is that saying anything, while believing in nothing aside from rallying to authority's writ, is a debilitating condition once the truth arrives.

As I emphasized throughout this volume, flak is always backed with power. In the contemporary moment, the intersection of economic, political, and symbolic power most driven toward flak is pursuing a deregulated neoliberal ("free market") economic program that facilitates intensified class division (Harvey, 2005). In turn, class division squares with the right-wing sublime of brutish, boot-on-the-face social striation (Robin, 2011). Neoliberalism and the right-wing sublime of pre-Enlightenment hierarchy as founts of flak run through this volume like a thread. The flak case-studies in this book implicate this right-wing vision in, for example, attacks on climate science and, by extension, on sunrise green industries that would disrupt established carbon titans. These flak campaigns assay to bind humanity to the corpse of carbon fuels, perhaps the world's most powerful complex of industries, and to a dystopian Malthusian future. In the case of universities, the advancement of knowledge itself as well as the opportunity for advancement through education for traditionally subaltern subjects is part of what is at stake in the flak assaults on the campus. Where elections are concerned, the opportunity for painfully slow, but palpable progress through elected representation that is accountable to the whole electorate is in play in attacks on the franchise. In contrast with this dead end, believe-in-nothing-beyond-bludgeoning-efforts-to-cancel-the-Enlightenment right-wing program, the vast majority of the public has an interest in continued and stepped-up progress toward dismantling, brick by brick, the hierarchies that have held most people back for millennia.

Backward-looking flak and its retrograde political project of rigidly pyramidal, hierarchal power places faith in nothing but crude expression of that power. By contrast, I posit that creating the facts on the ground of human advancement—for example, better housing, healthcare, meaningful work, sustainable economies, and education for all—is the correct thing to do. And doing so takes long strides toward defeating vulnerability to flak in the first instance. A figure such as Jones and his baleful message gain traction in an environment where many people feel, and are, subject to precarity; or, in the case of better-off subjects, harbor white-knuckle fear of slipping backward in socioeconomic terms into an abyss without sufficient safety nets. In this view, the flak battleground may regularly arise in mediated fora—but the confrontation is far wider, and implicates the everyday, material realities in which subjects are ensconced. Rather than reacting to flak campaigns, oxygen can be sucked out of them in the first instance by making the world a better place for more people, to fairer and more egalitarian specifications.

Everyone need not be become a fact-checker or an analyst of flak discourses and flak mills. Indeed, flak can be taken "too seriously" in this sense by distracting researchers and the wider public from keeping their eyes fixed on the quotidian issues and stakes that implicate fairness and justice. The strategic remedy is to resolutely stay on the path of betterment of sociopolitical conditions and not lose traction in the quicksand of flak. Media analysts, in this view, can support other consequential players in the sociopolitical sphere—scientists, educators, investigative journalists, voters, the public that seeks reliable information—in diverting the diversions of flak.

Third and finally, there is no space for polite deference, compromise or "triangulation" with flak campaigns. Indulging flak talking points in an inane gesture toward "balance" or simply to get flaksters off one's ass (even preemptively) may seem convenient—but it puts off necessary confrontation and degrades the countenance of truth. As I have suggested throughout this book, flak often emerges out of the shadows as it tries to insinuate itself into the mainstream. Flak campaigns regularly strive to keep their origins and funding obscured. On top of this, flak-mongers assume a variety of contrived disguises—"investigative journalism," "think tank," "expert"—that do not withstand even cursory scrutiny. Rather than passively enabling flak mills and flak merchants to gaze critically on those whom they would flak, the scrutiny needs to be turned preemptively back on the flaksters—*their* discourses, *their* professional training, *their* institutional funding streams, *their* unstated programmatic objectives, all of which tend to be enveloped in platitudes or haze and shadow.

Flak's foundational weakness is that it is a defective stream of discourse and activity, built on shoddy foundations, toward retrograde illiberal ends that require bully-boy tactics to succeed to the extent that they do. The weakness and weirdness of flak needs to be ruthlessly drawn out. There can be one, two, many Alex Joneses disavowing their own selves, shaken by the no-bullshit return of the repressed realities against which they have flaked. Compromise or effort toward "balance" and "symmetry" with flak is an affront to the power of truth in the first and final instance. When flak is in play, play to win against it.

References

Arendt, H. (2004). *The origins of totalitarianism*. New York: Shocken Books.
Decker, B.T. (2019). What a Kamala Harris meme can teach us about fighting fake news in 2020. *Politico*, 3 March. Retrieved from www.politico.com/magazine/story/2019/03/03/what-a-kamala-harris-meme-can-teach-us-about-fighting-fake-news-in-2020-225515.
Goodman, M. (2015). *Future crimes*. New York: Doubleday.
Harvey, D. (2005). *A brief history of neoliberalism*. Oxford, UK: Oxford University Press.
Herman, E., & Chomsky, N. (1988). *Manufacturing consent*. New York: Pantheon.
Jeong, S. (2018). *Internet of garbage*. New York: Vox Media Incorporated.
Robin, C. (2011). *The reactionary mind*. New York: Oxford University Press.
Sakuma, A. (2019). Alex Jones blames "psychosis" for his Sandy Hook conspiracies. *Vox*, 31 March. Retrieved from www.vox.com/2019/3/31/18289271/alex-jones-psychosis-conspiracies-sandy-hook-hoax.
Winston, B. (1995). How are media born and developed? In J. Downing (Ed.), *Questioning the media* (2nd ed., pp. 54–74). Thousand Oaks, CA: Sage.

INDEX

A

Abbott, Greg 112
Abraham, John 38–43, 71–72
Abrams, Stacey 145
Accuracy in Academia 181
Accuracy in Media (AIM) 5
Activism 45–47, 182–183
Affirmative action for the wealthy 168
Afghanistan 145, 149
Ailes, Roger 25
Alabama 119, 121
Alt-lite 171
American Association for the Advancement of Science (AAAS) 72
American Association of University Professors 189
American Civil Liberties Union 140, 169, 189
American Geophysical Union 73
American Legislative Exchange Council 64
American Pravda 105, 110, 118
American Spectator 142
American University 187
Americans United for Change 115
Amnesty International 45, 172
Anderson, Carol 145
Andino, Marci 137
Anti-Semitism 187
Arendt, Hannah 200
Arizona 156
Arlington, Illinois 59, 65
Arnaudo, Dan 36
Ashcroft, John 138
Association of Community Organizations for Reform Now (ACORN) 107–109
AstroTurf 45
Atlanta Journal Constitution 137
Audiences 11, 25–31

B

Baker, Scott 99
Ballot Access and Voting Integrity Initiative 138

Bard College 162
Barker, Molly 113
Bast, Joseph 58, 59, 66, 89
Battleground Texas 111, 113
Baylor University 173
Beard, Sterling 171, 184, 190
Beauchamp, Zack 162
Belarus 162
Belichick, Bill 72
Berelson, Bernard 26
Berry, Mike 48
Bethel University 38, 39
Bickmore, Barry 39–41
Big Government 109
Big Lebowski, The 200
Big Ten universities 166
Birtherism 34, 152
Biskupic, Steven 148
Blackwell, Morton 171, 172–173, 182
Blaze, The 64, 99, 181
Boburg, Shawn 118, 121
Boehlert, Eric 27
Boykoff, Jules M. 58
Boykoff, Maxwell T. 58
Bray, Dennis 75–76
Brazil 35–37
Breitbart.com 75, 89–90, 181
Breitbart, Andrew 68, 105, 109
Briles, Art 173
Broder, John R. 149–150
Brown, Jerry 108
Brulle, Robert 69
Business Insider 138
Brookings Institution 60
Buckley, William F. 165, 178
Budapest 162
Bullshit 6
Burton, Michael 90
Bush, George H.W. 8–12
Bush, George W. 18, 102, 117, 138–139, 144, 147, 149–150, 151, 178

C

Cable News Network (CNN) 132–133
Cadwalladr, Carole 9
Cai, Ming 70
Calgary, Canada 90
California State University at Dominquez Hills 183
Cambridge Analytica (CA) 9, 28–29
Campus Reform 102, 163, 168–192
Canada 146
Carson, Corbin 139–141
Carter, Robert M., see *Why Scientists Disagree about Global Warming*
Catholicism 39, 185
Cato Institute 64
Cecil the Lion 19
Central European University 161, 191
Central Intelligence Agency (CIA) 12
Centurion, The 102
Chafets, Zav 102, 104
Channel Four 123
Chapman University 187
Charles Koch Foundation 171
Charlottesville, Virginia 173
Chinese Academy of Sciences (CAS) 80–81
Chomsky, Noam 3, 5, 37, 44, 198
Chronicle of Higher Education 174, 175
Ciccariello-Maher, George 188–189
Cigarette industry 61–62, 66
Clapper, James 18
Clemson University 176
Clemson University Sexuality and Gender alliance 176
Climate change 38–42, 57–59, 61, 69, 92
Climate Research Unit at East Anglia University (CRU), see East Anglia University
Climate Truth 89
"Climategate", see "Hack-and-flak-gate"
Clinton, Hillary 11–19, 24–25, 106, 113–116, 152–153

Clinton, William J. 23–25, 33
Clinton Foundation 152
Colbert Report 44
Cold War 26, 164
College admissions scandal, 2019 168–169
College Republicans 171, 185, 186
Colorado 110
Commonwealth Academies of Science 73
Computational propaganda 30, 36, 45
Conspiracy theory 44, 197
Conway, Erik M. 61
Cooper, Anderson 106
Cooper, Roy 156
Copenhagen Summit, see United Nations Climate Change Conference, 2009
Cornell University 177
Cosby, Bill 47–48
Corsi, Jerome 15
Couldry, Nick 164
Coulter, Anne 178
Craido Perez, Caroline 32
Crawford v. Marion County Election Board 143
Creamer, Robert 115–116, 122
Crites, Alice 118, 121
Cuccinelli, Kenneth T. 87
Cultural Studies 26

D

D'Amato, Alfonse M. 24
D'Souza, Dinesh 46
DailyCaller, The 174, 181
Daley, David 155–156
David Horowitz Freedom Center 105
Davis, Aaron C. 118, 121
Davis, Wendy 111–113
Dawson, Michael 146
DCLeaks 14
De Posada, Robert 144

Del Prado, Christine 111–112
Dease, Dennis J. 39–40
Decker, Benjamin T 199
Democracy Partners 115–117, 122
Democratic Party (United States) 14–15, 110, 111, 115, 134, 152, 155, 156
DeSmogBlog 70
Department of Justice (United States) 134, 148
Dessem, Matthew 188
Digital, Culture, Media and Sport Committee of the House of Commons (United Kingdom) 44
Disinformation 44, 112
Does your vote count? 138–139
Dog Poop Girl 32
Donors Capital Fund 171
Donors Trust 105, 171
Donsanto, Craig 148
Double standards 181–182, 191, 200
Dowless, Leslie McCrae 135–136
Doyle, James 148–149
Drexel University 188
Drudge Report 25
Dude, The 200
Dukakis, Michael 8–11
Duménil, Gérard 167
Dumitrica, Delia 27
Dunlap, Matthew 153, 154

E

Eagleton, Terry 5–6
East Anglia University 81, 83, 86
Economidy, John M. 111, 112
Elections, 131–156, also see United States election 1988, 2000, 2016, 2018
Electoral College 131–132, 155
Environmental Law Institute 75
Environmental Protection Agency (EPA) (United States) 83, 84–85

F

Facebook 27–28
FactCheck.org 152
Fake news 43–44, 118
Faulk, Marshall 72
Faulkner, Neil 164
Federal Bureau of Investigation (FBI) 12, 148
Federal Election Commission 114
Fessenden, Ford 149–150
Feulner, Edwin 60
Fidesz 162, 192
Fields, James Alex, Junior 173
First Amendment, see Free speech
Flak, definition 5–7, 31–33
   contrast with scandal 33–37
   boutique flak 42–43, 61, 67, 90, 199
   faux (phantom) flak 15, 40–41, 72–74, 81–84, 152
   flak-in-action 36–41, 82–83, 87–89, 101, 111, 133, 135–137, 172, 174
   flak-in-discourse 37–41, 49, 72, 75–78, 82–84, 100, 111, 132–137, 142, 172, 174
   issue-oriented flak 41–42, 86
   meta-ideological flak 41–42, 86, 101, 121, 149
   personalized flak 41–42, 46, 48, 69, 75, 86–88, 167, 170
   vox pop flak 42–43, 61, 86, 171, 199
Flak mills 39, 43, 59–63, 98, 122, 169–170
Florida 46, 136, 146, 149–151
Flynn, D.J. 30
Flynn, Michael 19
Foreign Intelligence Surveillance Act (FISA) 30
Foval, Scott 115–116
Fox, Josh 101
Fox News 25, 46–47, 57–59, 174, 185
France 17
Frankfort, Harry 6
"Free market", see neoliberalism
Free speech 169, 176–177, 183–191

Freedman, Des 27
Freedom 65–66, 77
Freymiller, Dorinda 116
Friends of Science 90
Fund, John 136, 142–154
Furman University 179

G

Gabbatt, Adam 152–153
Gamergate 32
García, Ana 146
Gardner, Bill 153
Gateway Pundit 46
Gelfand, Michele 63
Geological Society of America 73
George Washington University 179
Georgia 145
Geraghty, Dana 97–98
Gerrymander 155–156
Giles, Hannah 108, 109
Gjoni, Eron 32
Gillmor, Dan 27
Ginsberg, Benjamin 164, 165, 167, 170
Gockowski, Anthony 178, 179, 182
God and Man at Yale 165
Golden, Daniel 168
Gonzalez, Emma 46
Goodman, Marc 199
Gore, Albert, Junior 90, 149–150
Goreham, Steve 71–72
Greenwald, Glenn 27
Guardian, The 9
Guccifer2.0 14–15

H

"Hack-and-flak-gate" 81–86
Hagel, Chuck 62
Hale, David 24
Hannity, Sean 108
Harris, Kamala 182–183

INDEX

Harris, Mark 135
Harvard University 47, 75, 168, 182, 199
Harvey, David 166
Hasen, Richard 110, 139, 141–142, 146
Hawaii State Health Department 34
Heartland Institute 5, 57–92, 142
Help America Vote 151
Heritage Foundation 60, 64, 136, 139, 143, 156
Herman, Edward 3–5, 37, 44, 198
Hitler, Adolph 91
Hogg, David 47
Hood College 186
Horton, Scott 147
Horton, William 8–11
Howard University 182
Hudson Institute 64
Huelskamp, Tim 64, 74
Huertas, Aaron 58
Hungary 161, 162, 192
Huvelle, Ellen 116

I

"Ice Ice Baby" 155
Idso, Craig D, see *Why Scientists Disagree about Global Warming*
Iglesias, David 139, 147–148
Ignatieff, Michael 161
Illinois 156
Inconvenient Truth, An 90
Independent Climate Change Email Review 61, 83, 85, 87
InfoWars, see Jones, Alex
Inside Higher Ed 175
Ingraham, Laura 47
Intelligence Community Assessment (ICA) 12
Intergovernmental Panel on Climate Change (IPCC) 77–81
Iraq 7
Israel 179
Ivy League 178

J

Jamieson, Kathleen Hall 8–11, 16–18
Jaschik, Scott 162
Jeong, Sarah 32, 199
Jesuits 185
Jones, Alex 39, 197–198, 202
Jones, Doug 119
Jones, Phil 86
Jordan, Elise 145

K

Kansas 64, 153–154
Kemp, Brian 145
Kennedy, John F. 119
Keynesianism 165–166
Khan, Natasha 139–141
King, Steve 46
Kirk, Charlie 169
"Kirk Myers" 41–42
Kobach, Kris 153–154
Korte, Roy 116
Kosinski, Marcel 28
Kreigsman, Rachel 58
Kushner, Jared 152–153, 168
Kuwait 78

L

Lamothe, Dan 120
Landrieu, Mary 106
Lava jato ("car wash" investigation) 36
Lazarsfeld, Paul 26, 29
Leadership Institute 102, 170–172
League of Conservation Voters 122
League of Women Voters 136
Left Exposed 66, 67
Le Pen, Marine 17
Levy, Dominique 167
Lewinsky, Monica 25
Lewis, John 142

Life Together Covenant 184
Liley, Betsy 99
Limbaugh, Rush 142
Lindzen, Richard 90
Lofgren, Mike 156
Lynde and Harry Bradley Foundation 105

M

Maass, Allison 117
MacDougal, James B. 23–24
Macron, Emmanuel 17
Mad, Mad, Mad World of Climatism, The 71–72
Main Directorate of the General Staff of the Russian Federation (GRU) 14–15
Maine 138
Manafort, Paul 115, 152
Mann, Michael E. 82–83, 84, 86–88
March for Our Lives 46
Marquette University 188–189
Massachusetts 8–11
Marjory Stoneman Douglas High School 46
Maryland 156
Mayer, Jane 18, 87, 97, 138, 139
Media Research Center 74
Mexico 146
MeToo 47–48
MI6 12
McAdam, John 189–190
McCain, John S. III 19
McCann, Michael 173
McCrory, Pat 156
McCaskill, Claire 122
McGinley, Bernard L. 140, 144
McKay, John 147
McKew, Molly K. 30
McSally, Martha 19
Michigan 131, 156
Middletown, Connecticut 181
Millbank, Dana 114
Minnesota Free Market Institute 38
Minnite, Lorraine C. 133–134
Misinformation 44, 112

Mnuchin, Steven 178
Monckton, Christopher 38–43
Moore, Roy 118–119
Motely, Seton 67
Mothe, Stephen 35–36
Mudde, Cas 161
Mueller, Robert S. III 12, 13–15, 44

N

Nagle, Angela 171
National Oceanic and Atmospheric Administration (United States) 58, 83
National Public Radio 99–100
National Review 142, 165, 174
National Voter Registration Act ("Motor Voter Act") 143
National Security Agency (NSA) 12
Nature 79–80
Neoliberalism 28, 163–164, 166–167, 179, 201
New England Patriots 72
New Era 110
New York Times, The 9, 17, 104, 149, 151
Newtown, Connecticut 197–198
Nevada 144
NewsMax 90
Nix, Alexander 28–29
Non-Governmental International Panel on Climate Change (NIPCC) 77, 79–81
Noon, Marita 63, 75
North Carolina 135
Northern Arizona University 177
Nunes, Devin 30
Nuzzi, Olivia 114
Nwanevu, Osita 121

O

O'Keefe, James 97–114, 117–118, 121–122
Obama, Barack H. 19, 34, 74, 109, 152, 155
Oberlin College 183

Occupy Wall Street 101
Olin Foundation 105
Onion, The 44, 176
Open Society Foundation 97–98
Orbán, Viktor 162
Oreskes, Naomi 61, 75
Oxburgh Panel, see *Report by the Lord Oxburgh's Independent Panel*,
Oxford University 30

P

Padden, David 59
Paglia, Camille 176
Palmer, Alicia 146
Palmer, Walter 19
Partido dos Trabalhadores (Workers' Party, PT) 35
Pedro-Carañana, Joan 164
Pennycook, Gordon 30
Pennsylvania 131, 140, 144, 156
Pennsylvania State University 82–83
Phillips, Cabot 117–178
Phillips, Gregg 132–133
Phillips, Jamie 118–120
Philo, Greg 48
Podesta, John 14, 16, 18
PolitiFact 46, 152
Pomona College 180
Power 6–7, 200
Poynter Institute 100
Preibus, Reince 134
Professor Watchlist 169–170, 181
Profscam 165–166
Project Veritas 98–122, 180
Project Veritas Action 103, 122
Propaganda Model 3–5, 7, 44, 48, 117
Putin, Vladimir 12

Q

Quinn, Zoë 32
Quintana, Chris 174, 181

R

Rand Corporation 7
Read, Brock 174, 181
Reagan, Ronald 10
Regnery Gateway 165
Reinhard, Beth 119, 121
Report by the Lord Oxburgh's Independent Panel 83–84
Republican Party (United States) 24, 63, 109, 133, 134, 144, 146, 156
Rhode Island 141
Ricci, David 59–60
Richman, Jackson 179
Robin, Corey 191
Rockwell, Norman 19, 147
Roosevelt, Franklin Delano 66
Rouseff, Dilma 35–37
Russell Review, see *Independent Climate Change Email Review*
Russian Federation 12–14, 16, 18, 46, 77, 81, 115
RT 13
Rutgers University 102, 133

S

Saint Louis University 185
Sanders, Sarah Huckabee 106
Sandusky, Jerry 88
Sarah Scaife Foundation 105
Sargent, Francis 8
Saudi Arabia 78
Scandal, see *Thompson, John B.*
Schattschneier, E.E. 131
Schiller, Ron 99–100
Schiller, Vivian 99
Schimel, Brad 116
Schmidt, Peter 174
Schuster, Paul F. 70
Science and Technology Committee of the House of Commons (United Kingdom) 82–83

Senate Special Committee to Investigate Whitewater Development Corporation and Related Matters (United States) 24
Shaft 109
Shirky, Clay 27, 101
Siddiqui, Sabrina 152–153
Singer, S. Fred, *Why Scientists Disagree about Global Warming*
Smith, Fred L. 60
Smithsonian Institution 88–89
Snyder, Timothy 66–67
Society of Professional Journalists (SPJ) 107, 112, 180–181
Soon, Wei-Hock "Willie" 88–92
Soros, George 97–98, 161
South Carolina 137–138, 182
Southern Company 88
Spencer, Richard 171
Stealing Elections, see Fund, John
Stern Review 62
Steyn, Mark 88
Stone, Chris 98
Stone, Roger 15–16
South America 17
Southern Poverty Law Center 173
Super Bowl XXXVI 72
Supreme Court, United States 143
Supreme Court, Virginia 87
Sykes, Charles 165–166
Swatting 47

T

Taylor, James 85–86
Temer, Michel 36
Texas 111–113, 141
Thematic analysis 48–49
Think tanks 6, 43, 59, 61–64
Thompson, John B. 33–35
Thomson, Riggan 141
Tompkins, Al 100
Townhall.com 64

Trump, Donald J. 12, 15, 15–18, 64–65, 74, 91, 105–106, 115, 118, 131–132, 152, 177–178, 190–191
Truth decay 7
Turkey 162
Turnbull, Mark 9
Turning Point USA (TPUSA) 169–170
Turzai, Mike 140

U

Ukraine 115, 152
Union of Concerned Scientists (UCS) 69, 78
"Unite the Right" 173
United Kingdom 9, 12, 31, 32, 38, 44
United Nations Climate Change Conference, 2009 81
United States Commission on Civil Rights 150–151
United States Elections, 1988 7–12
United States Elections, 2000 149, 151
United States Elections, 2012 140, 155–156
United States Global Change Research Program 73
Universities 20, 161–192
University of Alaska 190
University of Arizona 182
University of Chicago 149
University of Florida 176–177
University of Illinois 58
University of Rochester 182
University of Saint Thomas 40, 71
University of Texas 167, 169
University of Virginia 87, 173
University of Wisconsin 89

V

Vera, Juan Carlos 109
Vienna 162

Viscount Monckton of Brenchley, The, see
     Monckton, *Christopher*
Von Spakovsky, Hans 136, 137, 142, 154
Von Storch, Hans 75–76
Voser, Peter 62

W

Warpaint 37–38
Walker, Scott 156
Wall Street Journal, The 78, 90, 142
Washington Post, The 114–115,
     118–121, 152
Washington Times, The 64, 90
Watts up with that? 39–43
Weigel, David 106, 115
Wellesley College 187
Wemple, Erik 121

Wesleyan Argus 181
Wesleyan University 181
West, Allen B. 185–186
Winehouse, Amy 141
Whitewater 23–24
*Why Scientists Disagree about Global
     Warming* 74–76
Wikileaks 15, 18
Will, George F. 178
Wisconsin 116, 131, 148, 156
Wood, Diane 149
Woodward, Vann 132
World Bank 35, 79

Y

Yiannopolous, Milo 181
Young Americans for Freedom 183

Intersections in Communications and Culture
Global Approaches and Transdisciplinary Perspectives
General Editors: Cameron McCarthy & Angharad N. Valdivia

An Institute of Communications Research, University of Illinois Commemorative Series

This series aims to publish a range of new critical scholarship that seeks to engage and transcend the disciplinary isolationism and genre confinement that now characterizes so much of contemporary research in communication studies and related fields. The editors are particularly interested in manuscripts that address the broad intersections, movement, and hybrid trajectories that currently define the encounters between human groups in modern institutions and societies and the way these dynamic intersections are coded and represented in contemporary popular cultural forms and in the organization of knowledge. Works that emphasize methodological nuance, texture and dialogue across traditions and disciplines (communications, feminist studies, area and ethnic studies, arts, humanities, sciences, education, philosophy, etc.) and that engage the dynamics of variation, diversity and discontinuity in the local and international settings are strongly encouraged.

LIST OF TOPICS

- Multidisciplinary Media Studies
- Cultural Studies
- Gender, Race, & Class
- Postcolonialism
- Globalization
- Diaspora Studies
- Border Studies
- Popular Culture
- Art & Representation
- Body Politics
- Governing Practices
- Histories of the Present
- Health (Policy) Studies
- Space and Identity
- (Im)migration
- Global Ethnographies
- Public Intellectuals
- World Music
- Virtual Identity Studies
- Queer Theory
- Critical Multiculturalism

Manuscripts should be sent to:

Peter Lang Publishing, Inc.
Acquisitions Department
29 Broadway, 18th floor
NY, NY 10006

To order other books in this series, please contact our Customer Service Department:
peterlang@presswarehouse.com (within the U.S.)
orders@peterlang.com (outside the U.S.)

Or browse online by series:
www.peterlang.com